To Touch a Child . . .

At age two and a half, Anamaria was the size of a 15-month-old toddler. She was steadily falling away from the normal pattern of growth. Unable to walk or stand alone, she moved about only when she was rocking. She neither talked nor tried to communicate in any way with gestures, crying, or cooing. No one on the staff had ever seen her smile or heard her laugh. She rocked herself for most of her waking hours. . . .

"Your gigantic blue eyes are beautiful," I said to Anamaria, as I positioned myself on the mat beside her. "Unusually so, even in Romania, where beautiful, big eyes are the rule rather than the exception."

She stared at me with incredible intensity, holding her small body rigidly erect and keeping both hands in front of her face. All of my energy was focused on trying to read that stare. Immediately but almost imperceptibly, she began to connect emotionally. . . .

The session lasted nearly two hours and was like a dance. Sitting beside and slightly behind her, so as not to distract or upset her, I captured her attention with small toys . . . a shiny bell, small colored blocks, a cup, a fuzzy yellow tennis ball. . . . Finally she broke through enough to engage in manipulation of the toys. As she became more absorbed, Anamaria began to relax emotionally and allowed more touch. She was opening doors so rapidly that I found myself holding my breath. . . .

"Let's see if you'll let me pick you up," I said to her while I moved her to my lap. Despite the fact that her little heart was racing, she came into my arms as willingly as any child I had ever held. . . . As she nestled her curly head against my shoulder, I heard a little sound, guttural and hoarse at first, then stronger. . . . Anamaria was laughing for the first time in her life. . . .

THE COMPLETE GUIDE TO

FOREIGN ADOPTION

WHAT TO EXPECT
AND HOW TO PREPARE
FOR YOUR NEW CHILD

Barbara Brooke Bascom, M.D.
AND
Carole A. McKelvey, M.A.

Foreword by Janice Tomlin

POCKET BOOKS
New York   London   Toronto   Sydney   Tokyo   Singapore

"Childsong" by Neil Diamond is from *Taproot Manuscript* (1972), MCA Records, Inc., MCAD-31071. Copyright 1971 Prophet Music, Inc., Los Angeles, CA. All rights reserved.

Material from **The God Squad** © Paddy Doyle 1985. Extracted from **The God Squad** published by Corgi, an imprint of Transworld Publishers Ltd. All rights reserved.

Excerpts from *The 1995 Report on International Adoption*, Intercountry Adoption Chart from INS and personal quotes from Anna Marie Merrill appear with permission from the International Concerns Committee for Children.

An *Original* Publication of POCKET BOOKS

POCKET BOOKS, a division of Simon & Schuster Inc.
1230 Avenue of the Americas, New York, NY 10020

Copyright © 1997 by Dr. Barbara Bascom and Carole McKelvey

Bascom, Barbara B.
    The complete guide to foreign adoption : what to expect and how to prepare for your new child / Barbara B. Bascom and Carole A. McKelvey.
        p. cm.
    Includes bibliographical references and index.
    ISBN: 0-671-54646-5 (pbk.)
    1. Intercountry adoption—Handbooks, manuals, etc.   I. McKelvey, Carole A.   II. Title.
    HV875.5.B37   1997
    362.73'4—dc21   96-48425
                                                                 CIP

First Pocket Books trade paperback printing April 1997

10 9 8 7 6 5 4 3 2 1

POCKET and colophon are registered trademarks of Simon & Schuster Inc.

Cover design by Tai Lam Wong

Text design by Stanley S. Drate/Folio Graphics Co. Inc.

Printed in the U.S.A.

Contents

Authors' Note

International adoption had a turning point in 1990. After a steady decline that began in 1986 and continued through the cold war years, the numbers of children adopted from foreign countries suddenly reversed their downward trend and burst back into prominence when the plight of thousands of institutionalized children in former eastern bloc countries was exposed by the Western media.

By the end of the year, the hollow faces and pleading eyes of these children had entered the living rooms—and hearts—of every Western family that had a television set. For more than one million American families on waiting lists of adoption agencies—many having been there for years—the media blitz became a living advertisement for intercountry adoption. The results were predictable. Thousands of Western families rushed to eastern Europe to adopt its abandoned children. Returning airplanes were so full of adopted children and their new parents, they were dubbed "the baby flights." International adoption had begun its renaissance of the nineties.

In 1990, we, the authors of this book were experiencing turning points of our own.

Writer/journalist Carole McKelvey entered the Rocky Mountain Women's Institute to begin research on her second book, *Adoption Crisis,* an endeavor that would not only heighten her interest in this special group of high-risk children but would lead her into a new career path as a professional therapist and counselor.

Responding to an invitation from the minister of health (he had heard, somehow, of my previous work as developmental pediatrician/clinical program director) I (Bascom) stepped off of a plane in Romania to spend six weeks touring orphanages and conducting a needs assessment of children and staff. From the first time I set foot in an orphanage and met the children and staff, I knew my personal and professional life would never be the same. When the consultation grew into a proposal, and the proposal became a project, I stayed to direct the project. Six weeks turned into six years (soon to be seven) and not only joined two past career paths (program development and clinical work), but introduced a third. In 1993, I began to write about my experience with the children of Romania. In 1994, I met Carole McKelvey, who made me believe I could indeed write something other than scientific articles.

When we met, Carole and I discovered that we not only had a mutual interest in children of international adoption but also shared a mutual concern over the ongoing plight of these children and their adoptive families. By this time, we were aware that most parents who had adopted internationally were ill informed (by the adoption system) and had little sense of who these children were, what they had experienced, or what they, as parents, should or could do after adopting.

Too many parents had tragically brought home children who were difficult or seemed impossible to parent. Too many children were not able to realize their God-given potential, even when adopted by a loving home and family. Furthermore, too many children continued to live in foreign orphanages—abandoned and needing homes—while thousands of eligible families continued to wait. And waiting, in addition to being terribly frustrating, was beset with too many problems related to red tape and the bureaucracy.

As authors, we are convinced that international adoption's benefits far outweigh the risks and problems, many of which are addressed in this book. Despite the many uncertainties and unknowns, and despite the extraordinary complexity of many adoptees' problems, we believe that with love, knowledge, and the right interventions, even the most severely challenged child arriving in an American home can be helped to a useful and loving life. That belief is based on our own experiences as well as those of the parents and children who have "been there."

Through the stories of courageous parents and children who once rode home on a "baby flight," *The Complete Guide to Foreign Adoption* hopes to shed some light on the problems of today's international adoption and therefore reduce the stress of uncertainty for today's adopting parents. Although special attention is given to the problems, pitfalls, and unrealized expectations of international adoption, this book is not intended to function as an exposé or an indictment of the system. Instead, the information it contains is intended to inform and enlighten, and by so doing, help to prevent similar problems from occurring in future adoptions.

We cannot overstate the respect and admiration we feel for the many families who have shared their personal lives with us in the writing of this book. Without their stories of joy and sorrow, success and disappointment, dreams come true and unmet expectations, this book would lack the human quality that enriches its pages. Risking both embarrassment and the possibility of negative response that public scrutiny always involves, our parent contributors were unswerving in their determination to get the story out. Without exception, they told their stories so that other parents would benefit and the world would be a better place for children of intercountry adoptions.

The Complete Guide to Foreign Adoption tells the whole, true story of international adoption—a story largely untold until this time. Because it is dependent upon follow-up and outcome studies that could only be done after children have been in adoptive homes for several years, much of the information in this book has just recently become available. The stories told in this book are true and are neither edited nor embellished.

By allowing children to tell their story—through their behavior, their health and developmental status, and through their words, songs, and drawings—we have attempted to give a voice to the children and their adoptive parents. By preserving the honesty of the original, and by minimizing (as much as possible) our professional interpretations of the stories, we hope to give readers ample opportunity to draw their own conclusions.

This book is written for parents who have either been through foreign adoption or are interested in going through it. It is also intended for professionals and agency people, who play such a critical role in making adoption work. General readers, particularly those interested in the many difficult issues about the child and the family that confront American society today, will find much of relevance in the stories of these children and their adopting families.

We purposely focus on the highest risk children in this book: children of institutions (chapter 4), challenged children (chapter 6), and children at risk for attachment problems (chapter 5). Readers will be exposed to what these children are like both before and after adoption. Chapter 2 provides current information about the process of foreign adoption. Chapter 3 gives the reader an inside look at children, orphanages, and the inner workings of the adoption bureaucracy, using Romania as a model. Through case-illustrated discussions, the major issues in completing the process and establishing healthy child-parent relationships are explored in chapters 8–10.

In our attempts to address the complex and emotionally laden issues in the foreign adoption process, we may have raised more questions than we have answered. Finishing this book has been a learning experience for both of us. In retrospect, we recognize several important issues that were not addressed as fully as they need to be. There were two reasons for this:

◆ A critical issue surfaced that deserved further examination, and therefore required time and space that exceed the scope of this publication. For example: the nature/nurture issues inherent in adoption of children from foreign cultures.

◆ We were unable to obtain the data needed. For example, our attempt to obtain statistics on outcomes of adoption regarding disruption and dissolution was not entirely successful.

Every reader is entitled to accurate information, and it is our intent to deliver it as free of technical jargon as possible. We have attempted to demystify the complex, highly technical medical and psychological concepts behind many of our stories and make the information understandable without watering it

down or changing its meaning. Although lay language is substituted whenever possible, and definitions are provided, many
technical terms defy translation in that there is no concise, precise substitute for the terminology. Glossaries are provided.

Throughout this book, readers will find that we have attempted to avoid using gender pronouns, unless the sentence
structure absolutely called for this usage. The English language
lacks gender-neutral third-person singular pronouns. Impersonal singular pronouns in our language are masculine. So be
it. We deplore this constraint, but feel the repeated use of him/
her and similar artificial constructions would impede the flow
of the text. For readability and clarity, we have used "child" or
"children" where possible.

Apologies are offered for the abuse of English usage that is
inherent in writing about governmental and bureaucratic processes. Many of the words used in this book seem jargony—
disincentive, for example, or adoptive (the adjective) or parent (the
verb). It is advisable, however, for anyone involved in the process of foreign adoption to be familiar with the new language
of "bureaubabble." In international adoption, as in any human
transaction, the ability to communicate clearly is a most powerful weapon.

As authors who have lived and listened to the international
adoption story since 1987, we believe that finding homes and
families for abandoned children is the solution to one of the
world's oldest, most tragic problems. As the reported numbers
of homeless children continue to rise throughout the world, we
give priority in these pages to the neediest: children of institutions, challenged children, and children with special needs.

Through our own personal experiences and those of the families who have sought us out, we have learned the importance
of viewing adoption as a process that does not end when the
final decree is issued. An alarming number of foreign adoptees
experience problems attaching to their new families, and this,
from our point of view, represents the largest obstacle to any
successful adoption. Most of these problems are treatable or
respond to guidance and early intervention programs. Many
can be prevented when adopting parents are armed with appropriate information and guidance.

In a field as complex and uncertain as international adoption, parents not only need but are entitled to know as much as possible before embarking on the journey. As authors of this book, we feel obliged to withhold nothing, and to tell not only the truth, but the whole truth about foreign adoption. Based on the assumption that no adoption is complete until the child and family have made a strong, loving connection, we not only offer procedural how-tos but also include guidance on what can be done to foster healthy growth and development after adoption. We give special attention to attachment and why it is so important to understand attachment problems in intercountry adoption.

We believe that strong support of foreign adoption is one of the most effective ways to advocate for the multitude of children in this world who are being robbed of the opportunity to be all they can be because they are homeless. When children are deprived of the opportunity to realize their potential, or when that opportunity is fettered, whether by excessive red tape of a bureaucracy or by neglectful caregiving practices, the results are the same. These children are not only robbed of their childhoods, in itself a great tragedy, but can never fully develop as individuals, family members, or members or their communities. We take the position that without homes and loving parents, these children will never have that opportunity. Homes and families are the key.

—BARBARA B. BASCOM, M.D., and
CAROLE A. McKELVEY, M.A.

Foreword

by Janice Tomlin

Producer, ABC News *Turning Point* and *20/20*

In my 20-year career as a journalist, no other story has turned my life upside down like this one. No other story has taken hold of my head—and my heart—like the children trapped in Romania's orphanages and institutions.

Just days after the revolution in December 1989, I was in Romania with an ABC News television crew, filming a segment in warehouses filled with babies. In the "showcase" orphanage in Bucharest, there were more than eight hundred children under the age of three. As I entered one room after another, children would cry out "Mama, Mama" and raise their arms to be picked up. By the end of the week, I had traveled from orphanage to orphanage, and seen row after row of metal cribs, each one filled with children rocking back and forth to comfort themselves. For more than 100,000 Romanian children, this was the only life they knew.

After "Nobody's Children" was broadcast on *20/20* in April 1990, we were flooded with tens of thousands of letters and phone calls. It seemed everyone wanted to adopt one of these children. To be on the receiving end of this outpouring was exhausting, but gratifying. Every journalist would like to think they really can change the world, and this was one instance when I felt our program had made a huge impact. Americans headed over to Romania and children began to be adopted. We covered the homecomings in airports all over this country. These scenes were inspiring, yet the adoption situation in Romania was still a source of frustration. Some children were being rescued, but not in the numbers that I had hoped and prayed for.

The simple fact was that adoption in Romania wasn't easy. Prospective parents were forced to track down the birth parents who had abandoned the child in the orphanage and then obtain their signatures on court documents. Complicated paperwork and bewildering court hearings where required. Then entry visas from the U.S. embassy had to be obtained. It was a time-consuming, frustrating proposition in a country with over-whelming logistical obstacles. But several hundred children were brought to the United States by determined couples who refused to give up.

A year later, I was back in Romania. This time, we arrived unannounced in institutions all across the country, and found a horror show. Naked children, tied to their beds or crowded into cribs. Children drugged, covered with flies, lying in urine and feces. Children left to die in the basements. It was as if we had stumbled on Auschwitz. We left stunned. This time, I knew—I knew—there would be outrage around the world and the doors of these orphanages would be flung wide open. Finally, all of these kids would be rescued. In 1991, we broadcast "Shame of a Nation." In it, we told the story of Vasile, now Michael Goldberg, a child with a club foot who was deemed "unsalvageable" and destined for a life of institutionalized neglect. At age four, he was rescued by a Toronto couple. This is one of the success stories detailed in this book written by Barbara Bascom and Carole McKelvey.

But, I'm sorry to say that Vasile's story still isn't what usually happens. Vasile was in the right place at the right time. First, he caught Dr. Bascom's attention, who then made a plea for a family before our cameras, and a stockbroker who happened to be watching our broadcast "Shame of a Nation" decided to aggressively pursue his adoption. Only a handful of special-needs children have gotten out of Romania. Most of the faces you have seen on American television are still waiting for homes, or they have died.

As I write this in 1996, many children have been adopted but there are still 100,000 children in the orphanages and institutions of Romania. This is a "lost generation" of children who are growing up without families to love them. A committee has been set up in Romania to handle adoptions and, though it is a tediously slow process, one by one, children are being placed with families. There are more than twenty adoption agencies in the United States that are authorized to work with the Romanian Adoption Committee. This is the only way at the present time to adopt children from that country. Perhaps this is the most frustrating thing. I have had to accept that despite everything, including all of the reports on American television and the many people who want to adopt, the majority of the institutionalized children of Romania are still there. So far there is no happy ending to this story.

Still, I would like to end this on a positive note. I have personally talked with hundreds of families who have successfully adopted children from foreign countries, such as from Romania, Russia, China, Hungary, Korea, Peru, Paraguay, Vietnam, Mexico. I don't know of many cases in which the process was easy, but, in the end, the adoptions became reality. It takes patience and money, a translator you can trust, or an accredited adoption agency that will negotiate all the bureaucracy and paperwork necessary to adopt a child legally. Many prospective parents have called me to express surprise, and sometimes anger, after learning it can cost well over $15,000 to "save" a child.

Finally, a word of advice. If you are interested in adopting a child in a foreign country that you have never been to before, please beware of people who seem "too good to be true." If a stranger came up to you in the Atlanta airport and promised you a baby for $1,000, would you give him the money? Of course not. You should apply the same common sense to a similar situation in Romania and other countries. Most important, you should ask questions, review medical records, and realize that years of institutionalization can take a toll on a young child. I know many, many success stories, but I also know of heartbreaking cases where well-meaning, loving parents have discovered too late that giving a child "plenty of love and good food" doesn't always undo the trauma of abandonment and abuse.

I know these things because I am one of the many adoptive parents who have experienced foreign adoption firsthand. In 1992, I was in an orphanage in Romania that I had visited during my first trip after the revolution. Although the walls had been painted with Disney murals, there were still almost a thousand children inside. In the course of our filming, I picked up an infant who was crying, a little girl, it turned out, who weighed five pounds—despite the fact that she was five months old. She had spent her short life lying on her back, fed by a bottle filled with powdered milk propped up on a pillow. I don't know if she had ever been held before, but she grabbed my finger as if her life depended on it. Perhaps it did.

Three months later, I named her Marisa and she became my daughter. She is now a happy, healthy four-year-old who embraces life with a vengeance. But in her eyes, I see all the Marisas who continue to wait. As she grows, I am haunted by the thought that she might have been among the lost children of Romania—children I pray for every night as I close my eyes. I still hold on to the hope that one day all of these children will get a chance at life. But the rescue, it seems, will have to be one child at a time.

Dr. Barbara Bascom has dedicated the past seven years to the children of Romania. Through her efforts, children are finally getting a second chance. Perhaps her work will ultimately succeed in opening the doors of Romania's orphanages, and make certain every single one of the children who needs institutional care is treated with love and respect. As she talks about Vasile and Anamaria and all the children who have captured her heart, I have the distinct feeling she will spend the rest of her life trying.

THE COMPLETE
GUIDE TO
FOREIGN
ADOPTION

Introduction

Through the Golden Door

. . . Give me your tired, your poor,
Your huddled masses yearning to breathe free,
The wretched refuse of your teeming shore,
Send these, the homeless, tempest-tost to me,
I lift my lamp beside the golden door!

From "The New Collosus," 1883,
the Statue of Liberty poem by Emma Lazarus

If today is an average day, thirty children from foreign countries will step over the line at the arrival halls of America's international airports. If today is an average day, thirty children will pass through customs and immigration, held tightly by new parents, none of whom would look much like them. Their passports will be new and glossy, with only one visa stamp inside.

"Welcome to the United States," the customs official will say to one of the children.

"Welcome back," he will say to the child's parents.

If today is an average day, thirty children of foreign adoption will be "coming home" to a family for the first time in their lives.

More and more, the airplanes of today are transporting this special group of travelers from the world's developing countries. From Vietnam, Cambodia, Korea, China, Bosnia, Guatemala, and Russia, children are being brought into homes throughout America. If today is an average day, some will arrive at New York's JFK, several at Atlanta, two or three at Washington DC's Dulles, and a pretty big bunch at Los Angeles's LAX. But if they were all together, assembled for a group photo,

1

for example, the photographer would marvel at their diversity. There would be eyes of several shapes and skins of every color. Some of the children who were old enough to talk would be speaking in a language never heard before. A bystander would wonder where they were from.

If the children who come in today are an average group of thirty foreign adoptees . . . nearly half will be from Asia. Ten will be from eastern Europe, the Russian Federation, and the old USSR states, now called the NIS (New Independent States). Two will be from Central America. Five will be from South America. Although about two a week come from the Caribbean and Mexico, and an African child arrives about once every four days, none of today's children will have come from those countries.[1]

Of the ten children who come from eastern Europe, eight will be Gypsies. They will look much like the children from India, which is where the Rom (or Gypsy) culture originated before they migrated to Europe in the fourteenth century. None of the Gypsy children will be wearing a flowered scarf or brightly colored skirt. None of them will ever have lived in a painted wagon or danced the *hora* around a Gypsy fire. They will, instead, have come from institutions, and their birth families, most likely, are part of the impoverished Gypsy population of Romania, Ukraine, Bulgaria, or Russia.

All thirty children have lived at least part of their lives in some type of institution. Most have never lived in a home or slept in anything other than a crib, no matter how old they are. Several of the children (perhaps six or seven) will be rocking from side to side while they wait for the photographer to set up his camera. When he is ready, the children will smile, as if they are accustomed to having their picture taken.

Except for the babies less than nine months old (there will be three of those, all from China), all of the children will look small for their age. Three of the children (all boys) will have some type of physical disability. One will be older and sit quietly in a wheelchair. He might have on a new pair of cowboy boots.

If today is an average day, more than one-third of the arriving children will be from a former eastern bloc nation. Most of their new parents will have seen a television program or read a graphic article about the plight of children trapped in brutal institutions. They responded, instinctively, to human and spiritual motives and made the sacrifices necessary to provide a home and heal a wounded child. Nine of those ten families will experience the unique joy and fulfillment of watching that child heal and grow.

If today is an average day, however, one boy of the group from eastern Europe will be very fearful and keep apart from the others as well as his adoptive parents. When his mother attempts to bring him into the group, he will begin to cry. The scene will resemble one that took place several years ago, when another boy cried and could not be comforted by his new mother.

His name was Serge. He was five years old when he came to a childless couple from New Jersey. His country of origin was the Ukraine, where he had been institutionalized since infancy. Two and a half years after the adoption, his parents were interviewed:

"I think we went into the adoption very well informed, with the exception that nowhere along the lines of looking into adoption did we come upon any information indicating to us that something so drastically wrong could occur with what otherwise looks like a perfectly healthy child.

"I think," says his mother, "that we did what most parents do: we read lots of books, networked, researched, thought about it, jumped through all hoops, were ready, prepared, and wanted to do this.

"The adoption has gone badly from the beginning," his mother says. Serge had virtually no "honeymoon period" and burst into tears the minute he was introduced to his new parents. "Several times, during our stay in the Ukraine, we seriously reconsidered; but we didn't feel in any position to be able to refuse to take him.

"We said, 'Well, he is very small, the food is bad, his boots are too small and he has difficulty walking outside because of that.' It was easy to say to ourselves, 'Once he's out of this environment, he'll be fine.'"

But Serge has never been "fine." After arriving in his new home, evaluations would demonstrate that Serge was severely mentally disturbed. Currently, the child has so much self-abusive and aggressive behavior that the adoption is in jeopardy. He is considered a danger to himself and others in his household.

"We felt we were prepared for what we thought were difficulties of adopting an older child from overseas. We were ready for the trouble, but I don't think anyone could be ready for this," Serge's mother said, as she ended the interview.[2]

Serge's family did everything right. No one told them, however, about the mental health problems older children of institutions could have. All they had as far as background information on Serge when they adopted the boy was that he was "healthy." No psychological information was provided by the adoption agency or the orphanage. No one provided any guidance during the transition period while the family was in the Ukraine.

Although Serge's condition is unusually severe, the fact that he was not "just fine" or that his problems did not correct themselves after a few months in his new home is not unusual. If today is an average day, more than half of the children who arrive will still be struggling with health or developmental problems two years from now. And so will their parents.

The four most common long-term problems in all foreign adopted children—the ABCDs of foreign adoption—are:

Attachment disorders.

Hepatitis **B** leads the list of serious infectious diseases.

Challenged children: physical disabilities, acquired or due to birth defects, chronic health conditions, sensory handicaps.

Developmental disorders.

If today is an average day, all of the children in the group of thirty will have health problems except two. Over half (55–60 percent) will have "serious medical problems."[3] Nine will have intestinal parasites, all of which will clear with medication after a period of time. One out of ten who had positive skin tests for tuberculosis will test positive for the disease. Ten will have positive screens for hepatitis B antigen, and one will have active disease. Although the reported incidence varies from country to country, hepatitis B is endemic in all developing countries involved in foreign adoption. HIV or AIDS is not often seen in adopted children due to foreign, in-country screening and U.S. immigration restrictions. Some children with histories of repeated transfusions (common practice, for example, in Romania until 1991) with unscreened blood may develop seroconversion (conversion of a previously negative blood screening test to positive, sometimes months or years later).

Eye and ear problems top the list of noninfectious diseases and include strabismus (crossed eyes) and chronic otitis (ear infection). Three to 5 percent of foreign adoptees have some degree of hearing loss. Neurological conditions, if lumped together, occur in 15 percent. They include seizure disorders, mental deficiency, and cerebral palsy (CP). Birth defects and postpolio syndromes (residual weakness) lead the list of diagnoses in physically challenged children. The most common birth defect is limb abnormality. Cleft palate is also common and is seen in greater frequency in regions where there was prenatal radiation exposure; for example, older children from Chernobyl fallout regions of eastern and central Europe. Renal (kidney), gastrointestinal (other than hepatitis), orthopedic (bone and joint), and cardiac (heart) problems are seen in higher frequency among foreign adoptees than in U.S.-born children. There are recent reports that some children with severe gastrointestinal symptoms may have rare but virulent infections.

Correctable nutritional deficiencies are very common and include: protein/calorie malnutrition, poor weight gain ("organic failure to thrive"), vitamin deficiencies (rickets most common from vitamin D deficiency), and iron deficiency anemia. Persistent growth deficiency with growth hormone deficiency related to psychosocial deprivation ("psychosocial dwarfism") is not uncommon in children who have been emotionally deprived.

Developmental delay is the most common problem in all foreign adopted children, although some exception should be made for children under the age of six months and children raised in loving homes (true orphans, for example). Most (60–70 percent) *true delays* in development are reversible within twenty-four months of placement, but information is insufficient to make long-term predictions regarding this group. Outcomes are related to the age of the child and the length of time in institutions. Overuse of the term "delay" is rampant in eastern Europe, NIS, and Russia. It is most often misapplied to children with developmental *disability*, including older children with moderate to severe mental retardation.

Mild developmental disabilities, such as borderline mental (cognitive, intellectual) functioning and learning disability with hyperactivity are very common. Because language and communication is the most sensitive area of development in deprived children (sensory and/or emotional deprivation), residual language deficits and language-based learning disorders lead the list of more severe developmental learning problems in children after adoption. Although the severe developmental disorder "autism" or "pervasive developmental disorder" (a psychiatric disorder) was previously reported in only a small percentage of cases of foreign adopted children, the reported incidence has significantly increased since eastern Europe became a major source of adopted children. Some of the children with this diagnosis, however, are assigned the label in order to qualify them for services. Autism is an "official" developmental disability— and many disturbed children are called autistic because their symptoms bear the closest resemblance to already described diseases.

Although not classified (technically) as a developmental problem, there are several reports of foreign-adopted children who are intellectually gifted and/or exceptionally talented, particularly in music. This group of children have special needs and entitlements of their own. The relative degree of social immaturity that many gifted American children display is much more significant in foreign-born children. Therefore, the gap between intellectual and social skills is much wider in this group of children, raising many issues in educational planning and programs.

Dominating the mental health problems in foreign adoptees is "reactive attachment disorder" (failure of the adopted child to make emotional attachments to his new parents) and a combined disorder of attachment failure with pervasive developmental delays. In this book, the latter problem is referred to as "developmental attachment disorder" because this condition does not satisfy criteria for previously described definitions. In its developmental components, language is always most severely affected.

Other mental health conditions include: PTSD (post-traumatic stress disorder), ADHD (attention deficit hyperactive disorder), conduct and character disorders, oppositional behavior disorder, and childhood psychoses. PTSD is seen more often when there is a history of abuse (experienced or witnessed) or when the institution was severely neglectful, committed atrocities or had high mortality rates, and the children in question repeatedly witnessed the events associated with those conditions. There are increasing numbers of reports of sexual abuse in postinstitutionalized children over the age of three.

Since 1990, both professionals and parents have been caught unaware by the complexity and severity of mental health problems, like Serge's, in the post-institutionalized child. To compound the problem, the various disorders that fall under this category are still undergoing classification and reclassification, and precise diagnosis is often difficult. Multiple disciplines are involved, including psychology, psychiatry, education, social sciences, occupational therapy, and developmental pediatrics. Each has its own language (terminology) and approach to intervention. Because the professional community remains divided in both opinion and theory, particularly regarding attachment disorders, parents are frequently subjected to conflicting opinions and advice.

Although the condition is very old, the field of study utilizing current standards is very young. Other than "strictly medical" surveys and several developmental studies, there is a paucity of current research on the topic of institutionalization and its effects on the mental health of children. It will be years before we do know the long-term results or outcomes of today's children from intercountry adoption. Parents, however, have formed networks and organizations and have achieved some solidarity in approaching the many problems their adopted children present.[4]

In follow-up surveys of limited numbers, however, patterns are emerging that provide a window to the future. Current case follow-up material, for example, strongly suggests that the child with a combined developmental disability and attachment disorder but no secondary or additional psychiatric problems has a better prognosis for response to therapy than the child like Serge, who has multiple psychiatric diagnoses, including so-called conduct or character disorders. This is particularly true if the former child receives *appropriate* intervention for his developmental problems. Appropriate therapy may include, for example, sensory integrative therapy for the symptomatic, sensory-deprived child, language therapy (*not speech correction or articulation therapy*), and specialized early education or play therapy for developmental or learning problems.

The critical factor in intervention, and the necessary service upon which all else depends, is guidance for the family. In seeking guidance, however, adopting parents should know that issues remain in both diagnosis and intervention. Still controversial are:

- ◆ Diagnosis: When to do the first evaluation, how to evaluate and which assessments or measurements are valid, appropriate disease classification (the label), when to rely on allied health practitioners or interdisciplinary teams, when to refer to a "subspecialist" such as a developmental pediatrician, pediatric psychiatrist, or child neurologist.
- ◆ Intervention and/or treatment: method or mode of therapy, traditional versus "nontraditional" therapeutic approaches, use of psychopharmacologic agents, multi- versus unidisciplinary approaches, access to therapy for children with severe language/communication deficits, whether "alternative" therapies are snake oil or sometimes helpful, denial of access to therapy for financial reasons.

Despite the knowledge and experience gained during the past four years in both sending and receiving countries, countless children continue to arrive in the countries of their new parents with inadequate medical records. While most of the records are just inadequate, there are reports of deliberate falsification of records to enhance a child's adoptability or to cover up conditions in the sending country. Some items that may be deliberately removed or never included in a child's record are:

◆ Exposure to environmental hazards, such as radiation or lead exposure.

◆ Failure to complete immunizations (donated vaccines have been diverted to black market).

◆ Use of "developmental delay" instead of mental deficiency because of Western country quotas or immigration restrictions.

◆ The true scope of communicable disease conditions in institutions, even when the epidemiology is known, is not included; hepatitis B is one example.

The political sensitivity of many of these issues only adds to the pattern of suppression. Deprived of vital information and embroiled in day-by-day efforts to help the children, caregivers, both parental and professional, often find it difficult to be politically correct. As a result, the gap between government bureaucracy and the caregiving community tends to widen rather than narrow.

It is undeniable that marked improvement has been made in the condition of the world's children since 1990 when the story of Romania's orphans broke and a new age of intercountry adoption began. The tragedy has had far-reaching impact: Foreign-aid programs have reestablished priority on long-term development, with children and youth as beneficiaries. Social change is beginning in the larger arena of human rights for the child and the disabled.

Still:

◆ More than a hundred million children are living on the streets of the world's cities. It is not yet known how many of these children are legally adoptable. Most of them, however, are abandoned.

◆ War in Bosnia, Afghanistan, Rwanda, and other countries has created another generation of orphans and children with traumatic physical and psychological injury. Amputation, for example, is one of the most common physical injuries seen in war orphans and most often occurs when children play in fields where mines were buried. Children of war often suffer psychological injury as well; many, like veterans of Vietnam, suffer from post-traumatic stress disorder.

♦ Despite the major improvements in Romania's orphanages since 1992, admissions remain high due to socioeconomic conditions and a persistent "mentality" to institutionalize the disabled child. Most of the children pictured in 20/20 and other major media productions of the early nineties *are still there*.

♦ Despite worldwide improvement in maternal-child care, the frequency of low-birth-weight births remains high throughout the developing world. Most of these babies are *not* premature. Low-birth-weight babies, however, are almost always misdiagnosed as premature; as a group, they are at higher risk for many health and developmental problems and are a hundred times more likely to end up in institutions where their failure to thrive worsens.

♦ Gypsy families continue to be persecuted, incarcerated in concentration camps, and forced to live in severe poverty throughout the world. In eastern Europe, especially, a disproportionate number of Gypsy children are institutionalized.

♦ Gender bias and prejudice continues throughout the world.

If today is an average day, how many unwanted Chinese girl babies will be born on this date? How many of those will be taken to orphanages? If a total of 856 were adopted into American households in 1994, and if the current trend continues, how many will come home to America in the next five years?

If today is an average day, three of the thirty children who stepped over the line at immigration will be Chinese children or babies. All of them would be girls, and one might be a little girl like Hayley Rose QiaoQiao Lansing, who hails from Hunan Province, China. Her new parents tell quite a story:

The Lansings had been flirting with the idea of adopting since the early years of their marriage, but along came Lauren and then Justin, now ten and twelve years old. "We had thought about the idea of adding to our family, but with age and the risk, we decided against another natural child," says Pete Lansing, CEO of a lending company in a large midwestern town.

"I do volunteer work on the boards of two organizations that help troubled, high-risk children, and we had thought about adopting one of those children. But we wanted to be able to keep our busy lifestyle and we weren't sure we could do that with a child who had such severe problems."

With their family very settled and happy, Suzanne and Peter rekindled their fascination with the idea of adopting a foreign child when a close friend of Suzanne's, Marie, told them she was adopting from China.

"We heard what Marie was doing, and it intrigued us," says Peter. His wife, Suzanne, had been a reference for Marie, her lifelong friend, when she decided to adopt. "These were children who needed help. Then, Suzanne came to me, asking if we couldn't also do this.

"All along it had been my desire to adopt and take care of another child as a father. I really enjoy parenthood. And my first reaction was—YES! YES! YES! Let's do this. Hey, I go off every day and go to work. The majority of this work [child care] will be her mother's job. I would have done this five years ago, but when it was *her* idea, that did it.

"It [adoption] was something we had talked about a lot as a couple. We felt this was the perfect opportunity to help someone, bring love to someone, change someone's life. We felt we could make a life better for another little person. I guess it's kind of the prejudiced, American way—to feel it is the better way here. But as you go through the process of adopting a foreign child, you start to become more realistic. We became part of this wonderful process that I would tell everybody to do. Once we started thinking about the idea we plunged in, finding out everything we could."

Approximately six months of paperwork later, and a lot of investigation and fact-finding, the Lansings—all four of them—found themselves on a plane to the Far East. They were on their way to pick up their new daughter, a baby named QiaoQiao from a rural community in the south of China. They had seen only a small picture of her when they left for China. Because of the remoteness of the area, the family wasn't able to visit QiaoQiao's orphanage, but were to meet with orphanage workers and finally see their new baby in the larger community of Changsha.

After some official meetings and with the paperwork completed and the adoption official in China, the family set off with agency workers in two taxicabs to rendezvous with QiaoQiao and three of her caregivers in a small hotel. Pete says that in the excitement of the moment, he left a satchel in the taxicab, with *all of their paperwork!* This included:

◆ four American passports
◆ four visas
◆ five airplane tickets
◆ all their cash, amounting to $1,300
◆ the official adoption documents

Pete Lansing realized the error just as the cab drove away. "There was major panic. We didn't know, first of all, whether or not we were going to be able to get our daughter. Also, we didn't know if we could get out of China. I went nuts. I had this terrible vision of us becoming missionaries in China, *all of us.* What a disaster, what a stupid mistake," he says in retrospect.

"Of all the things that can go wrong in the process of adoption in a foreign country," thought Lansing, "this is probably the worst scenario. Stuck in China with no baby, no papers, no proof of American citizenship, and no money." The family even went on local television in China to try to find their missing paperwork. "But," Lansing says, "in such a third-world country there is virtually no infrastructure. There was no local police station to go to so we could not trace the cab. Everything was gone and stayed gone."

The Lansings give full credit for their "rescue" to their adoption agency. The Chinese Children's Adoption International in Littleton, Colorado, came through like champs. They convinced the hotel to loan the family $1,000 in American cash, sent duplicates of all the missing paperwork, and made sure all the adoption papers were reissued.

"One lost day later, we finally were able to meet our beautiful daughter and receive her," Pete says.

Once the Lansings saw Hayley they were in for quite a surprise. The birth date they had received was February 21, 1994. This was July 1995, and they had expected a toddler. What they had was an infant, a very small infant. Hayley, it turned out, was ten months younger than they expected. Instead of a seventeen-month-old toddler, they had a seven-month-old baby.

"The joke was on us; her birth date had been translated incorrectly. Oh, she was adorable, but the suitcase of seventeen-month-old clothes that we took just drooped on her. It was comical. We just decided to stay flexible. Because of others in our group who had taken the trip at the same time, we received instant supplies and support.

"I still had my video camera and I took pictures of everyone. So that Hayley could see who she had been with her first year, I asked the orphanage caregivers to say good-bye to her into the camera and give their wishes for her future. It was such a wonderful moment. Here was this dad, behind the camera, crying."

The Lansings have nothing but praise for the way the Chinese people treated them as Americans who had come to China to adopt. "Everyone was so great to us, particularly after the taxicab fiasco. And the orphanage workers, they were so thoughtful. One of them was wearing a particular perfume. Before she handed Hayley to my wife, she sprayed Suzanne with some of the perfume. Then, when Hayley was handed over, my wife smelled familiar."

Baby Hayley was very confused when the couple first met her. She had been out of the orphanage for the first time and there was all this commotion. Despite this "Hayley bonded with us right away," Pete says. "We all took turns giving her a bottle and she loved it. Within hours she was laughing and giggling with us."

Pete Lansing says the most moving piece of film he shot that day in Changsha, China, was of a young fifteen-year-old orphanage worker with the group. "She was young enough to be an orphan herself. When I asked her to say what she wanted for Hayley, she said: 'I want for you to go to America and have a good life and grow up and learn English and some

Chinese and then maybe someday you can return to China and be an ambassador so our two countries can be closer.'

"The experience of adopting this child has been wonderful. Our family is so excited to have another grandchild, particularly one from China," says Hayley's dad. "We feel so lucky to have Hayley in our lives today."[5]

Except for the adventure in the taxicab, the Lansing adoption is a happy story, just like most foreign adoption stories. Hayley arrived with only a few residual problems due to malnutrition and those are quickly resolving. A hepatitis scare turned out to be false. She is quickly attaching to her new family.

Hayley Lansing will be a welcome addition to her midwestern community. Like Ana Dorr, the physically challenged child from Romania (chapter 6) who now rides her horse in Indiana, or Michael Vasile Goldberg (chapter 1) who has no hint of disability when he walks into his special education class, the children of foreign adoption are adding a richness and diversity to American culture. Disability is as much part of that diversity as ethnic and cultural differences.

Hayley may not grow up to be an ambassador. Michael Vasile may not go to Harvard. Ana Dorr, whose birth defects left her without hands, may not consider her new "bionic arm" from Shriners Hospital as perfect as five real fingers. All of these children, however, and thousands of others like them, have been given the gift of a family and have thus reclaimed their childhoods. All of their parents, and thousands of adoptive parents like them, would agree with Gene Goldberg when he said "It's a wonderful thing to save a child." Even parents like Lori Eisinger (chapter 4), who came to Romania too soon to take advantage of today's knowledge, would do it over again, knowing what she knows today. Although Di Di Eisinger cannot be completely healed and her family struggles daily with the pain of her illness, all of us are "better off," including Di Di, because of their experience.

∽

It is estimated that the names of more than five million people are on waiting lists of the world's adoption agencies. By the end

of 1996, if this is an average year, two million Americans will
have applied to adopt a child. Faced with diminishing domestic
options, many will join the waiting parents of other Western
countries—Ireland, France, Italy, Scandinavia, to name a
few—to seek an international adoption. And, if this is a typical
year, many will be successful. Each year of the past decade,
more than eight thousand children from more than fifty foreign
countries have been adopted by American parents.

Since the early eighties, international adoption has represented a rising percentage of total adoptions in the United
States.[6] The increasing incidence of infertility is only one factor
in the recent growth of international adoption. Historically,
American families have long responded to the needs of the
world's disenfranchised and neglected children through volun-
teerism, child sponsorship, and donor support to humanitarian
organizations. During the past twenty years, foreign adoption
has been a significant part of that humanitarian response.

Since 1980, airplanes have carried increasing numbers of foreign babies and children to the United States from strange cities
like Bucharest, Lima, Beijing, Seoul, and Kiev. Instead of tour-
ists and businessmen, the flights' passenger lists are now dominated by adopted children and their new parents. Throughout
the international community, these flights are called "baby
flights."

On any "baby flight," passengers observe the entire spectrum
of foreign adoption: joy, fear, frustration, fatigue, relief, and fulfillment. Dressed in American clothes and often the first pair of
shoes ever worn, babies and children are getting to know their
new parents. The scene is rife with new beginnings and happy
endings to stories of hopelessness. For most parents, the baby
flight is a joyful experience, similar to the beautiful, early bonding of new mothers with newborn babies.

For others, however, the baby flight is the first step into a
maze of uncertainty and unmet expectations. On these occasions, bewildered and terrified children are seen being held
tightly by exhausted, frightened new mothers. Their concerns
of the past few weeks have abruptly switched from the frustrations of foreign travel and the adoption process to a frantic

worry about the deeper problems the child may harbor as a result of deprivation and neglect.

Despite the huge humanitarian effort taking place in foreign orphanages, and despite the advances made in child development and rehabilitation technologies in the West for the past few decades, most parents feel ill prepared to meet the challenges of parenting high-risk and wounded children from abroad. The majority of adopting families receive very little information or guidance about their new children—before, during, or after adoption. Almost none of them are given guidance to assist them through transition. Misinformed, ill informed and uninformed, it is not surprising that adopting families have found it so difficult to parent their new children.

Foreign adoption is doing its part to deinstitutionalize the world's children. Foreign-aid programs continue to do the job they came to do and establish the kind of programs that will prevent the wounds suffered by Di Di and Serge and so many others described in this book. Children who need intervention, like Anamaria (chapter 5) are well on their way to healing long before leaving the country.

If these current trends continue, children will no longer continue to deteriorate while they wait through a series of six-month delays imposed by adoption regulations. In many orphanages, today's adoptive parents have the added benefit of knowing about the child's response to intervention while they were institutionalized. This not only provides help in making final adoption decisions but also provides invaluable clues to future case management and long-term prognosis for both the adopted child and his new adoptive family.

Foreign-aid workers who have lived and worked in institutions are accustomed to "miracle stories"; they are, for example, everyday fare in Romania's institutions. Children who previously lived in inhuman conditions have repeatedly demonstrated an inner spirit and a resilience so astonishing that rational, scientific explanations are impossible. Miraculous outcomes, however, are not so much a product of what has been done *for* children as they are products of what has been discovered *within* the children themselves. Said Greti Dorr, in an interview about Adriana (Ana Dorr), her adopted daughter: "I could tell just by her face in the picture [in *People*] that she had a spirit about her."[7]

When that human spirit is allowed its fullest expression through adoption, as it is most of the time, international adoption is successful. That "spirit about them" is the promise of foreign adoption.

It will be years before professionals can unlock the secrets and meet all the challenges of postinstitutionalized children. The day may never come that all their problems are solved. With the help of enlightened, well-informed parents, however, tomorrow may be an average day: Thirty more children will walk or be carried out of institutions, board a baby flight with their new adoptive parents, and each of those thirty children will have a better chance at recovery when they pass through the golden door.

On July 4, 1995, more than two hundred families who have adopted Romanian children gathered in Orlando, Florida, to hold their third biennial reunion. After three days of workshops and activities in the Disney theme parks, they held a final ceremony to celebrate the nation's birthday and their children's U.S. citizenship. Most of all, on that final day, they came to celebrate their children.

The day's festivities began in the early morning with ABC's *Good Morning, America* broadcast. While conference participants were interviewed, pictures flashed across the screen of a pretaped performance of children who remained in Romanian institutions. These children, many of whom couldn't talk four years ago, reached out to their Romanian American cousins and sang the same song to be performed by the Disney Choir and the adopted children that afternoon. Although the program was interrupted, and most of the American public had no idea that the children who were singing were still in Romanian orphanages, what was obvious was that the children knew the meaning of what they were singing. As if the songwriter had known beforehand, it was a perfect expression of the spirit within them. It showed in their faces and rang in their voices.

When the concert was held that afternoon at EPCOT Center, "Childsong" was sung again by the Disney Choir. As the adopted children joined in from the audience, a tiny girl stood up on her chair and did the sign language to the song. Permanently silenced by her past, she had learned to communicate her thoughts and feelings with her hands.

Finally, it had happened. Children who had been sung about, talked about, interpreted, misinterpreted, analyzed, and publicized for five years were able to express themselves. The children sang their song:

> *Weeping sky*
> *We bring the sun*
> *To make you glad*
> *And fill you with the day*
>
> *Quiet tree*
> *We have the wind*
> *To make you dance*
> *And fill you with our play*
>
> *And you shall be glad!*
> *And you shall dance!*
> *And you shall come*
> *To hear our song*
> *And learn its tune*
> *Before it fades away*
>
> "Childsong," from *Taproot Manuscript*[8]
> Words and music by Neil Diamond

GLOSSARY

Allied health practitioners: Nonphysician professionals in the health field.

Attention deficit hyperactive disorder (ADHD): Attention span deficits of problems with hyperactivity. Usually results in or is associated with learning disability.

Autism: A psychiatric disorder of infancy and early childhood characterized by self-absorption, profound withdrawal from contact with people, severe communication deficits, a preoccupation with inanimate objects and developmental language disorders. Classified as a *perva-*

sive developmental disorder; usually present at birth, becomes symptomatic by age three; 75 percent of autistic children have mental deficiency. Treatment is psychotherapeutic and special education. Prognosis is related to cognitive (intellectual) ability.

Baby flight: The colloquial or slang term for international airplane flights in which passenger lists are dominated by newly adopted children and their parents.

Cleft palate: A congenital birth defect in which a child is born with an opening or fissure in the palate or roof of the mouth. Often associated with cleft lip ("harelip"). Due to failure of normal closure of tissue in embryonic life. Multiple causes; may be associated with other abnormalities or syndromes or radiation exposure in early fetal life (first trimester of pregnancy); increased incidence in eastern Europe following Cernobyl disaster. Causes secondary problems with feeding, speech. Treatment is surgical repair and long-term medical therapy for associated problems.

Conduct disorders: Special behavioral disorders of childhood in which the child exhibits undesirable and antisocial conduct; disturbed behavior in one or more of following: aggression, deceitfulness, destructiveness, severe violation of rules.

Deprivation: Denial or lack of adequate stimulation to the degree that development is impaired in the sphere of deprivation. *Sensory deprivation* refers to deprivation of touch, movement experience, or special senses—auditory, visual etc. *Emotional deprivation* refers to withholding or denial of affection and social interaction. Social and sensory deprivation are usually combined in grossly neglectful circumstances, such as institutions.

Developmental delay: Slow or late development in one or several areas of development. When all areas (i.e., motor, language, mental or cognitive and social) are delayed, is referred to as *global developmental delay.* Causes may be environmental (i.e., deprivation), physical (chronic illness) or constitutional ("late bloomers," late walkers, etc.). If persistent, becomes *developmental disability (DD).* Development usually normalizes within two years if appropriate intervention is provided. Occasionally resolves spontaneously. The most common problem among all foreign adopted children.

Developmental attachment disorder: A combined disorder of attachment and developmental deficits; used in this book to describe the constellation of problems seen in post-institutionalized children from grossly neglectful environments in infancy and early childhood. As an attachment disorder, incorporates developmental sequelae not seen in reactive attachment disorder alone. Previously undescribed as a single entity.

Honeymoon period: In adoption, refers to the time period following the child's arrival in the new home and family; interval during which the child is usually on his/her best behavior and is not exhibiting disruptive behaviors. Some children never go through this period, others can be on a "honeymoon" with the family for almost a year. The average time ranges from three to six months.

Interdisciplinary teams: Professional teams, made up of multiple disciplines, who practice (work) together in a common setting. Commonly found in child development centers, for example, where an occupational therapist, developmental pediatrician, educator and psychologist, etc., work together for purposes of diagnosis and/or treatment of a child with developmental disabilities.

Language therapy: Speech therapy with children with developmental disorders involving language and communication.

Learning disability (LD): Disorder of learning in which school achievement is lowered; may be restricted to one area of learning or development, i.e., dyslexia—reading disability, language learning disability—language LD, etc. Multiple causes, including "minimal brain damage," deprivation, congenital or inheritable conditions. Excludes mental deficiency, although IQ is often in borderline (75–100) range. Often associated with hyperactivity and or attention deficits, perceptual problems, poor self-esteem and poor coordination. Common in post-institutionalized children. Intervention usually involves special education in school-age child. Rarely diagnosed before children enter school.

Oppositional behavior disorder: Behavior disorder of childhood characterized by a recurrent pattern of negativistic, defiant, disobedient and hostile behavior.

Otitis: Inflammation (usually infection) of the ear; most often refers to *middle* ear conditions (*otitis media,* or middle ear infection). Acute otitis is almost always infectious. Chronic otitis usually refers to persistence of fluid in the middle ear cavity (*serous otitis media*) and is related to chronic congestion. Severe recurrent or chronic otitis may result in hearing loss. Treatable. Extremely common in childhood. Often goes undetected and untreated in children in neglectful or institutional settings.

Post-traumatic stress disorder (PTSD): A delayed anxiety disorder, reactive to extreme (i.e., life-threatening), psychologically or physically traumatic circumstances experienced or witnessed by the individual. Occurs in both children and adults. Onset is usually within three months of traumatic event(s), but may be delayed months or years. Duration varies; complete recovery within three months occurs in 50 percent of cases. In children, symptoms may include recurrent nightmares, night terrors, recurring flashbacks during which reenactment of traumatic events occur, detachment from or impaired ability to form attachments to people, extreme pessimism about future, and feelings of betrayal or abandonment of social contacts left behind. (See chapter 4).

Psychopharmacology: The use of various drugs to treat mental health conditions.

Psychosocial dwarfism: A persistent growth deficiency with related growth hormone deficiency caused by emotional deprivation. Usually diagnosed by ruling out any other physical or constitutional causes of growth deficiency. Affects height due to depression of growth centers located in long bones. Treatment is environmental change and emotional nurturing. Usually self-correcting. Some children remain permanently short despite treatment. Growth hormone replacement may be useful in some cases.

Reactive attachment disorder (RAD): The failure of a child to make emotional attachments to parental figures, usually due to neglect or abuse during the first two years of life or from repeated bonding breaks with caregivers, such as multiple moves within the foster-care home system.

Sensory integrative therapy: A type of therapy usually done by occupational therapists for perceptual problems.

Seroconversion: The change of a blood test from negative to positive, indicating the development of antibodies in response to immunization or infection. Sero (serum) conversion.

Strabismus: Crossed eye or eyes. Mild forms often referred to as "lazy eye" in which the eye wanders but is not fixed in the crossed position.

Transition: In adoption, refers to the time period during which a child is moving from the institutional environment (or previous home) to the new family. Involves many events such as making and breaking attachments, separation and loss, adjustment and adaptation, behavior change or modification.

REFERENCES

1. U.S. Immigration and Naturalization Services, Report on Intercountry Adoptions (1985–1995).

2. Pat Donahue, New Jersey, personal interview, fall 1995.

3. M. K. Hostetter, S. Iverson, W. Thomas, D. McKenzie, K. Dole, and D. Johnson, "Medical Evaluation of Internationally Adopted Children," *New England Journal of Medicine* 325, no. 7 (August 1991), pp. 479–484.

4. Parents Network for the Post-Institutionalized Child, T. Tepper, director (see appendix).

5. Peter Lansing, personal interview, September 1995.

6. C. A. McKelvey and J. E. Stevens, *Adoption Crisis: The Truth about Adoption and Foster Care* (Golden, CO: Fulcrum Publishing, 1994), chapter 8, "Foreign Adoptions."

7. CBS, "Where Are They Now?" May 1995.

8. Neil Diamond, "Childsong," from *Taproot Manuscript* (1972), MCA Records, Inc., MCAD-31071. Copyright 1971 Prophet Music, Inc. Los Angeles, CA. All rights reserved.

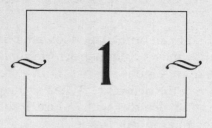

An Overview

Dear Lord
Be good to me
The sea is so wide
And my boat is so small.

Children's Defense Fund, 1991

On October 5, 1990, ABC's newsmagazine *20/20* broadcast a documentary program entitled "The Shame of a Nation." For fifty minutes, more than twenty million U.S. and Canadian viewers watched, stunned, as the story of Romania's so-called unsalvageable orphans graphically unfolded on their television screens.[1] Beyond gates and walls where signs were posted reading "Camin Spital for the Deficient and Irrecuperable," ABC's cameras revealed the shocking, inhuman conditions in which more than 150,000 Romanian children were incarcerated.

In building after building, children fought to survive in cement halls and caged-in rooms without food, warmth, medical care, or any semblance of emotional nurturing from their adult caregivers. Although the program featured the end of the line in former Communist dictator Ceausescu's torturous system of institutional care, the message to the viewing public was clear: Unless these children found loving homes, thousands of them were doomed.

Watching the TV screen in Toronto, Canada, were Eugene and Susan Goldberg. The story of one little boy in a Romanian orphanage captured Gene Goldberg's heart. Vasile, about three, had been admitted to an orphanage soon after birth because of a birth defect known as a club foot deformity. During his first two years, he had undergone a series of unsuccessful attempts to surgically correct the deformity. When subsequent efforts to rehabilitate the child also met with failure, it was evident that time was running out for little Vasile.

Knowing that Vasile would never survive a Camin Spital, or that if he did, he would live in misery, I (Bascom) had encouraged (insisted, maybe) 20/20 to film him for the show. He sat very still while I told the camera crew about his foot problems and tried to explain, in regular language, that much of the deformity was due to the heavy scarring from repeated, unsuccessful surgery. 20/20 reporter Tom Jarriel said it in a few words. He called it "botched surgery," then talked about my "crusade" to find a home for Vasile. Tom was right. Despite the improvements under way at Vasile's orphanage, there was little I could do unless someone adopted him.

Knowing that the complex surgery Vasile needed was not available in Romania, I put out a plea, saying this one small child needed a home and expert medical attention. "Without intervention this child will be sent to an institution for the unsalvageable," I told the TV audience.

"I found the show very painful," Eugene Goldberg said later, "but between my pain and anger and the plea from Dr. Bascom saying this child needs to be out of here, I turned to Susan and said, 'We can do this, we can adopt this child!'

"I knew I was definitely going to go over there and get that child, come hell or high water."

~

I (Bascom) first met Vasile in April 1990, three months before they shot the 20/20 program. In preparation for setting up the ROSES (Romanian Orphans' Social, Educational, and Services) project, I was completing a needs assessment study in Romanian orphanages and was screening children in the Leagane de Copii (Cradle for Children) in the Moldovan city of Iasi.

Vasile was brought to me while I was touring the section of Iasi's orphanage that housed most of the children who were labeled "handicapped." He was hand-carried by a physical therapist, Alice, who put him into my arms and stepped back, waiting for me to respond. Her eyes seemed to seek a solution for this child she had cared for, as best she could, for the past two years.

Alice knew what she was asking. Not only was she the only fully trained physical therapist working in a Leagane in the entire country, but she was also the parent of a beautiful, bright, but physically disabled daughter who could not attend school in Romania because she was wheelchair-bound. She knew both sides of the agony of disability in Romania: the impossible future of institutionalized children and the denial of opportunity to homebound, disabled children in the community.

Like Alice, the plight of Vasile had a personal connection for me. As the adoptive mother of a child born with a club foot deformity, I had experienced the joys and rewards of seeing a son grow up healthy, strong, and free of disability. My son had his first cast when he was only ten days old. A series of surgical procedures had been completed successfully by the time he was seven years old. Today, he can hit a home run for his local softball team and run the bases without a hint of disability. It is no wonder that bright-eyed Vasile touched my heart. There, but for the grace of God, went my son Erich.

Although the United States had its institutions when Erich was adopted, and although he might have gone to a children's home had I not adopted him, there was nothing in America that approached the atrocity of Romanian Camin Spitals.

I didn't know much about the institutions for the so-called *irrecuperable* when I first met Vasile in April 1990. At that time, my focus was on the Leaganes (orphanages) where my project was being developed. Words like "irrecuperable" were not in my vocabulary until three months later, when I was invited to join 20/20 for "The Shame of a Nation." During that tour, I saw my first Camin Spital and met the children who were called irrecuperable. It was a week of unspeakable horror.

Until that week, I had not fully understood why Vasile's physical therapist, Alice, had been so eager to have me "consult" on his case. When I held him on my lap for the 20/20 filming, however, I realized what she wanted. She wanted me to help her rescue him. He was nearly three years old, and when he turned three he would be labeled "irrecuperable" and sent to the Camin Spital that Romanian doctors called the Auschwitz of Romania.

On October 7, two nights after "The Shame of a Nation" aired in the United States, I returned to my hotel room in Boston, where I was attending the annual meeting of the American Academy of Pediatrics. When I dialed in for my messages, a machine voice told me, "You have forty-seven messages." Message number one was Eugene Goldberg. So were messages twelve and twenty-three. He wanted to know if he was too late to "speak for" Vasile.

In 1990, most Romanians couldn't believe a family would want to adopt a handicapped child like Vasile. Such children had long been considered defective and "unadoptable" in the formerly Communist country. Most disabled children and children with birth defects were institutionalized from the time of birth. Because rehabilitation was seldom provided in institutions, their names rarely, if ever, appeared as adoption candidates. Furthermore, if disabled babies and young children survived until age three in the orphanages, they were usually sent to Camin Spitals, where they received no services at all. When the meager attempts to "repair" Vasile's foot failed, he was considered and truly believed to be "unsalvageable" in the minds of most Romanians. This attitude, often referred to as "the mentality," prevailed throughout eastern Europe and the Soviet Republic.

Because there were (and still are) woefully inadequate resources for disabled children in Romanian communities, nearly all children with special needs were institutionalized soon after birth. Average Romanian families were and still are confronted daily by the specter of poverty, hunger, cold, and lack of opportunity. Families who were marginal in their ability to meet the basic needs of healthy babies were overwhelmed by the birth of a child with special needs.

In 1990 Romania, physically disabled children could not go to public school—even in the cities. The level of poverty and hardship experienced, day after day, by rural families was indescribable. Many rural Gypsies were denied access to village schools. The only alternative for a disabled Gypsy child was institutionalization, and in most institutions, there was no education at all.

Disabled children and adults lived on the periphery of Romanian society. Neither school nor workplace accepted them. When children like Vasile tried to attend school, they were usually ostracized. Gene Goldberg, however, said he was drawn to this one child *because* he was handicapped. "We have two gorgeous, perfectly normal children," he said. "But I thought, we need to get this kid!"

We need to get this kid!

Fueled by this need, his limitless energy, and unswerving determination, Eugene Goldberg was a man with a mission when he came to Romania in December 1990. As he waded through hip-deep mud in the remote villages of northern Romania and searched out maternal relatives to sign papers during one of the coldest winters on record, Goldberg needed every one of those resources.

Once located, Vasile's birth family stirred everyone's compassion. Living in a small village with no paved roads, no public utilities, no access to adequate medical care for nine months out of the year, and no schools for Gypsy children, his father's struggle to provide the barest necessities for the family was enormous. He had many strikes against him. Like Vasile, he had been born with a club foot deformity.

Unlike Vasile, however, Vasile's father had lived a lifetime of disability because of lack of treatment. His challenges had multiplied when his first son, Vasile's older sibling, was born with the same club foot deformity. But the family had somehow met the challenge and kept the older child at home. When Vasile was born with the same condition, however, the overstressed family had simply given up and relinquished him to "the care of the state." Soon after Vasile's admission to the orphanage, his mother disappeared.

Six weeks after his arrival in Romania, Eugene Goldberg accomplished his mission to adopt the little boy who had won his heart six months before on 20/20. Vasile, dressed in padded snowsuit and "moonboots" to fit over his misshapen foot, left the orphanage with his new father. Soon after, father and son boarded the Air Canada baby flight headed for home. Susan Goldberg and the two Goldberg birth children were at the Toronto airport, awaiting their arrival.

Vasile, soon to be renamed Michael, was initially frightened by all the attention at the airport. Then one of his new siblings, Jessica, handed him a bag of popcorn. "This," said 20/20 reporter Tom Jarriel, in another ABC program, "apparently convinced him this group of strangers might be worth getting to know."

Vasile remained convinced. After Michael was in their home a few months, his mother Susan told 20/20, "As much as we've claimed him, he's claimed us."

In May, four months after Michael's arrival in Toronto, he was taken to the Toronto Sick Children's Hospital for surgery on his foot. Because of complications from his previous operations in Romania, the procedures planned were very complex. His medical care required a level of expertise and technology found in few places in the world. Toronto was one of those places.

For months, doctors had puzzled over Vasile's case, seeking the best solution to his problem. Finally, they sat down with the Goldbergs to make some difficult choices. The circulation to Michael's foot had been damaged, and risks were involved in the surgery. Without the surgery, however, the child would never be able to wear a shoe or walk and run and play normally. Doctors told the Goldbergs there was a possibility Michael could lose his foot. "But," they said, "he could do almost as well with a prosthetic."

The Goldbergs chose the surgery.

"We knew this would happen when we adopted him, but it's one thing knowing and another thing living through it," his father said as he and Susan waited out the twelve-hour-long operation.

Sharing the tension in the operating room that day was 20/20's crew and camera. Roll after roll of film was shot as surgical teams did their meticulous work. Tendons were transferred, bones realigned, and tiny, fragile blood vessels were repaired. Finally, skin grafts were applied to cover the area that had been marred by disfiguring scars. As the long operation drew to a

close, surgeons demonstrated for 20/20 cameras that Michael
Vasile had "matching feet" and that all his toes were pink. The
doctors not only managed to save Michael's foot, but they also
were able to return it to a normal position.

When the cast was removed a month later, Michael Goldberg
began walking with his two feet flat on the ground for the first
time in his life. Not only did he walk, defying all expert predictions that it would "take some time," he ran down the hall of
the clinic. 20/20's crew was again present to capture the jubilant
response of hospital staff and family. When asked what was
next, his father smiled and replied, "Harvard, Harvard!"

Even the most skeptical professional experts called it a "miracle." 20/20 agreed. The title of their prizewinning 1991 Christmas special (filmed in May and June and aired in December)
was "A Miracle for Michael."[2]

MICHAEL'S MIRACLE

The miracle for Michael was made possible by a combination
of factors: the miracle of Western technology and its dedicated
professionals, the Western mentality that no child is unsalvageable or *irrecuperable,* and the determination and drive of families
like the Goldbergs to give a desperately needy child a home
and a chance at life.

There is also the miracle of Michael: his resiliency, his un-
quenchable thirst for life, and the joy within him that always
refused to die. Reflecting on the victory with this child, Gene
Goldberg commented on his family's fulfillment "to see an exceptional, special child like this" . . .

"It's true!" he added. "He really swallows . . . well, gulps life
down."

In Canada, Michael's struggles are far from over. He is confronted daily with the challenges of his residual developmental
disabilities: persistent language delays, learning disabilities, hyperactivity, and impulse control. Although Harvard may not
be in his future, he continues to make steady progress, and he
continues to gulp life down.

"You don't get a chance to do something like this in life very
often," his father said. "I had to grab it."

Part of the energy that drives families to complete adoptions of children—as Goldberg said, "come hell or high water"—comes from the miraculous resilience within children themselves. There is often an indefinable spark in their eyes or a glow in their faces that says: "I am salvageable, I want to live." The other part lies within the hearts of families like the Goldbergs who watched television one night, were deeply moved, and acted upon their instincts, saying, "We could do this; we could adopt that child!" and did just that, knowing full well that adoption was just the beginning.

$\sim$

Improvements in institutional care are still under way in Romania. In many of the orphanages, remarkable progress has been made, and the severe developmental deficits seen in 1990's children are now being prevented in most orphanages. If 20/20 were to return to Romania for a follow-up today, most of the institutions they visited originally would be unrecognizable.

Today's improvements and progress, however, would have come too late for Michael Vasile Goldberg. One has only to look at the children who are like Michael and were left behind. For those children, and the thousands like them who are still institutionalized in Romania, any possibilities for rehabilitation and future, independent living remain severely limited.

Although schools are improved and teachers better trained, there is no special education. There is no occupational therapy, no highly technical orthopedic care, and no pediatric physical therapy. Hyperactive "orphans" have no access to medication or behavior therapy. Birth families are still unable to bring their children home. By the time these resources are developed in Romania (if development continues at its current rate), Michael Vasile Goldberg will be at least twenty years old.

The miracle for Michael now is that he has a home, medical care, a school with special services, and a loving "forever family." The miracle of Michael—his special toughness and remarkable resilience—never stops. To the delight of all his caregivers, professional and personal, he continues to "gulp life

down." When he summed up for 20/20's "A Miracle for Michael" in December 1991, Eugene Goldberg said it best:
   "It's a wonderful thing to save a child."

TODAY'S HUDDLED MASSES

The Statue of Liberty would be a "Mother of Exiles," welcoming the outcasts of other nations to a "sweet land of liberty." More and more in the United States, these immigrants, the poor and the homeless from other nations, are children. Children are the "huddled masses" from war-torn streets, cold institutions, or poverty-stricken homes abroad. Children are the "wretched refuse" of tragically deprived circumstances. Cold, starving, abandoned, and unloved, they are coming to America.

Invading our shores from far and wide, these children are of every shape, color, and ethnic group. Robbed of their early childhoods, they yearn to breathe free, to know the sweetness of love and liberty. They are in desperate need of homes.

These children are coming to adoptive homes in America from such foreign places as:

Russia	Honduras	Mexico	India
Romania	Guatemala	Latvia	China
Ukraine	Vietnam	Korea	Paraguay

and they are coming by the thousands. Statistics on these children, available from the INS (U.S. Immigration and Naturalization Services), show:

INTERCOUNTRY ADOPTIONS, 1994*

Europe	2,406	North America	846
Asia	3,641	South America	1,204
Africa	91	Central America	628

*All Countries Total   8,195

Intercountry adoptions in the U.S. for fiscal year 1994; U.S. Immigration and Naturalization Service (INS).

Why are so many foreign children finding their way home to America?

As the globe shrinks and mass media is readily available to every American household, more and more families are exposed to the plight of homeless children in countries less fortunate than ours. Although many Americans contribute to various charitable and humanitarian organizations that benefit the world's children, more and more families are responding as the Goldberg family did. After seeing a television program or reading a magazine article, they are saying, "We could do this! We could adopt this child." As a consequence, many, if not most foreign adoptions are motivated by the humanitarian instincts of these families to bring a needy child into a loving home.

There are many children in need of adoption. They come from many different circumstances:

- Children orphaned by war, disease, or by virtue of their abandonment ("legal" orphans whose parents have deserted them).
- Adoptable children with special needs that cannot be met in their communities. Most are institutionalized and will never leave institutions.
- Children without parents, living on the streets or in refugee encampments. An estimated 150 million children live and die on the streets of the world's cities. Most of them are abandoned.
- Children whose names are lost on endless lists of bungling bureaucracies.

Some of these lost children have names that have never made the "waiting children" lists. In 1994, for example, there were sixty-seven thousand abandoned and legally adoptable children, all between ages three and seven, who remained in Romania's institutions. Despite the new adoption law's mandate to report all abandoned children, most of those children had not been reported to the Romania Adoption Committee. In America alone, there were thirty qualified applicants for each of those three- to seven-year-olds.

A WORLD OF OPTIONS

Adoptable, small children and babies in Western, industrialized countries, including the United States, are in short supply. In most Western countries, the number of babies who are given up for adoption has become increasingly limited in recent years. Several factors are responsible for these increasing limitations, among them legalized abortion, contraception, and the increasing tendency of single parents to keep their children. Even when babies are available, applicants are increasingly frightened by the reported cases of birth parents showing up—sometimes years later—to reclaim their child. They do not want to risk the heartbreak of repeating the story of Baby Jessica.[3]

Thousands of adults from the seventy-five-plus million baby boom generation are seeing their childbearing years slip away from them. One out of every five of these adults is infertile. Many of them have spent fortunes on fertility methods and experiments. Some have fallen prey to hustlers and charlatans. When their efforts to conceive a child fail, they join the lengthening line of other waiting parents on adoption agency lists.

Many of America's waiting families are willing to adopt a child with special needs. However, today's couples who consider adopting a U.S. child with special needs are often confronted with changing demographics. Most of the adoptable, special-needs children in this country are older, disenfranchised youth from our flagging foster-home system. More and more, these children have psychological problems of almost overwhelming complexity and severity.[4] Most adoptive parents don't feel able to take on the major challenges such adoptions entail.

More than half of the children awaiting adoption in America are children of color. Due to recent changes in domestic social policy that prohibit (or discourage) adoption of racially different children, many of these children are unavailable to the majority of parents (primarily white, middle-class couples) who are seeking a child to adopt.

Thousands of childless American couples will soon be ineligible to adopt within this country due to age restrictions. (Although variable from state to state and from agency to agency, this age restriction usually applies to individuals in their early to mid-forties.) When they find no babies to adopt in their hometowns and wait endlessly on agency lists, they become desperate to start a family. In increasing numbers, they are turning to foreign adoption.

Foreign adoption, however, represents more than a last-chance alternative to couples who have exhausted their options in the domestic adoption system. It is an increasingly attractive option for any family or individual who wishes to adopt a child. As stories spread about the fulfillment and rewards of foreign adoption, many adoption candidates consider it the preferred option.

WHERE HAVE THEY BEEN?

Over the course of this past decade, more than eighty thousand American parents have found "their child" in one of a growing list of foreign countries where children are abandoned and have no other possibilities for home or family.

These countries have one thing in common: They are members of the so-called third world; they are all developing or re-developing nations. If adopting families understand some of the socioeconomic and political history of the countries they visit, they are better armed to cope with the frustrations associated with the intercountry adoption process.

Developing countries are different from those of the industrialized world. They are gridlocked by poverty and a shortage of both natural and human resources. Most of their governments are unstable and are dependent on the outside world for assistance, relief, and development. Lacking resources and technology, they are especially vulnerable when either man-made or natural disaster strikes.

Redeveloping countries, most notably the emerging democracies brought to the forefront by the collapse of Communism during the 1980s, have a second set of problems. They are often torn by wars, both hot and cold. Their economies have collapsed. Having fallen prey to tyrannical leadership in the past, they are often forced to live with the legacy those leaderships left behind. Their histories are often marred by multiple violations of human rights. Despite their avowed cultural values for family, their children always seem to suffer the most when human rights are violated.

Developing and redeveloping countries are always deficient in community resources. Health care is woefully behind that which we have in the United States and is often dependent on outside help to meet the lowest standards. The child with known mental deficiency will not receive special education. There is no special education. The deaf child will not be diagnosed; there are no facilities for early diagnosis of hearing loss.

When resources are scarce or nonexistent, priorities are different. When hunger is the problem, starvation must be abated. The child with a complex biochemical disorder that prevents him from absorbing essential nutrients will take a backseat to the child who is simply starving. The deaf child will not be taught sign language or reading when illiteracy in the general public is still the issue. The elderly or disabled will not be picked up by an ambulance where there is an accident. Basic health care will take precedence over rehabilitation.

Redeveloping countries don't always find redevelopment easy. When reform and reconstruction begin, they must struggle to survive at the same time they seek democratic and economic reform. The introduction of free-market economies often brings unemployment, inflation, and a new kind of poverty in the beginning. New democracies, extremely fragile, are vulnerable to the social unrest that ensues when the breadlines shorten, but few can afford the bread that is available.

The necessities and cold realities of years of oppression, totalitarianism, and poverty have forged new, hardened cultural attitudes in many redeveloping nations. Old ways of thinking and ancient prejudices often resurface. Despite political reform, health care and medical education continue to rank low on the government's budget priorities in most redeveloping countries. Rehabilitation, when it is offered, will focus on the injured, otherwise normal adult who has the capability to lead a "productive" life. Children born with birth defects or physical disabilities will not be rehabilitated. They are not considered potentially productive members of society. If they survive at all, they will be placed in institutions.

INSTITUTIONAL CARE

The majority of children adopted from foreign countries come from institutions. Frequently mislabeled as orphanages, these institutions are more often the leftovers of a fragmented child-welfare or social protection system. Children in such facilities, therefore, are wards of the state. Rarely, even in postwar situations, are they true orphans.

When socioeconomic conditions deteriorated in Communist bloc countries during the eighties, and when everyone was cold and hungry, neither survival nor any semblance of normal development could take place in an institutional environment. Virtually none of the children raised in institutions had any hope of reaching their God-given potential, and few will ever be productive members of society without intensive, highly specialized care. Their development was arrested long before their countries emerged into the free world and opened the adoption door.

Today, most of the old state facilities that were discovered in the early nineties are still open and are operated under the authority of a government struggling through a reconstruction process. Although reform and foreign aid measures have accomplished many improvements, children continue to suffer negative effects from institutionalization. Despite the improved attitudes and level of training of many institutional caregivers, children continue to suffer emotionally from the loss or lack of a parent. A home, even an impoverished home, offers more hope than any renovated orphanage. A loving, lifelong caregiver or, best of all, a parent offers more hope than an institutional caregiver, however well trained she might be.

Most health professionals from the West were ill prepared to cope with the widespread, tragic crisis of abandoned, institutionalized children in eastern Europe. Although we were theoretically familiar with the various syndromes and clinical profiles associated with institutional deprivation in children, very few of us had any recent experience with institutions or institutionalized children. The reason for this inexperience was rooted in our own history of human rights legislation and social policy change. By the late-1970s, America and most of the world's industrialized democracies had undergone deinstituti-onalization. Soon after deinstitutionalization, the enactment of U.S. legislation (PL 94-142 of 1975) requiring "education for all handicapped," without discrimination and in the "least restric-tive environment," became reality throughout America.

Over the course of the next fifteen years (1975 to 1990), cul-tural attitudes changed in the United States. Institutionalization was considered the most restrictive environment imaginable. No child was considered unsalvageable. When previously insti-tutionalized populations were reunited with families and rein-tegrated into community life, disabled persons were viewed as part of the rich diversity of American culture.

The developmentally disabled, therefore, reentered Ameri-can society. Only those requiring constant, skilled nursing care remained in institutions. Buildings that were once institutions were abandoned or renovated to serve other community pur-poses. Professional staff took other jobs or pursued "second ca-reers," and new trainees acquired skills more relevant to current problems and issues. By the time America's "experts" were called on to provide assistance in eastern Europe, the old problems posed by institutions had long been replaced by new problems of inner-city decay, homelessness, and America's ail-ing foster-home system.

When eastern Europe opened up, the search for solutions to the problems of institutionalized children in developing nations meant, literally, that everything old was new again. The para-dox was that Western professionals lacked experience with the institutionalized but had the advanced technology. In the devel-oping countries, the opposite prevailed: They had the experi-ence but no technology. Out of this paradox grew a new professional collaboration with the unified mission to provide services to institutionalized children and apply the lessons learned to generate new solutions to a very old problem. The enhancement and elevation of standards for intercountry adop-tion was one of those solutions.

BUREAUCRACIES, OLD AND NEW

When ideal solutions present themselves for massive social problems and those solutions are not being implemented, serious questions arise. Why, for example, does foreign adoption move so slowly when so many adoptable children are waiting, along with so many qualified parents? The very question defies logic, particularly when one considers that neither children, who progressively deteriorate in orphanages, nor parents, whose age will soon disqualify them, can afford to wait much longer.

Part of the answer lies in the bureaucracy surrounding inter-country adoption. When the nineties began and international governing bodies (the UN, for example) began to set forth new policy, eastern Europe became the standard bearer for how that policy would be translated into law. Ironic as it may seem that countries like Romania (which was in such gross violation of human rights with its institutions) would lead the way into the new era of international adoption legislation, it was indeed the case.

Unfortunately, and often tragically, development of a functional law and system had more delays than working months. Despite the urgency the international community felt in getting children out of eastern Europe's institutions, the bureaucracy often seemed to impede rather than facilitate the process. Problems multiplied when other eastern bloc nations failed to learn from Romania's mistakes. History began to repeat itself within months—sometimes weeks—of the initial events. In country after country, the drama went like this:

A totalitarian government collapses—borders open—press and media rush in—children, thousands of children, are discovered in institutions—foreign aid pours in—thousands of foreigners arrive to adopt the children who are abandoned and are deteriorating in environments of neglect and abuse—chaos reigns while adoption remains unregulated and wide open—unscrupulous practices develop—scandals are publicized—adoption shuts down while the emerging democracy writes a new adoption law—a new bureaucracy develops to implement the new law—adoption reopens, but functions very slowly—the new bureaucracy is cumbersome—periodic shutdowns occur due to loopholes in the new law, abuses, poor management, and overpublicized scandals, many of which are isolated events—laws, when perfected, cannot be enforced or monitored—waiting lists grow and grow and grow . . .

Despite the chaos and inefficiency that permeated this scene, the passage of laws and development of the adoption bureaucracy had many positive effects. When used legally, the word *orphan* was expanded to include abandoned children; abandonment itself was given legal definition. Specific criteria were developed to define abandonment as desertion of parental responsibility for a given period of time (usually "no show of parental interest for six months") and failure of birth parent(s) to respond after a reasonable attempt at notification (often another six months).

Although legal definitions were helpful in rendering abandoned children adoptable, the application of the law often entailed a series of waiting periods. It was not unusual, for example, for an abandoned newborn infant to be eighteen months old before being legally declared adoptable. Most of the new laws entailed further waiting periods while efforts were made to place the child in adoptive homes in his country of origin. In this frustrating situation of prolonged waiting periods, many adopting parents sought shortcuts or ways around the system. A second black market soon developed when unscrupulous "facilitators" reappeared, offering shortcuts for a fee to unsuspecting adopting parents.

It only takes one scandal or abuse of the law to stop adoption for months. In Romania, for example, a desperate British couple tried to smuggle their chosen child over the Hungarian border and were caught by local authorities. When they were arrested and imprisoned, adoption closed for months.

Sadly, tragically, when abuses do occur, a gleeful foreign press will often hype the event out of all proportion. When this occurs, a climate of secrecy and suspicion quickly develops, and the new adoption system is hampered. Children and parents continue to wait until the story dies or diplomacy intervenes.

HUMAN RIGHTS ISSUES

Adopting parents should know that real abuses of the system do occur.

In April 1992, a foreign press agency (Agence France Presse) reported a press interview with the Geneva-based organization Defense for Children, International (DCI). Spokesman Nigel Cantwell said that "the practice of international adoption has degenerated into a form of child trafficking . . . with many organized syndicates profiting in adoption deals."

Corrupt and shady practices in foreign adoption are not restricted to eastern Europe. In 1990, Guillermo Carranza of Guatemala reported that unscrupulous baby brokers had invaded clinics and hospitals in poor villages throughout the country. They were looking for women who could be coerced into selling one or more of their children for adoption. Prostitutes and poor girls were also being hired to act as surrogate mothers. Adopting parents were charged up to $15,000 per child on this burgeoning black market. Guatemala lawyers legalizing such an adoption were receiving most of the money.[5]

Although there are many false, inflated, and bogus stories about child trafficking, many reported incidents have substance and are accurately reported. These fall into three major categories:

- ◆ Syndicate adoptions, or independent, illicitly brokered deals in which children are trafficked for purposes of adoption. Sometimes referred to as the "black market of adoption."
- ◆ Child trafficking for purposes other than adoption, but done under the guise of adoption. In these instances, phony "adopting parents" act as a front for child-trafficking rings. The so-called adopted children are then exploited for other illicit purposes, such as prostitution, child labor, or child pornography. (Many of these children were never legally adopted, but were illegally removed from institutions under the pretense of adoption. False adoption documents were often presented to dupe institutional staff.)
- ◆ Outright kidnapping of children for purposes of trafficking and exploitation but without the phony adoption front.

Americans may wish to join advocacy groups to help stop the corruption and criminal practices that have invaded the foreign adoption arena. Such corruption is deplorable; its continuation not only has tragic consequences for children but also places a shadow over foreign adoption in general when the perpetrators use adoption as a front for their criminal practices.

Although it transcends adoption issues, a proactive stance on the part of adopting parents will not only will help to stop the victimization of precious children but will also identify foreign adoption (and adopters) as part of the solution to these problems. There is more than one way to save a child. Putting a halt to criminal child trafficking and thus preventing future occurrences of this nature is the first step in saving countless numbers of victimized children.

Many of these problems are being addressed by children's advocacy and human rights groups around the globe. Advocacy has been given teeth by the UN Convention on the Rights of the Child, adopted in 1989. The convention contains specific articles that address intercountry adoption and others that protect disabled children and guarantee their rights. Most of the developing countries and "emerging democracies" have ratified the convention (Romania was one of the first) and are accountable to the UN in carrying out its tenets.

Soon after the UN convention on children's rights was adopted, the Hague Convention on Intercountry Adoption was drafted. The Hague Convention provides refinement of international adoption laws and uniform standards for all social policies and legal practices regarding intercountry adoption. Interested adopting families may obtain copies of either convention from United Nations offices.

AMERICA'S FUTURE PARENTS NEED TO KNOW

Every foreign adoption should be considered a special-needs adoption. Every foreign adoptee should be considered a high-risk child.

Developing or redeveloping countries, with their thousands of waiting, adoptable children, are the prime example of why enlightened international adoption is needed. Most of the children in these countries are waiting in environments that jeopardize their future growth and development. Because of the deprivation that is characteristic of those environments, most adoptable children have special needs:

- Acquired developmental disabilities that stem from deprivation during early childhood.
- Health conditions their countries cannot treat.
- Growth and nutritional deficiencies.
- Psychological problems that jeopardize normal attachment to adoptive families.

Nearly all (more than 95 percent) are conditions that could have been prevented or cured. Most (more than 80 percent) are conditions that still can be treated.

Except for its unusually high numbers, Romania is no exception to other developing (or "redeveloping") countries where children are institutionalized or placed in "orphanages." Russia, for example has numbers that far exceed Romania's and the system is the same. China institutionalizes its baby girls in numbers that defy logic. Although they are reputed to be "better places" (generally higher standards and better physical appearance), South and Central America have hundreds of institutions housing homeless and abandoned children.

Despite claims to the contrary, there are no five-star institutions. Any child in the world who is institutionalized is disadvantaged and more at risk for developmental disabilities than children living in homes. At highest risk are babies and children who are born with birth abnormalities (some of them very minor), low-birth-weight babies, and physically challenged children who are institutionalized soon after birth.

The global response to children's rights issues in the nineties will undoubtedly have a positive effect on both intercountry adoption of abandoned children and reunification of nonabandoned institutionalized children with their families.

We the authors, are firm in our support of international adoption as a top priority in relieving the ongoing crisis of abandoned children. We are equally firm in our position that adopting parents must be informed parents. If adopting parents are well prepared to meet the challenges their children pose, they are better able to be good and stable caregivers of the children placed in their charge.

The importance of informed, enlightened adoption is just now coming into the consciousness of those involved at all levels of international adoption. If adoptions are to be truly successful, it is important that adoptive parents have as many facts as possible before beginning the process. When parents are deprived of complete and accurate information, there is always the risk that adoption will fail and that family integrity will be painfully ruptured.

When foreign adoptions fail, through dissolution (legal termination of adoption) or disruption (interruption of adoption before finalization), a foreign-adopted child is often relinquished to the American system of foster homes and/or long-term care in our residential treatment system. When this happens, two tragedies can occur:

- ◆ Internationally adopted children fall through the same cracks that swallow U.S.-born children in our nation's social services system. Once the foster-home cycle has started, however, foreign-born children are at particularly high risk to never find a compatible family. Although statistics are not available, many state agencies report that it is much more difficult to find a second home for a foreign-born child than one born in America.

- ◆ The integrity of the adopting family is broken, leaving the family members with feelings of failure and grief that often go unresolved.

Although accurate statistics are not available, the success rates of foreign adoption in the United States are extremely high. The most widely accepted figure is 90 percent, which exceeds the reported success rate of U.S. special-needs adoption by 3 to 10 percent.

MOST LIKELY TO SUCCEED

It is generally believed that nine out of ten foreign adoptions succeed to the extent that they do not end in disruption or dissolution. These figures are estimates, however. As suggested by our background research for this book, it is probable that accurate statistics do not exist.

In preparing the research for this book, we designed a brief survey and mailed it to every state's social service agency. The survey was simple. We asked how many foreign adoptions in the state had failed, been disrupted, or dissolved. We asked how many children had made their way into the American social services system.

When we received no replies, we attempted a telephone survey. We spoke to each of the fifty states' social service departments. The results of the two weeks' work were both alarming and fascinating. In summary, the information we sought does not exist—not in retrievable form. This is because virtually no one tracks international adoption—no private agencies, no international agencies, no national agencies, no one.

Like silence, questions not answered can often tell as much as those that get replies. Below, we have listed some of the answers derived from our survey, beginning with the conclusion:

1. There is no single agency, government body, or organization that is responsible for tracking or monitoring international adoptions.
2. When/if a foreign adoption fails, the adopting family may seek assistance from any one of a large number of agencies, both private and public. Many families make private arrangements with another family and never involve an agency.
3. Private agencies are very hesitant to release the information they have within their own agency. They have no official requirement to do so.
4. It is likely that only a small percentage of internationally adopted children make their way into the state foster-home system. Those who do, however, are not reported separately from other (U.S.-born) children in the foster-home system.
5. Most state social services agencies are divided into districts or regions. Fewer than 10 percent of agencies have a specific desk or office that deals with services to families of foreign adopted children.
6. Of the agencies surveyed, none were able to refer us to another system that might have the information we sought. To their knowledge, the information would not be available through INS, public health, schools, or the state juvenile court system. In other words, precise follow-up information does not exist in the form of *a single database* about foreign adoption and its outcomes.

7. Throughout the public sector, foreign adoptees are treated no differently than any other children. To the statisticians, a child who was born in Lisbon, Peru, is no different from a child born in Cedar Rapids, Iowa.

MAKING THE FIRST DECISION: HOMEGROWN OR INTERNATIONAL?

Before going abroad to adopt a child who is likely to have special needs, adopting parents are often asked the question, "With more than one million American children and youth currently in out-of-home care,[6] why would an adoptive parent go overseas?"

Although many adoptive parents have carefully considered this issue, there are no easy answers. It is not our intent to try to provide those answers or to impose a point of view on adopting families who are grappling with this issue. Instead, we would like to provide some information that may assist adopting parents in making this first and most difficult decision.

Home-front adoptions are not an option for many American parents for the following reasons:

♦ *Eligibility:* Potential parents do not qualify to adopt domestically because of age restrictions, financial reasons, or marital status; criteria for foreign adoption qualification may be broader or more lenient.

♦ *Availability:* Many children in American foster care are not available for adoption. Of those in either temporary or long-term placements, many have a permanency plan that clearly states goals of reunification with his/her parents sometime in the future. The majority of U.S. foster-home children have neither been relinquished by their parents nor have their parents' parental rights been terminated by the courts.

♦ *Compatibility:* In recent years it has become increasingly difficult for U.S. couples to find a compatible match between their preferences for a child and the U.S. children available for adoption. In the early 1990s, American couples who flooded into eastern European countries in droves, looking to adopt, often did so because these children looked like children they might have given birth to themselves—they looked like they "belonged" in the family—or were innocent victims of man-made disasters and desperately needed homes.

◆ *Preferences:* Adopting members of the baby boom generation, many of whom are infertile, often want younger children or babies. Because of their increasing age, they are not able to wait for a baby in the United States; domestic waiting lists are much longer than those for intercountry adoption.

Adopting families who are seeking a child of another culture or race find that while interracial adoption is discouraged at home, it is encouraged abroad. Prospective parents who wish to open their homes to a child with special needs feel better equipped to deal with the special needs of abandoned, foreign children than the problems they see in adoptable children from U.S. foster homes.

When adoptive parents look at the children in American foster care, they can't imagine them fitting into their families or lifestyles. For one reason or another, these are predominantly older children who have developed emotional problems. They have been moved repeatedly from one situation to another. There is often a history of abuse in the birth homes from which they have been removed. The few babies available may already have become physically or mentally challenged due to drug abuse while in utero. Many times, therefore, foster-care wards are not the children parent hopefuls are seeking.

The U.S. news media have been very influential in indirectly promoting foreign adoption. Scarcely a week goes by that a news special isn't broadcast featuring the plight of needy children abroad. From Romania to Somalia to Bosnia to China, adoption hopefuls have followed the media exposure of abandoned children in need of homes. American foster children are not made a media priority, despite their needs and desperate circumstances. The image of the needy waif is not there to draw the adopter in.

This is not to say that American children who have been relinquished for adoption don't need or deserve it. In my book, *Adoption Crisis: The Truth Behind Adoption and Foster Care,*[7] I (McKelvey) explore domestic adoption in depth, and anyone wishing more information on this issue is referred to that book. It is my opinion that all children should have equal opportunity at adoption and a chance for a new, happy life.

In this book, however, the focus is on international children who are also deprived of their families. One can argue that these children are just as needy as American foster children—or more so. Many foreign children do not have access to health care or proper food or education, for example. Even our troubled foster care system provides those elements of care.

I strongly believe any child who is in need of a permanent home should be a candidate for adoption, domestic or foreign. True, it is time the abuses and failures of our own foster care system not be ignored. But our foster-home system and its many troubled children is a larger social problem and domestic adoption is only a part of its solution.

When families who have decided to adopt a child sit down to make their choice of that child, the overriding factor in that choice should be their ability and commitment to meet the needs of the child and the potential for compatibility. When the process is individualized and personal, the erasure of borders only increases the options for all would-be parents, and the adoption has a better chance of success.

MAKING THE RIGHT CONNECTION

Within these pages, you will find a series of stories, each of which illustrates the spectrum of joys, promises, frustration, success, and failures that could be experienced in any foreign adoption. The book deals both with procedure, the external process of foreign adoption, and the complex, inner psychology and philosophy that drive the process forward. The procedure of international adoption ends when adoption is legally finalized. Its product is a final decree. The real goal of adoption, however, is not a legal document. It is the establishment and solidification of a parent-child relationship. The process involved in reaching that goal is the inner core of any adoption.

Although extraordinary, the story of Michael Vasile Goldberg is exemplary of the joys and promises that can and do occur thousands of times a year when foreign adoptions take place.

Many parents see a child in an adoption exchange book, on a television show, or in a magazine article and have an incredible *pull* to that specific child. It is a phenomenon child therapist Connell Watkins of Evergreen, Colorado, says she doesn't understand, but "is something we must pay attention to; these parents just instinctively know they can parent that child and it is something we professionals need to listen to."

As an adoptive parent, I (Bascom) understand this phenomenon called the pull or the chemistry and sometimes referred to as "instant bonding." Had I not experienced it when I first held my adopted son, Erich, I would not have this understanding. As a young doctor, halfway through internship, I had been summoned to the newborn nursery for a pediatric consultation on his case. When it came time to put Erich back in his bassinet, I noticed his little fists tightly gripping handfuls of my hospital gown. Well, . . . I couldn't let go either. So we just stood there together, holding on tight, and made the decision that we were in this thing together and forever. It was, most definitely, a mutual decision.

It was not my compassion for his situation that led me to adopt him. Nor was it my background (in pediatrics and physical therapy) that might give me some added-on value as his mother, nor a recent fertility scare (later proved false), nor the fact that he was being sent to an orphanage (Children's Home, they called it) and would stay there until his foot was "fixed" (which would have been seven years later). All of those things were elements, no doubt. But it was this phenomenon they call the pull (or chemistry), and the strong feelings that went along with it, that cemented my decision to adopt him. And his to adopt me.

When I see it occur in other adopting parents, as I often did in Romania, I always pay attention. It is probably the first positive sign of a successful parent-child attachment in the making. One of the negative aspects of adoption legislation and bureaucratic matchmaking is that fewer and fewer adopting parents can have this personal opportunity.

TWO SIDES OF FOREIGN ADOPTION

Institutionalized children come with no strings attached. This has a good and bad side. Once a foreign adoption of an institutionalized child is legally completed, those ties are severed forever. The risk of an institution director or birth parent showing up to challenge the adoption in later years is nil. This is the good side.

But having no strings attached has a deeper, more significant meaning for children of institutions. Most of these children suffer from some degree of faulty attachment. Children locked up in cruel—or even benign—orphanages rarely have the opportunity for attachment to any caregiver at all. Devoid of this vitally important experience, they often have difficulty forming attachments after their adoption.

Research has proven how vital touch, play, and talk are to children's healthy growth and development. Orphans cut off from words and loving caresses may never develop their capacity for communication and affection. Early neglect and sensory deprivation may cause a host of learning and developmental problems. For example, a study of Romanian adoptees from orphanages found that 90 percent were developmentally delayed.[8] With intervention, proper nutrition, and emotional nurturing, however, adoptive parents have made all the difference in the lives of most of these small victims. Developmentally delayed children can usually catch up, given proper attention. Emotionally deprived children can usually learn to love, given time, understanding, and the nurturing love of a parent.

For many of these children, however, scars are deep and needs so primitive it is necessary to provide more intense and specialized intervention. When these children are brought into nurturing environments for the first time, there is a natural tendency to shower them with affection and attention. Both parental and professional caregivers need guidance on how to approach these children. Even basic human touch, the intuitive response of most caregivers, can send some of them into overload and hinder their further progress.

BEHAVIOR

Many institutionalized children coming to America from distant countries exhibit habitual behaviors. Although predictable, when one considers their origins, these behaviors are difficult to control or tolerate in a new family, unless the family has had anticipatory guidance on what to expect, when to worry, and how and when to intervene. In one survey of Canadian parents who had adopted children from eastern Europe, the persistence of rocking, sometimes for months after adoption, topped the list of parental concerns.

In professional terminology, the term "behavior" has a broader definition than common usage implies; both the physical and emotional responses that are characteristic of a child's behavioral repertoire are included in this definition. Behaviors, however, are not diseases but are symptoms of underlying problems, like rashes in chicken pox or convulsions in meningitis. For children of orphanages, these "typical" behaviors are often the outward sign of inner turmoil. At the same time, they are reflections of sensory deprivation and the child's need for stimulation.

Children will always react in some way to deprivation, neglect, abuse, or rejection. They telegraph their sensory deprivation and replace what is missing by self-stimulation. They show and tell their emotional deprivation through a variety of habitual responses that protect them from the pain that any unloved human being experiences. Although deprived children vary widely in their individual responses, each sends a powerful signal. Silence can be as communicative as screaming. Both indiscriminate affection and profound withdrawal can signal problems with attachment as a result of emotional deprivation. "Frozen watchfulness" is as indicative of underlying problems as frenzied hyperactivity.

CHILDREN

Children are defenseless in fighting for their rights. Because they are children, their small voices cannot and will not be heard unless adult members of society speak out on their behalf. It is largely immaterial whether that voice comes from Lima, Peru, Bucharest, Romania, or Brooklyn, New York. They are children.

Foreign-born children who come from nations that do not have human or material resources have a particular need for a voice. We believe that international adoption, when done properly and in the best interests of children, can contribute significantly to the provision of that voice.

When children are abandoned to environments that cannot meet their most basic needs for affection, health care, nurturing, or education, not only are their rights being violated by a country, a government, or a group of individuals, but society in general has let them down. When prizewinning author Paddy Doyle was asked to comment about his 1988 book, *The God Squad,* he wrote:

> It [the book] is about a society's abdication of responsibility to a child. The fact that I was that child, and that the book is about my life, is largely irrelevant. The probability is that there were, and still are, thousands of me's.[9]

Other than the fact that his numbers were too modest, Paddy Doyle knew what he was writing about. Orphaned at the age of four, he was sentenced by an Irish court to be "detained" in an industrial school for the next eleven years of his life. During those years he was ostracized because of his physical disability, and assaulted and sexually molested by his religious custodians. When he began to show signs of worsening disability, he was transferred to hospital care, where he spent years of boredom and agony in the company of aging, dying men until finally, without his consent or knowledge of what was happening, he was subjected to a series of experimental brain surgeries. The experiment was unsuccessful, and may even have been harmful. In the months and years that Paddy Doyle was undergoing and convalescing from more than eight complex neurosurgical procedures on his brain, his condition deteriorated, resulting in permanent, crippling deformity and severe physical disability. When the experiment was finally deemed a failure, he was transferred out of the hospital to yet another set of institutions.

Things took a turn for the better. His final round of institutions were convalescent homes and offered him both educational opportunities and the companionship of a peer group. He developed friendships and learned to function independently. Finally, when Paddy Doyle left the institution, in his early twenties, he had the fortune to be placed in a good foster home. Given his background of abuse, neglect, disability, and no one to speak on his behalf, his eventual transition to independent living, successful career, marriage, and fatherhood seems nothing short of miraculous. He was a successful survivor of Ireland's institutional system.

Although institutions in developing countries are given most of the publicity, Paddy's story illustrates the fact that the tragic situation is universal. Ireland is a Western country, an industrialized democracy, and the Irish people are renowned for their sentimentality. Their love and belief in family and children are unquestioned. Despite these cultural assets and the fact that books like Paddy Doyle's are having a major impact in effecting change, Ireland, and many countries like it, still have a system of institutions. And although many of us would like to forget, it was not so many years ago that the United States institutionalized many of its developmentally disabled children.

Underlying our commitment to children who live beyond our borders is a deep appreciation for the freedom and plentiful resources American society offers us and our children. It doesn't take much experience in the halls of a developing country's orphanage to reaffirm that appreciation. It doesn't take much time there, however, to discover how similar are most of the issues we face and how much we need each other to work effectively toward solutions. Although our social and economic problems in America seem small by comparison to those of Romania, or Rwanda or Guatemala, they stem from the same root causes and have many similarities. We (the authors) don't view the issue of child neglect as one of "here versus there." From our point of view, it is not a mutually exclusive issue, and the problem of homeless and disenfranchised children knows no national boundaries. Therefore, we believe, neither should its solution.

Furthermore, we believe that:

No child is unadoptable.
No family having the desire and personal resources needed by homeless children should remain childless.

No family having the personal means and humanitarian motivation to help a desperately needy child should be denied the
opportunity to become that child's family.

Families who have adopted a foreign child deserve the full support of both lay and professional communities, both public
and private sectors of the receiving country—the child's new
home.

Priority should be placed on dedicating our resources to securing and preserving the integrity of families and preventing
the problems that may jeopardize that integrity.

When so many children are homeless and so many families
are either childless or have the desire to reach out to homeless
children, foreign adoption represents an ideal solution to two
of the world's most pressing needs: children in need of homes
and families in need of children.

GLOSSARY

Attachment: The establishment of an emotional bond between parent
and child.

Camin Spital: Romanian institutions housing disabled children and
adults.

Club foot: A birth defect causing characteristic foot deformities (foot is
turned in, drawn into a pointed-toe position); *talipes equino-varus*.

Developmental pediatrician: A pediatrician who has received additional training (usually two years) in child development and developmental disabilities; often called a "subspecialty."

Disruption: Interruption of the adoption process after the child has arrived in the home, but before the legal adoption is finalized.

Dissolution: Legal termination of adoption; equivalent to divorce in
marital relations.

Frozen watchfulness: A descriptive term referring to the hypervigilance
and immobility of severely deprived children.

Irrecuperable: The Romanian term assigned to disabled persons who
are considered hopeless cases and are not perceived as candidates for
rehabilitation. Most Camin Spitals were designated "care" facilities
for "the deficient and irrecuperable."

Leagane de Copii: Literally translated to "Cradle for Children," a Leagane is an institution for infants and young children who require institutionalization for reasons of "social protection." Although
officially designated for children up to age three, many Leagane kept
children until ages five to seven.

Mentality: Commonly used term meaning the mind-set of individuals or societies that reflects basic attitude and values; often based upon long-held beliefs and philosophies in the society.

Moldovan city of Iasi: Moldova is one of Romania's seven states; located in northeast Romania. Iasi (pronounced *Yahsh*) is its capital city.

Resilience: The ability to bounce back and/or overcome adverse circumstances; thought to be due to a combination of constitutional and psychological factors, some of which may be genetically determined.

ROSES project: Acronym for Romanian Orphans' Social, Educational and Services project; a program designed and developed by author Bascom to provide child development services and rehabilitation to institutionalized children and service-based training to Romanian health professionals.

Social protection system: The term used throughout Europe for child welfare and protective services.

REFERENCES

1. ABC, 20/20 newsmagazine, "The Shame of a Nation," Janice Tomlin, producer, and Tom Jarriel, reporter, October 5, 1990.

2. ABC, 20/20 newsmagazine, "A Miracle for Michael," Janice Tomlin, producer, and Tom Jarriel, reporter. Barbara Bascom, guest. December 1991.

3. This sensational case of an adopted child, caught between her adoptive and birth parents, caught the hearts of America in July 1993, when the U.S. Supreme Court agreed that two-and-a-half-year-old Jessica be taken from the home of her adoptive parents and returned to the birth parents she had never known.

4. K. Magid, and C. A. McKelvey, *High Risk: Children Without a Conscience* (New York: Bantam Books, 1989).

5. Bascom, op. cit., ABC 20/20.

6. McKelvey, C., and Stevens, J. E. *Adoption Crisis: The Truth About Adoption and Foster Care* (Golden, CO: Fulcrum Publishers, 1994).

7. McKelvey and Stevens, *Adoption Crisis*, page 106.

8. B. Bascom, various sources, including *The Romanian Orphans: A Child Development Crisis* (May 1990) and *Report to the Minister of Health* (May 1990). Self-published by The Brooke Foundation, ROSES Project files.

9. Paddy Doyle, *The God Squad* (London: Corgi Books, 1989).

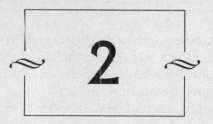

International Adoption: The Process

I will follow the right even to the fire—
but avoiding the fire if possible.

Michel de Montaigne, *Essays II,* 1580

The process of international adoption is both challenging and rewarding. As soon as a family has made the decision to adopt a child from a foreign country, the challenges begin. They are confronted with mountains of paperwork, each piece of which is absolutely necessary to achieve their primary goal of adoption. They must simultaneously pursue another paper trail to ensure that their adopted child can immigrate to the United States. Finally, they must follow yet another document-littered procedure to see that their adopted child becomes an American citizen. Before they begin, however, adopting couples (or individuals) must prove that they are deserving and competent parents. Their privacy is often invaded as they document this proof.

The first challenge and most of the frustration that adopting parents encounter is making their way through the tangle of rules, regulations, and laws that govern the process. Confronting this unique set of requirements is often referred to as "dealing with the bureaucracy." Foreign adoption is enmeshed, controlled, enhanced by, and dependent upon the phenomenon we call the bureaucracy. When things go wrong in foreign adoption, the problem can usually be traced to some aspect of the bureaucracy. When things go right, the success can often be traced to a set of rules, standards, policies, regulations, or a law being implemented by the bureaucracy.

When applied to international adoption, "*the* bureaucracy" is a misnomer. American families who travel halfway round the world to adopt a child must deal with at least *four* bureaucracies. Additional regulations in their state of origin may represent a fifth:

1. The U.S. government bureaucracy: Department of State and INS (Immigration and Naturalization Services).
2. The domestic, nongovernment organization (NGO) bureaucracy surrounding U.S.-based adoption agencies.
3. The foreign government bureaucracies that govern and control intercountry adoptions.
4. The international bureaucracy: policy and international law on intercountry adoption set forth by the Hague Convention on Intercountry Adoption (1994) and the UN Convention on the Rights of the Child (1989).

To meet the challenges and avoid the frustrations embedded in the bureaucratic process, it is best for American parents to know the strengths of different bureaucracies and how they can assist and protect you. It helps to know their weaknesses and how they can frustrate you, obstruct you, and even turn you into a victim. It is best to know their attributes, the principles and laws they defend and implement. It even helps to know their seamier side and hidden agendas. It helps to learn their history and try to understand how that applies to the present.

Learn how to cope with them and when to avoid them. Use them. Make them into a set of tools, not a monster. It is the first big step in the process of enlightened adoption.

Adopting parents may learn better to manipulate bureaucracies if they understand more of how they developed. A detailed discussion, using the Romanian paradigm, is included in chapter 3. Although we have found that it is applicable in almost any country, readers may find it particularly useful in eastern Europe and Russia.

PURSUING THE PAPER TRAIL

As we explore the procedural process of adoption in this chapter, adopting parents may wish to know what a typical dossier of documents looks like. This list, reprinted with permission from the *Report on Intercountry Adoption,*[1] will give adoptive families an idea of what is required:

- Birth certificate(s) of parent(s), certified copy.
- Marriage certificate, if applicable (certified copy).
- Financial statements from competent authority (bank, employer, 1040)—three copies, notarized.
- At least three letters of recommendation from people with impressive-looking letterheads (letters from lawyers, town clerk or councilperson, clergyman, or teacher, for example). Letters must speak to the parents' personal qualifications. Originals, typed and notarized.
- Adoption home study report, notarized.
- Physician's statement of good health, and, if applicable, certificate of infertility.
- Power of attorney, typed and signed by parent(s), required by some agencies to adopt in a foreign country.
- At least two photographs of the family (parents and children already in family) and two of the home.
- Affidavit of Support form from the INS, with all required documents (listed at the bottom of the back page of the form) attached.
- Letter to the agency that will find the child; the document that introduces yourself(selves) and children briefly; the letter should also give information on the kind of child desired (general age, sex if a strong preference) acceptable medical problems, etc.
- Translated copy of documents, if agency requires it.

These documents are only those required to complete a foreign *adoption.* The next step is *immigration.* In addition to the adoption dossier, there are at least thirteen forms to be completed legibly and submitted to the Immigration and Naturalization Service (INS). This action must be taken before the adopted child can immigrate to the United States. After (and only after) submission of this paperwork to the U.S. embassy or consulate in the child's country of origin, a U.S. entry visa may be obtained for the newly adopted child.

One of the common misconceptions in international adoption is that once the child is found and adopted in the foreign country, all the new parents have to do is get on an airplane and bring their child home. This is where many adoptive parents slip up. An entrance visa is not automatically provided for adopted children. It must be applied for. Even when paperwork is in order, there may be a wait while visas are processed by the American embassy's offices. Foreign embassies usually observe both American and host country holidays.

Immigration attorney Rumi Engineer of Denver, Colorado, stresses how vital it is that returning American parents make sure they have completed all the proper documentation for their new child. Not only is documentation needed to complete adoption proceedings in the foreign country, it is rigidly required to obtain an entrance visa into the United States. The process doesn't end when the new family leaves the country, however. Once back in the United States, parents must file for citizenship for their new child.[2]

The final step adoptive parents must take before they can be assured their child is fully protected is applying for citizenship. Until this step is taken, the child is an alien in the United States. Obtaining U.S. citizenship is more than a formality, however. It is important to consider the child's future as a U.S. citizen. Situations can arise, sometimes years after adoption, where the protection of U.S. citizenship is vitally important. Some adoptive parents who have not taken this step have learned the hard way.

As an immigration attorney, Engineer is aware of many such instances when U.S. citizenship became critical to the safety and well-being of an adopted child. One recent case is particularly illustrative of his point:

The adoptive parents had "forgotten" or neglected to obtain citizenship (or even permanent resident status) for their adopted son. Now an adult, he had been adopted at an early age after being brought to the United States legally from another country while still a baby. He was then adopted. Like many other couples in these circumstances, the parents never got around to doing anything about their son's immigration status. The child grew up, married, had children of his own, and then committed a felony. He was imprisoned. Because his parents had never applied for his citizenship and he could not prove any legal status in the United States, immigration authorities put him on an immigration detainer and sought to deport him.

"But to where?" asks Engineer. "To his country of origin? He had no visa, no passport, no status. He has no ties to his native country, no family, etc. He doesn't even speak the language. He is a man without a country, without hope.

"In this case," Engineer added, "I believe something was worked out. But this scenario can happen."[3]

Engineer says he cannot emphasize enough how important it is for all the legal paperwork to be completed and properly executed for a child to become an American citizen with all the privileges therein.

He knows of one case, for instance, in which this point became a major problem for an adoptive mother. Although this is a story of a woman who adopted from a Muslim country, readers need to know that generally adoption is forbidden in Muslim countries and this is a very unusual case.

AN ADOPTION

An American woman working in a Middle Eastern country as a nurse fell in love with a severely disabled child in the hospital where she worked. Born into a poor family, the child had been hospitalized because of a severe birth defect involving his stomach and intestinal track. Although his medical condition was operable in the United States, it could not be handled in the country of origin.

Knowing that the child's condition could be treated in America, the nurse convinced the child's birth parents to let her have the child and return to the United States for the required surgeries. The parents of the baby had already decided they could not care for him with the disability. In fact, without the surgery the child surely would have died in infancy.

When the birth parents consented, the American nurse, who had no children of her own, said she could only do so if they would allow her to adopt him. Again, the birth parents consented and they went into court for permission. In Muslim countries there is no law for "adoption." The father, however, is considered to have all power over the children. The court said the father could give the child to the woman and it would be official. The nurse then brought the child into the United States on a medical visa and, soon after, adopted the child in a U.S. court. Nine or ten years went by, during which she had raised the child as her own and saw him through all but one of the necessary surgeries to repair the birth defect. By this time the nurse was married and had two birth children of her own.

The child's mother (the nurse) decided it was time, after about nine or ten years, to see to the child's immigration status. So she went to the Immigration and Naturalization Service offices to file a petition for the child. A few months went by as the child was in and out of the hospital with surgeries. The mother finally took the paperwork back in and, unfortunately, Engineer says, she got some bad advice. A worker on duty told her the child was in the country illegally. Furthermore, the INS worker advised the mother to go outside the United States, get a proper visa, and then reenter. This advice was wrong. But the mother had not contacted an attorney so did not know her rights.

She contacted some relatives of her son's birth family in the United States whom she had befriended, suggesting he might go for a vacation with them to the native country. And, since the child was going to visit the native land, perhaps it would be good for him to see his birth parents so he could maintain ethnic roots.

The child's mother did not, and could not have anticipated what happened next. Seeing their child and recognizing that he was almost completely well and healthy, the birth parents changed their minds.

They decided to keep their child and not return the ten-year-old to his American mother. In the meantime, the relatives who had accompanied the child inquired about obtaining an entrance visa into the United States for the child, explaining he had been adopted. But, by Muslim law, no child can be adopted. And, by this time, the father had reneged on his original pledge to let the woman have the child.

Frantic to have her child back, the mother finally retained immigration attorney Engineer. After ten years in her home, she and the child had bonded, loved each other, and were truly mother and child. Now she faced the prospect of never seeing her eldest child again.

The natural parents were called into the American consulate to explain the situation. In an attempt to keep his now healthy child, the father denied any knowledge of an adoption. Lying, he told the consul that the nurse had taken the child to the United States for surgery and that he, the father, had been supporting the child all along and paying for the costs of medical care. He further stated that he had expected to get the child back all along. The father said the child was not the American woman's but their child and they would not give the child back.

The frantic American mother had asked Engineer to intervene and get her child returned from the Muslim country. All the time she kept in contact with her child, trying to explain to him what had happened and that she was still his mother. Understandably, this child was very confused and didn't know what to think. Had his mother abandoned him? Why had she sent him away? Would he ever see her again?

Listening to the mother's pleas and the attorney's arguments, INS authorities in the United States and the foreign country acted. They said there was no reason for the child to have originally been ordered out of the United States, and that it should not have happened. They understood the child desperately needed the remaining surgery. They said the mother had met the requirements by filing the original petition for status. She had received bad advice and the whole crisis had been created through this mistake. Moved by the unfolding horror story, the Immigration Service promptly acted on the petition and informed the U.S. consulate in the foreign country that the mother's petition was approved.

The consulate, however, was still haggling over the statement of the birth parents that they had not approved relinquishing their child to the American woman. The consulate would not issue a visa to the child because this paramount issue needed to be resolved.

On the advice of her counsel, the mother talked back and forth with the birth parents for the next six months. Finally, she established enough rapport with them to convince them the child would have a better life with her in the United States (which was true since the child needed one final surgery to be totally well and functioning). The birth family finally acquiesced. Agreeing to the pleading of the mother, they said they would give up the child, but only with the stipulation that the mother and child keep in touch and inform them of how the child was doing.

Six months of legal work was required for the attorney and mother to show that the child's adoption was valid in the United States and Muslim law did not apply. Through the intervention of the government of the Muslim country, the U.S. consul finally gave a visa to the child.[4]

Since the child's return to the United States, the birth family has continued a relationship with the child, and the youngster now goes back and forth to his birth country for visits in a type of "open adoption." The child is in the United States "legally" in his adoptive family, and, it seems, all parties are satisfied with the arrangements.

Although it has a surprisingly happy ending, Engineer notes: "This story cannot reflect the nightmarish months that went by as we tried to bring this child back to the only mother he had ever known." Certainly, the adoptive mother suffered enormous stress during the six-month ordeal, as did her other children. The emotional damage done to the child, a very bright ten-year-old, is hard to assess.

Engineer warns that, in the United States, adoption laws can vary from state to state. Satisfaction of all the federal requirements does not necessarily mean that the job is over. States may have additional paperwork requirements and they may vary from state to state.

Wherever the adoption takes place, however—in California, Texas or overseas—U.S. immigration and naturalization laws are uniform. A foreign, adopted child *is not automatically a U.S.*

citizen, nor will the child automatically be admitted to the U.S. once adopted.

"It simply does not make sense," says Engineer, "to go and get a child, go through the adoption willy-nilly, and then say, 'Now let's find out how to get our child into the country.' This is where people run into problems."

THE DANGER OF OMISSIONS

The above discussions and case histories illustrate the two most common, serious omissions that adoptive parents can make during the international adoption process:

- ◆ Failure to complete and/or submit the necessary documentation to obtain a visa for the foreign-adopted child to enter (immigrate to) the United States.
- ◆ Failure to secure U.S. citizenship for the adopted child, after the child has arrived in the country.

Either or both of these omissions can have serious consequences for both the child and his adoptive family. To prevent similar problems, it is helpful to think of international adoption as a three-step, sequential process: adoption, immigration, and naturalization as a U.S. citizen.

Because laws may vary from state to state, and because federal regulations and laws governing adoption, immigration, and naturalization are constantly being added to and changed, the authors offer the following recommendations:

- ◆ Always consult a reliable immigration attorney or an adoption agency before beginning the adoption process.
- ◆ Consult, and preferably enroll with, an approved international adoption agency (this guidance is also the recommendation of the American Academy of Pediatrics Committee on Intercountry Adoption).
- ◆ Don't forget to plan for immigration and naturalization of your adopted child.

WHAT IS AN ORPHAN?

Before an adopted child enters the United States legally, the parents must file what is known as an "Orphan Petition." A new law passed by Congress in 1994 requires that an adopted child must meet the legal definition of "orphan" before he or she is eligible for full citizenship privileges as the immediate relative of a U.S. citizen. For an Orphan Petition to be filed, two requirements must be met according to the code of federal regulations 204.2-204.3:

1. The prospective adoptive parents must prove their ability to provide a proper home environment and their suitability as parents. This determination is based on a home study and fingerprint checks.
2. An Orphan Petition (Form I-600) must be filed, which focuses on whether the child is an orphan under section 101(b)(1)(F) of the Immigration Act. Prospective adoptive parents may submit the documentation necessary for each of these two determinations separately or at one time, depending on when the orphan is identified.

For a child to obtain "orphan" status, several requirements must be met. The child is legally an orphan, if (1) both birth parents have unaccountably and inexplicably passed out of the child's life, (2) if their whereabouts are unknown and there is no reasonable hope of their reappearance, and (3) there has been a reasonable effort to locate them by a competent authority in accordance with the laws of their country. In some cases this will mean the parents are dead; in others, the child has been abandoned or deserted by parents who have refused their parental rights and have not carried out their obligations and, furthermore, the child has become a ward of a competent authority in accordance with the laws of the foreign-sending country.[5]

If a child is not an orphan (as defined in the above paragraph), a valid adoption can be done legally in another country, but the parents must show that the child has been in their custody for two years before the child is eligible to receive a visa as an immediate relative.

PROCESS PLANNING

It is often valuable for prospective adoptive parents to mentally rehearse the process of international adoption before beginning down its path. To accomplish this, you may find it helpful to develop an *adoption plan*, following this list of activities:

- *Pull together* as much information as possible from many resources. Then sift through and evaluate the information.
- *Determine the kind* of child you hope to adopt.
- *Turn to a parent group* for support and join.
- *Understand* how the adoption process works.
- *Learn* about various options in adoption and how they relate to the child you hope to adopt.
- *Decide* what is of major importance to you in your quest.
- *Determine* your monetary situation. What can you afford to assume in the way of costs?
- *Maintain* your flexibility.

In the process of adoption, the potential parent is confronted with several major decisions. The first of these is determining what process to use. There are two basic options:

1. To adopt independently, by making application directly to orphanages, maternity homes, or lawyers abroad.
2. To adopt through an intercountry adoption (placement) agency.

Adopting parents who choose to go with an agency need to explore which programs best meet their needs and which agency's qualification requirements best match their capabilities. Many U.S. agencies have intercountry adoption programs for several different countries. Each of these programs may have different requirements established by the child's country of origin.

For example, through one program in the African nation of Liberia, single women may apply for adoption, but single men may not. Across the world, regulations vary, for example in the Philippines, one program allows couples age twenty-five to forty-five to apply for adoption and specifies nonsmokers only, while another agency's program qualifies couples age twenty-one to forty-five, who have been married at least three years and places no restrictions on smoking. Another program in the Philippines says those adopting can be no more than forty years older than the child they are seeking.

As adoptive couples explore placing agencies and their programs, they are likely to discover that they are eligible for some and not others. Those who are single or an older couple must be prepared to spend more time searching for the right match. It is important to understand the playing rules.

Anticipate, also, that when you start making the initial phone calls to find an agency, you might wonder if you'll ever be able to adopt. Age may not be the only determining factor; others are religion, geographic location, and financial capability. Often the first responses can put you off. But by consulting the yellow pages, adoptive parent support groups, and other sources of adoption information, such as your place of worship, you will eventually be able to evaluate the possibilities from a realistic point of view and make an informed decision.

Once you are officially qualified as a "waiting parent," you will spend a lot of time doing just that—waiting! In addition to the usual waiting periods, there may be one or a series of unanticipated delays. Most of these delays are related to activities in the foreign country. An adoption in process can be put on hold, or terminated, because of government policy changes or even a change in governments. While waiting, expenses can soar with extra costs at home and abroad.

MANAGING DIVERSITY

It is important to understand some of the risks. When an agency describes a healthy child, for example, they may be describing a child who is undernourished, who has an acute infectious disease that requires treatment on arrival, or a child who will show developmental delays in comparison to American children their age. What the agency is most likely saying is that the child was, to the best of their knowledge, born free of disease and with normal potential, that his delays will reverse in time, and that none of these conditions are necessarily long-term problems.

Parents who are familiar with the pitfalls of adopting domestically often find it easier to adopt internationally. This is especially true for those seeking to adopt children of a different ethnic or racial background. In the United States, most states discourage the adoption of black, American Indian, or other racially mixed children by white couples, despite the fact that studies of adopted children of a different racial background than their parents have proven these children usually grow up feeling good about themselves and have adjusted to the adoption positively.

Positive evidence on the well-being of children reared by parents of a different ethnic background is contained in a study by Rita Simon, a sociologist at the American University in Washington. She tracked two hundred parents and children from interracial families for twenty years. In 1971 she found the youngsters understood their race was different from that of their parents, but did not seem bothered by the fact. Twelve years later, the children, by that time teenagers, perceived their parents as being "very, very committed" to informing them about black issues.[6] When Simon returned again in 1991, the then grown children continued to do well: "We are not Oreos," they said, pointing out that they were as black as children raised in ghettos.

The majority of adoptable children from foreign countries differ racially from the majority of American adopting families. Even in Romania, where the orphans are described as "Caucasian," many, if not the majority, of institutionalized, adoptable children are of Gypsy origin.

In central Asia, there is a town where some tiny, helpless victims of ethnic hatred live. These children, who were conceived despite racial differences and later abandoned because of the stigma, face bleak futures unless they are adopted. KUSA-TV in Denver, Colorado, reported that for the orphans of Karaganda, who are of unique ethnic descent, there is a glimmer of hope. Some of these children from "one of the last outposts of civilization," somewhere between Siberia and China on the plains of central Asia, are being adopted by American parents.[7]

These children come from a part of the world with a tortured history. Karaganda, Kazakhstan, is a town built by victims of Soviet oppression. Today, more ethnic Russians live in Kazakhstan than Cossacks, and that is a source of racial tension. After Stalin's reign of terror ended, millions of slave laborers were freed and stayed in Karaganda, only to produce another generation of victims. Because of the shame associated with having a mixed-race child, many of the grandchildren of the slave laborers have been abandoned to institutions. Still others are institutionalized because of birth deformities.

Says KUSA: "These are the tiniest victims of a society that now discourages mixed-race families—beautiful children with the light Russian skin of one parent and the Asian, Cossack eyes of the other. In many cases, the shame of having a mixed-race child led their mothers to abandon them."[8]

In Kazakhstan, as in other countries where the borders of formerly Soviet Union countries have opened for adoption in the 1990s, hundreds of American parents have rushed to embrace these ethnically mixed children. They are children who will have a much better life in the United States than they could possibly expect in their native land, where cultural attitudes of nationalism, prejudice, and deep hatreds prevail, forcing innocent children into lives of oppression and misery in institutions.

Parents wishing children of a mixed ethnic background or any background unlike their own would benefit from joining other families who have parented children of a different ethnic group or race. By this kind of networking before adopting such a child, parents not only gain in knowledge and understanding but can actively prevent later problems.

Most American families who adopt have never personally experienced the pain or humiliation of racial prejudice or discrimination. It is predictable, however, that they will have this experience, once they have a child of a different race or color in their lives. This being the case, it is best to be prepared. Not only do parents need support and guidance on these issues; they need to have their own feelings resolved well enough to be capable of helping their adopted children. Adoptive parents will face challenges helping ethnically different children develop confidence in themselves as being worthwhile people. Although this is a challenge any parent faces with any child, it is particularly intense for parents of foreign adopted children, who may have a diminished concept of self-worth related to neglect and abuse before adoption.

PREJUDICE AND DISCRIMINATION

Despite the strides we have made in our culture to eradicate racial prejudice and discrimination, these are very real issues and persist in American society today. Parents who are adopting children from Asian, African, or South American countries will, most likely, encounter this phenomenon repeatedly. When light-skinned mothers take a Gypsy, African, Asian, or Hispanic child into the supermarket, they must be prepared for the stares, absurd questions, or crude remarks of strangers. When children go to school, they themselves must have some preparation for the questions and teasing many of them will experience—even in America today. Physically disabled children or children with visible physical deformities are as vulnerable to prejudice and social affronts as racially different children.

Parents often learn a great deal from the responses of their children in these situations. When confronted with an embarrassing question or even a racial slur, it is often best to see how the child responds. The sincerity and honesty of their responses often carry a very clear message to both insensitive offender and embarrassed parent. I (Bascom) recall an early experience with my son Erich that illustrates this point. Like most mothers of children who appear different, I have a supermarket story.

He was very young, a toddler, and we were in the midst of a series of corrective procedures for his club foot deformity. This wasn't much fun for either of us, and I always tried to follow up visits to the orthopedist with some kind of treat for Erich. We had gone to the supermarket to shop for that treat and were in the checkout line. Erich had a new long-leg cast, a huge white plaster affair with a bent knee, put on just hours before. It was a "custom cast," designed by the orthopedist to discourage my adorable son from playing Houdini in the middle of the night and wriggling out of his cast before morning. With its extra layers of plaster, the cast looked bigger than he did. His pants had been split to the hip, so there was lots of exposure, and the fact that Erich's leg was different was pretty obvious. He added to the spectacle by banging it gleefully against the sides of the metal cart. I added to the spectacle by getting him stuck when I tried to extract him from the cart.

A woman in front of me turned to offer assistance, then recoiled when she saw the problem. It had grown very quiet, when she said in a booming voice, "Oh, you poor little boy, what happened to your leg? Did you break it?" It stayed very quiet when Erich responded "NO!" then added proudly, "I have a club foot."

"See?" he said, pointing to his wiggling toes, which had been painted with an iodine-containing substance and looked slightly green. The lady's complexion turned pale and she quickly withdrew her hand, which had been patting the cast sympathetically. After glancing at the staring crowd that surrounded us, she turned to me and said, "I don't know what to say."

She *didn't* know what to say. She didn't understand why she was so embarrassed and immobilized by a birth defect when she had been so comfortable with a serious injury just moments before. And she had been totally disarmed by a child's frankness.

What I learned from that experience was how very uncomfortable and inappropriate people are when they are confronted with differences in other people. Responses of this nature do not always reflect ingrained attitudes or prejudice. They are more often an expression of embarrassment and discomfort, and people don't like to be uncomfortable. Avoidance of discomfort, however, quickly gives birth to intolerance, and intolerance, to prejudice and discrimination.

What else I learned was that children are often more effective (and appropriate) in dealing with these circumstances than their parents are. Thereafter, I always let Erich take the lead when people asked questions or made inappropriate comments. He was very good at it, and it seemed to strengthen his own ability to deal with difference and disability. Over the years, his direct approach and the honesty with which he expressed his feelings, whatever they were, made us closer as parent and child.

It wasn't always easy. Not all of our confrontations had the humor or positive resolution of our day in the supermarket. Sometimes, the episodes were painful, and occasionally they left me enraged. I had to fight my tendency to gloss things over, or to make very sad times funny or entertaining, thinking I was protecting him. Fortunately, Erich was too honest in his self-expression to let me get away with it.

One day we were watching a movie on TV. Sort of watching—Erich, about age five by then, was finger painting on his PlaySkool easel and I was ironing. The film being shown was based on Somerset Maugham's novel *Of Human Bondage*, the story of an orphaned boy, Philip, who was born with a club foot. I wasn't paying much attention until I noticed Erich had left his easel and was sitting as close as he could to the television set. He was crying. The scene being shown was one in which school chums were cruelly taunting Philip in the school-yard, mocking his limping gait and hooting with laughter.

I reacted inappropriately, rushed to Erich's side, and smiling, told him "That's just a story someone made up a long time ago. That didn't really happen." He looked at me straight, still cry-ing and said, "NO, Mommy. That's not true It happened." Then, pointing to the screen, he shouted, "That's ME!" We watched the rest of the film together. Both of us cried a lot that day.

So, other lessons were learned about the importance of allow-ing a child to have and express his feelings honestly and the immense importance of respecting those feelings. In children like Erich, feelings that are not sincerely respected are quickly suppressed.

Each time discrimination or prejudice, or even discomfort, is expressed, a tiny impression is made on the child. Children, even very young children, are never insensitive to these occur-rences. They accumulate, like layers of dust, on budding psy-ches. It doesn't take very long for children to see themselves as different and to sense that, somehow, that difference represents a flaw. A marred self-concept quickly leads to more significant problems in self-esteem. And when self-esteem begins to erode, it becomes increasingly difficult for any child to relate to others or realize their own potential.

The process of helping a child make a happy, secure adjust-ment, particularly when that child is physically different from others around him, is a growth experience both for parent and child. Parents who have adopted children from races different than their own or children with recognizable disabilities are doubly challenged as they work through this process.

Here, I (McKelvey) provide a list of goals/challenges/issues that I have found to be good guidelines when parenting a child who is ethnically from another culture.

1. Helping the adopted child have confidence in themselves as being worthwhile people (self-esteem issues).
2. Helping the child have a positive attitude toward adoption.
3. Helping the child be comfortable with their physical appearance.
4. Helping the child be comfortable with his heritage.
5. Helping the child develop the ability to handle racial incidents appropriately.

There is no "how-to" list regarding these issues. Based upon our experience, personal and professional, and based on that of the parents who have adopted internationally, the following may be helpful:

1. *Observation, awareness:* When incidents occur, observe closely the child's response. Allow the child to try to resolve things without stepping in too soon. Observe also the response of the offender. Learn from the experience.
2. *Cues and their importance:* Follow the cues the child provides (behavioral, verbal, delayed, immediate). Learn to read those cues and respond appropriately. (Seek guidance, if needed.) Don't overanticipate or provoke responses that may not be natural.
3. *Facilitate self-expression:* Encourage creative experiences and expression, such as art, theater, music, play, and storytelling. If tolerated, expose your child to the folklore (bedtime stories, songs, etc.) of his native culture.
4. *Provide a good model:* When unpleasant incidents occur, stay in control; protect your child by removing him quietly from threatening circumstances. Discuss feelings (anger, fear, etc.) later and on cue.
5. *Respect and empathy:* Be empathetic with the child's expressed feelings. Don't try to "talk him out of it." Share private expe-

riences emotionally when they occur (crying, laughing, etc.). Never be phony or dishonest. Children, especially wounded children, have built-in radar for dishonesty or insincerity.

6. *Become an advocate:* Advocacy training and informative workshops are widely available. Adoptive parents with children who are at risk for discrimination and equal opportunity violations can benefit from attending these sessions and becoming a trained advocate.

JUST HOW DOES INTERNATIONAL ADOPTION WORK?

Let's go back to the procedural process. Although it appears very complicated, international adoptions are governed by a certain set of laws and regulations. Understanding the regulations and where they conflict or are redundant can make the process easier. Be informed, so the heartache and financial disaster of attempting to adopt a child that cannot be brought into the United States can be avoided. Each country, state, and agency has its own requirements. Become familiar with them.

Be aware the rules in each country can change overnight. Dealing with mercurial changes and unannounced halts in the process requires flexibility and patience. The first step is to check with the State Department of Social Services to make certain that your individual state allows foreign adoptions. If so, a home study done by a licensed social worker is the next step. All adoptions require this step; in some states it must be done by a licensed adoption agency; some agencies require that it be done by agency caseworkers while others will accept home studies done by any licensed social worker. Work with a reputable agency to smooth the way. They can guide adoptive parents through the process, step by step:

1. Apply to a private, state-licensed agency or an individual social worker in your state to have a home study done. Before choosing an agency, you will probably find it useful to check with other adopting families who have used that agency.
2. Contact the placing agency. Be certain to inform them that the adoption is for a foreign-born child. After your agency of choice has received your home study and approved you for

their lists of waiting parents, it will obtain information on a child (usually including a picture) and send it on to you. This action is called a referral. If you accept the child, the child's birth certificate and proof of abandonment or relinquishment will be sent and immigration proceedings can begin.

3. Use advance processing (ask your agency). This can shorten the time if it is necessary for there to be an adoption proceeding in the child's country of birth. (More and more countries are going this route. In previous years, many sending countries simply released the child for adoption once abandonment or relinquishment was determined; the U.S. government then issued a special visa, allowing the child to be admitted to the United States for purposes of adoption.) If in-country adoption is required, the agency will also send a list of papers needed for that, along with the necessary power of attorney.

4. The placing agency will send the paperwork to the child's country to begin proceedings there.

5. When the papers have been approved, the visa granted, and the adoption completed within the child's country (if necessary), the child will be flown to the United States and the wait will be over.

6. After the child's arrival, you must complete U.S. adoption proceedings, as prescribed by state law. It is *essential* to re-adopt any child who was legally adopted abroad to prevent a later challenge to the adoption or to your child's inheritance rights. Check with your caseworker and/or attorney to find out about this procedure.

In all likelihood, you will have to spend some time abroad (in the child's country) completing the adoption. Some countries require that one or both adopting parents must physically see the child (not just view a photograph or video) before their selection of that child is confirmed. In many cases, a parent (or both parents) are required to travel to the child's country to complete the foreign adoption. Although the requirement may cause frustration and additional expense, it may offer a hidden benefit.

Children often profit from a more gradual period of transition from orphanage to home than most foreign adoptions provide. Adjustments to a new family are much easier, and adopting parents have an opportunity to get to know their child in an environment that is familiar to the child. This transition time is an important (but often overlooked) piece of helping the new child adjust. Both authors highly recommend it. (Transition is addressed more fully in chapters 9 and 10.)

REQUIREMENTS AND REGULATIONS

Receiving Country—U.S. Immigration Regulations

1. The child must be younger than sixteen years of age.
2. The child must be an "orphan" by definition. (Remember the discussion above regarding orphan status and the Orphan Petition?) You must apply for "Orphan Petition." If an adopted child is other than an orphan, the parents must have legal custody of the child for two years before they can apply for the child.
3. At least one of the adoptive parents (filing the petition) must be an American citizen. A single person must be a citizen and must be at least twenty-five years old.
4. If the child is adopted abroad, the adoptive parents must have both personally seen and observed the child before or during the adoption process, or it will be necessary to readopt the child in the United States after his arrival. Some countries permit proxy adoptions in which neither parent travels to the country; if documentation is in order, the INS will then issue a visa and allow the child to enter the United States for readoption here.

STATE AND AGENCY REQUIREMENTS

Adoption agencies are governed by the states in which they operate. Although each agency has its own rules and regulations, modification or additional requirements may be added to comply with the laws of the state(s) in which they operate. If adopting parents are planning to change geographic locations, it is best to be informed about the rules and regulations of their future location as well as those of their current home state.

All agencies have individual, basic requirements that adoptive parents must meet to qualify for adoption through the agency. Although they vary from one to another, agency criteria may include any or all of the following:

♦ Age of parents and/or age difference between parents and child.
♦ Marital status; some will consider singles.
♦ Religious preference; some require proof of active affiliations.
♦ Sexual preference. Gay couples are not accepted, for example. (Most sending countries are not comfortable with gay parents adopting children.)
♦ Family size and/or the length of time since birth or adoption of another child.
♦ Leave of absence for one parent if both parents work.
♦ Proof of insurance coverage for adopted child.

A little known provision in the Omnibus Budget Reconciliation Act of 1993 may benefit foreign-adopted children. The provision puts adopted children on an even keel with children born into a family regarding insurance. In effect, the law says that if a health plan provides coverage for birth children, then it must also provide identical coverage for adopted children from the moment the parents assume "total or partial" financial obligation for the child and not when the adoption is finalized.

Parents should be aware, however, that any insurance program can disallow preexisting health conditions and that most insurance programs have a cap or ceiling on the amount they will pay for mental health conditions.

It is advisable for adopting parents to know the rules and regulations affecting eligibility for medical coverage *before* adopting. Policies and restrictions should be reviewed regarding all potential providers—Medicaid, HMO, and insurance company. Some insurance programs or health care plans disallow payments for preexisting medical conditions.

Be Aware: Some U.S. states (Texas, for example) require an adopting parent to sign a waiver that would make the adopted child ineligible for Medicare, Medicaid, or SSI payments. The waiver is required before the state will approve the U.S. adoption (or readoption).

Each agency is responsible for the child it places. Adopting parents should anticipate several inquiries, requests for documentation, and some follow-up activities, including scheduled home visits by caseworkers assigned to their agency. When both parents work, some agencies require that one parent make adjustments in their work schedule or take leaves of absence during the adjustment and transition periods following the adoption. When an adoption does not work out, the agency usually (but not always) has some obligation to resolve the situation.

SENDING COUNTRY—FOREIGN COUNTRY REQUIREMENTS

1. Some countries have minimum or maximum ages for parents or age differences between child and parents.
2. Some countries require adoptive parents to be willing to adopt a child of either sex.
3. Few foreign countries knowingly approve adoption of a child by a gay couple. Some allow adoption by singles, others will not. Sometimes couples must be married a specific length of time.
4. Some countries allow adoptions only to infertile couples or those with limited numbers of children in the home.
5. Families whose original ethnic origins are in the foreign country are often given preference.
6. Many countries allow exceptions to policy for those willing to adopt special-needs children. Definitions for special needs differ by country.

REGIONAL CONSIDERATIONS AND VARIATIONS

Not all agencies handle adoptions in all countries. Although most agencies specialize in certain areas of the world, there are several large adoption agencies that handle adoptions in every region. The following samples of information, taken from an information book on foreign adoption, are an example of how the rules, expenses, and policies of a single agency may vary in different regions of the world:

KOREA

AVAILABLE: ages 0 through school age; full Korean; occasional special needs and siblings.

COST: $9,400, including local service and transportation of child to port of entry.

TIME: usually under twelve months for infants, longer for toddlers and school age.

FACTS: parents must be between twenty-five and forty-three with annual income of at least $25,000; marriage—minimum three years; religion must accept conventional medical care; prefer no sex preference for first child; usually no more than four children already in family; weight restriction; parent home six weeks after placement for infant and toddler; no smoking.

MALI (IN AFRICA)

AVAILABLE: ages 0–5, usually healthy; children are in an orphanage; tested twice for AIDS, TB, hepatitis B, and syphilis over several months.

COST: $4,750, not including child's one-way airfare, shared escort expenses, or translations (into French).

TIME: Six to nine months.

FACTS: single women, yes; no single men; parent(s) thirty or older; prefer infertile, childless (will consider one or two children already). Parent(s) select sex and approximate age.

CHINA

AVAILABLE: ages 0–2, AIDS-tested.

COST: $13,000, not including transportation or local service.

TIME: one to two years.

FACTS: parents twenty-five to forty-five for infants; married five years; Christian; one parent Chinese or parent of Chinese child; with certified infertility; no more than one child already; travel one to two weeks for one parent.

We provide these as samples of the kind of information you will be provided with by adoption agencies. We are not providing a complete list here because the rules and regulations change from month to month and country to country. The adoption agency you work with should have the most up-to-date material on the countries that interest you.

BE PREPARED FOR SUDDEN CHANGES

Foreign adoption, its policies, procedures, and the politics that surround it are in a constant state of flux. In general, it is best for adopting parents to assume that any information can change at any time. Be prepared to see at least one such change during the course of your adoption.

Those adopting from South American countries, for example, will find that the rules and regulations there are constantly under revision. Peru is an outstanding example of the fickle nature of adoption. In reviewing charts on adoption trends, we became curious why intercountry adoption numbers in Peru had fallen so dramatically:

INTERCOUNTRY ADOPTIONS IN PERU: 1989–1994

1989	269
1990	440
1991	722
1992	324
1993	230
1994	37

We learned that this drop coincided with the time that Peru changed its adoption laws and drafted new regulations that extended the required length of stay in the country for adopting families. Peru was requiring all foreigners who were adopting Peruvian children to stay a minimum of seven weeks before being allowed to leave with their new child. This was acting to discourage potential adopters who could go elsewhere in either South or Central America and accomplish adoptions in less than two weeks.

For a family with other children at home or working parents with job obligations, prolonged stays in foreign countries can create significant hardship. One of the most unpleasant surprises for Americans adopting children in developing countries is the exorbitant cost of decent hotels. In many of these countries, there are few, if any, reasonably priced alternatives for lodging.

Length of stay is not the only determining factor. Peru, like many other countries, has revised and tightened its regulation of adoptions by foreigners in several ways. Currently (as of this book's publication date), only licensèd adoption agencies are allowed to work in Peru. Private parties and self-directed adopters are not permitted to apply. Bolivia is another country where only licensed agencies are allowed to operate within the borders. This means private adoptions through adoption attorneys had ceased.

Whether the restriction of private adoption is a growing trend or isolated to a few countries is unknown. (It appears to be a growing trend.) Therefore, it is advisable for adopting parents, particularly those who have initiated private adoptions, to always be prepared for change in law and policy and to have a backup plan.

Adopting parents should ask their adoption agency to plan for a contingency in case their country of choice shuts down adoption. We heard from one family, for example, that was headed for Russia when that country unexpectedly halted adoptions. Rather than come home empty-handed, they and their adoption agency, which operated in another nearby country, arranged for the family to fly on to the second destination where they found the child of their dreams.

Russian adoption, which was closed down for legal revision and new regulations, was reopened in spring, 1996. The revised adoption law in Russia has decreed that all information about all the children in all the orphanages be placed on a database before intercountry adoption reopens. That process has been understandably slow. The law also mandated that new children coming into the orphanage system must be held for a certain period of time before adoption is opened to foreigners.

In addition to Russia, several other countries shut down adoptions in fall, 1995. Paraguay, for example, was closed for new laws to be enacted to counteract corruption in the adoption industry. Also in Paraguay, it is expected the country will move to an agency-only rule soon. The Ukraine was also closed down for legal revision and new regulations. Nepal has been closed for some time.

THIRD-WORLD TRAVEL ADVISORY

It is important for uninitiated parents to remember that travel to a developing or redeveloping country is, in many ways, like entering another world. Returning Americans often liken their journeys to "a step back in time." Apart from differences in dress, language, and social custom, however, there can be a darker side to the so-called third world.

The level of desperation caused by years of poverty and hunger is impossible to overestimate in third-world and developing nations. A climate of suspicion and mistrust prevails in many redeveloping countries where the entire population has never experienced anything other than secrecy and betrayal to secret police. In underdeveloped countries with high degrees of illiteracy, ignorance and superstition reign. In redeveloping countries, even the educated have been deprived of information and modern technology for decades; this has created a relative degree of illiteracy in the academic and professional communities. In Romanian medical schools, for example, Western literature was cut off in the mid-1970s. When foreign adoption invaded eastern Europe in the early nineties, medical reports of adopted children often contained archaic language and serious omissions regarding current technical knowledge. Improvements have been made, but the problem still exists in many institutions and clinics.

Development and reform in the field of intercountry adoption, however, has been more troubled than redevelopment in the field of health sciences. When waves of westerners who were desperate to both rescue and adopt children invaded the shores of developing countries in the early nineties, a new kind of culture shock ensued. The receiving country was as shocked by this special group of visitors as the outsiders were by the conditions they found when they arrived in the country to adopt a child. Understanding was often lacking. The plight of an infertile, American woman who had undergone several unsuccessful attempts at uterine implantation was as incomprehensible to the host country as the desperation of a street beggar who was willing to sell a baby in order to feed her starving family was to the visitor.

Against this backdrop of cultural disparity, lack of common experience, and widespread misunderstanding, to say that the actions of westerners who arrive to adopt children are "misunderstood" is a sad understatement. They are, instead, often not understood at all. In many instances, they are deeply resented. This is particularly true of Americans, even those of modest incomes, whose relative degree of affluence appears rudely ostentatious.

In this climate of resentment and suspicion of outsiders, it is easy to see how vicious stories and rumors begin to take their toll. This is particularly true when there has been substantiated corruption or illicit adoption taking place in the foreign country in question.

RUMORS AND THEIR RISKS

For several years, a chain of ugly rumors has run rampant through many of the countries where foreign adoption is particularly active. More than tall tales or even malicious gossip, these rumors have dealt specifically with scandals, illicit child trafficking, and exploitation of children under the guise of adoption. Although the rumor mill has been most notable in Central and South America and eastern Europe, very few countries doing intercountry adoptions are exceptions. Americans are usually implicated in these stories.

Because many of these stories are inflated, sensationalized versions of real scandals involving illicit adoption syndicates (operating primarily in Europe and the Middle East), any rumor, however bizarre, is often believed to have a thread of truth. These include false reports that children are being adopted for such macabre reasons as medical experimentation or to be used as organ donors for surgical transplant programs.

The wide belief of rumors is *not* restricted to the illiterate and or superstitious populace. Many members of the professional community and the so-called intelligentsia have become very skeptical and suspicious. The major reason for this is the common practice of unrestricted, scandal-sheet journalism in many of these countries. Literally anything can be reported and printed at any time. Many of these papers make our worst tabloids read like comic strips. Since 1990, there has been a proliferation of new newspapers throughout the "emerging democracies." Today, in Romania, for example, there are more newspapers per capita than in any other country in all of Europe.

Adopting parents should be aware of these rumors, if for no other reason than to be prepared to deny them. Rumor has often been the source of temporary adoption shutdowns while government officials investigate the story. While it is rarely openly acknowledged, delays in adoptions in progress are often traced to official reactions to these rumors.

When rumor or scandal is behind the shutdown, an undercurrent of suspicion and tension envelops the international community in sending countries. U.S. government employees of foreign embassies or consulates are particularly sensitive to both rumors and inflated news stories of adoption-related scandals. On several occasions, adopting parents have been openly threatened or attacked.

It was into this atmosphere of distrust and corruption that an Alaskan woman walked in March 1994. The rumors that foreign-born children are being adopted so that their organs can be removed and used for transplants in the United States was responsible, in part, for the severe beating she suffered in Guatemala. June Weinstock, a Fairbanks, Alaska, environmentalist was touring Guatemala after leading a river trip in southern Mexico. She was beaten into unconsciousness after a crowd accused her of kidnapping a Guatemalan child whom they believed she planned to traffic to illicit organ donor groups. The child in question was later found unharmed, according to press reports.

Weinstock, fifty-five, was attacked by hundreds of Guatemalan peasants in the town of San Cristóbal Verapaz when she tried to take photographs of some children. She suffered head injuries and fractures of her arms. Weinstock was airlifted in critical condition back to Anchorage where she remained in a coma for months.

In addition to Weinstock, Reuters news service reported two other U.S. citizens and a Swiss volcanologist have been attacked since the rumors took hold in early March 1994.[9] A Philadelphia woman, Janice Wogel, was whisked to safety by U.S. embassy security guards in May 1994 after a group of Guatemalans accused her of stealing a baby she had recently adopted.

Weinstock's attack was among four others that had occurred in Guatemala since rumors began circulating that Americans were traveling to the country to steal or adopt babies and children and then sell them for organ transplants. Americans have been the target of rumors concerning bizarre child-kidnapping plots. Although the Guatemalan government had said the rumors were groundless, the U.S. State Department issued a warning for American citizens to avoid all nonessential travel to the country.

There is a simple way to defuse such rumors and that is to keep in touch with those from whom the child or infant was adopted. For example, those who have adopted children from a foreign country should write regularly to the source from which the child was adopted (such as the institution) and tell them, with photographs when possible, just how well the child is doing. Writing updates every six months or so establishes a rapport and shows how well adopted children can do in the United States. Adoptive parents who come after you will be helped by this correspondence.

TRENDS AND THE BIG PICTURE

For the past ten years, an average of more than eight thousand U.S. families (or individuals) have completed foreign adoptions each year. After peaking at 10,097 in 1987, numbers gradually declined until 1991, when the explosion in eastern Europe, primarily in Romania, brought the total to 9,008. The low figure of 6,536 in 1992 (before the Russian Federation opened) was almost entirely due to Romania's shutdown of adoption to write its law. From 1992 to the present time, numbers have steadily risen.

As we reviewed the big picture of foreign adoption for this book, the authors noted general trends that should be of interest to adopting families.

INS reports Intercountry Adoptions by region, listing only the major countries in each region individually. There are five regions: Europe, Asia, Africa, North America (includes Mexico and Central America), and South America. Oceania is a sixth, but numbers from there are very small.

The following tables list regions and rank the countries by numbers of children adopted. A separate table is provided for each of the following years—1988, 1991, and 1994.

U.S. INTERCOUNTRY ADOPTIONS—1988

Rank	Region	Number Adopted	Country	Number Adopted
1	Asia	6,484	Korea	4,942
2	South America	1,757	Columbia	735
3	North America	844	Guatemala	209
4	Europe	99		
5	Africa	15		

U.S. INTERCOUNTRY ADOPTIONS—1991

Rank	Region	Number Adopted	Country	Number Adopted
1	Asia	3,194	Korea	1,817
2	Europe	2,761	Romania	2,552
3	South America	1,949	Peru	722
4	North America	1,047	Guatemala	347
5	Africa	41		

U.S. INTERCOUNTRY ADOPTIONS—1994

Rank	Region	Number Adopted	Country	Number Adopted
1	Asia	3,641	Korea	1,741
2	Europe	2,406	Russian Federation	1,798
3	South America	1,204	Paraguay	483
4	North America	846	Guatemala	436
5	Africa	41		

INTERNATIONAL ADOPTION TRENDS, TEN YEARS (1984–1994)

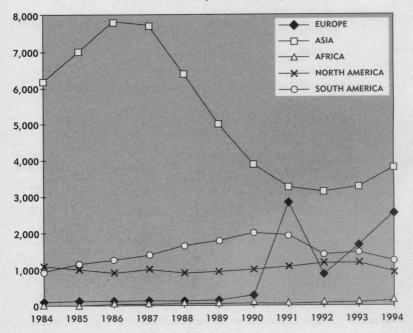

INTERCOUNTRY ADOPTIONS (1984–1994)

	1984	1985	1986	1987	1988	1989	1990	1991	1992	1993	1994
All Countries	8,327	9,286	9,945	10,097	9,120	7,948	7,093	9,008	6,536	7,348	8,195
Europe	79	91	103	122	99	120	262	2,761	874	1,521	2,406
Romania	0	0	0	0	0	0	121	2,552	145	88	199
Russia	0	0	0	0	0	0	0	0	0	0	1,530
Other Former USSR	0	0	0	0	0	0	0	12	432	1,107	268
Other Europe	79	91	103	122	99	120	141	197	297	326	409
Asia	6,251	6,991	7,679	7,614	6,484	5,112	3,779	3,194	3,032	3,163	3,641
P.R. of China	6	16	10	15	52	81	29	62	201	330	787
Taiwan	56	72	90	66	56	81	29	62	201	330	787
Hong Kong	30	51	40	56	49	47	0	40	27	27	34
India	468	496	588	807	698	677	348	448	348	342	406
Japan	45	57	46	64	69	74	57	83	71	59	49
Korea	5,157	5,694	6,188	5,910	4,942	3,552	2,620	1,817	1,787	1,765	1,795
Philippines	408	515	634	593	476	481	421	417	353	358	314
Africa	8	11	22	22	28	36	52	41	63	59	91
North America	1,026	1,012	885	973	844	910	959	1,047	1,136	1,133	846
Mexico	168	137	143	178	123	107	112	106	104	97	85
Carribean	93	118	102	124	140	202	156	159	134	150	132
Central America	756	746	626	654	568	595	683	770	892	878	628
El Salvador	364	310	147	135	88	92	103	122	115	97	38
Guatemala	110	175	228	291	209	208	257	324	428	512	436
Honduras	148	181	135	114	161	191	197	244	253	183	77
South America	954	1,172	1,235	1,363	1,650	1,757	1,995	1,949	1,418	1,471	1,204
Brazil	117	242	193	148	164	180	228	178	139	178	149
Chile	153	206	317	238	252	254	302	263	176	61	79
Colombia	595	622	550	724	699	735	631	527	403	416	351
Paraguay	8	15	32	90	300	254	282	177	244	405	483
Peru	31	34	71	84	142	269	440	722	324	230	37

Foreign adoption continues to increase in the redeveloping nations that were once part of the Communist world. Despite the inefficiency of the new bureaucracies and the frequent halts in adoption while laws and regulations undergo revision, thousands of children have been given "orphan status" by virtue of their abandonment and are making their way onto adoption lists. In late 1995, adoptions were still going strong in Romania, Latvia, Lithuania, Georgia, and Bulgaria. In addition to children in orphanages, many adoptable children who are older and more challenged are coming out of long-term stays in institutions.

In other parts of the world: Adoptions continue to flourish in Guatemala and are strong in Honduras and Panama as well. Adoptions in Africa are also on the rise, and are particularly strong in Liberia, Ethiopia, and Uganda (on both African coasts). Despite increased restrictions and fees that have gone up considerably, intercountry adoption continues to thrive in India.

Another area in which there has been furious growth and change (as this book went to press) is mainland China. In late 1996, the estimates were that more than one million little Chinese girls were available for adoption in China. Americans and adopting families from other Western countries, like England, Ireland, and France, were flooding the borders in search of infant girls.[10]

The current adoption boom in China has a history. When adoption first reopened to the West (after 1990), only infertile couples of thirty-five years of age plus were allowed to adopt. Furthermore, they could only adopt one child. After several years of experience with the adoption process, however, the rules were relaxed, previous restrictions lifted, and the current rush to the Chinese adoption front began. In addition to newcomers, many families who had adopted previously returned for another child.

The numbers from mainland China from 1990 to 1994 show the trend clearly:

INTERCOUNTRY ADOPTIONS FROM MAINLAND
CHINA: 1990-1994

Year	Total
1990	29
1991	62
1992	201
1993	330
1994	787

It is anticipated that the numbers of Chinese adoptions will jump even higher in the future. The only cloud on the horizon is the recent worldwide exposure of China's human rights violations with respect to women. The selection of infant girls for institutionalization in state orphanages and the deprivation and neglect of many of them in those orphanages are only part of the larger issue of Chinese women and their role in society.

By law, Chinese families are permitted to have only one child. Despite the political changes of recent years, these legal restrictions—part of the population control measures instituted by the Cultural Revolution—have persisted. When coupled with centuries-old negative cultural attitudes about the role of women in Chinese society, enforcement of these laws has resulted in thousands of young mothers giving their girl babies to orphanages so that they might conceive again and have a son.

With no social security system, this gender preference for newborns is a strong reinforcement for Chinese mothers to give up their little girls and keep trying to give birth to a boy. In Chinese tradition, it is the eldest *son* who is to provide for his parents in their declining years. Women, therefore, are discriminated against from the time of their birth onward and continue to hold a low position in society throughout their lives.

Chinese human rights issues were brought to the forefront in 1995 when foreign adoption began to boom and stories about Chinese adoptions flooded the American media. Major pieces appeared in *Family Life, Parenting* magazine, numerous local newspapers, and on major network television programs. The subsequent discovery of inhumane conditions in several orphanages pumped fuel on the growing media fire. Reinforced by the worldwide publicity surrounding the United Nations 4th World Conference on Women at Beijing in September 1995, the story of China's baby girls became front-page material and continues to dominate press and media releases about intercountry adoption in Asia.

If reports of human rights violations in orphanages continue to mount and if China remains overly sensitive to world criticism in this area, the long-term effect upon intercountry adoption of Chinese girl babies is uncertain. Unless China makes some effort to correct their human rights practices, there is some danger that continued public scrutiny may have a negative effect and China will tighten up on foreign adoption to avoid further exposure. On the other hand, any effort toward positive change and correction of violations will have a positive effect. There is early evidence that some positive change is occurring, particularly in orphanages where conditions are beginning to improve as a direct result of media exposure and ensuing humanitarian assistance.

In the meantime, intercountry adoption is undeniably an important part of the immediate solution to China's problems with its institutions overcrowded with unwanted female infants. Hundreds of thousands of Chinese baby girls remain in the orphanages and are available for adoption by Westerners. Hundreds of Americans are returning home with children like Hayley Rose Lansing, whose story was told in the introduction. Almost without exception, adopting parents have happy stories, and their adoptions of China's baby girls seem to be going well. As for the numbers of children coming out of China, we personally can't think of anyone who hasn't heard of a friend or family member who is either headed for China to adopt or has already been there and returned with a story like Hayley and the Lansing family's (from the Introduction).

Despite the attention it has received in 1995–96, China doesn't totally dominate the Asian adoption market. Korea remains the champion and adoptions there are still going strong, despite earlier predictions that they would drop. Since the postwar trade embargo was lifted in 1989, Vietnam has also reappeared as a major Asian adoption market. In late 1995, China, Korea, and Vietnam all had infants and children up to about age fifteen ready for adoption. The Far East, therefore, is the hot spot where potential parents are turning for adoptable infants and young children.

DOLLARS AND SENSE: A WORD ABOUT FEES

Many adoptive couples want to know, up front, how much they can expect to spend on an international adoption. There are a number of expenses to consider. The following figures are current estimates and represent averages compiled from agency and parent organization literature.

1. The *agency fee*, which can run from $3,000 to $12,000 and usually includes:
   - *Home study and post-placement home visit fees* (usually part of the agency fee), which pay the social worker and typically cost from $450 to $1,500 each.
   - *In-country fees*, covering such things as attorney fees, court costs, translation, expediting fees, miscellaneous filing fees, etc. (These often vary widely, depending on the country. In some countries, so called "expediting fees" are really official bribes under the table.)
   - *Fees to foreign governments or agencies* can be as high as several thousand dollars.
2. *Travel costs*, (often not entirely covered by agency fees) covering travel for the child to come to the United States, as well as round-trip travel and food and lodging costs for the adoptive parent/parents. This cost is highly variable, depending on the country of choice, the length of stay, and many other factors.
3. *Miscellaneous costs* (not covered by agencies), including initial application fees, notary fees, supplemental document translation and preparation fees, fingerprints, visas, etc.

Total out-of-pocket costs, costs that are not part of the agency fee, usually run in the area of $10,000.

In late 1995, all costs and fees for foreign adoption were rising just as the demand was rising. Beginning in the 1990s with the influx of the baby boom generation, the trend has continued. In November, 1995, the cost of international adoptions ranges from $5,000 up to $25,000 for agency fees alone. Today, more and more fees were being quoted in the $20,000 range.

Intercountry adoption, therefore, is not as inexpensive as we wish it were. "We're not all Daddy Warbucks," one new father lamented, "and most of our children are not Little Orphan Annies either. Ours have lots of extra expenses after adoption."

FINDING EXTRA SUPPORT

Adopting parents need to know about resources that may help (financially) with the adoption of a foreign child. The following may help reduce the costs of adoption fees:

Nonrecurring adoption programs: Existing state programs, federally mandated to include foreign-born children adopted by American couples or singles. A program of the U.S. Department of Health and Human Services, nonrecurring adoption assistance allows up to $2,000 of nonrecurring (one-time-only) expenses involved in adopting special-needs children whose adoptions were finalized after January 1, 1987. The rules were written into the Tax Reform Act of 1986.

Military, nonrecurring program: A one-time subsidy program for full-time military personnel. Adopting couples or singles can receive up to $2,000 per child or $5,000 maximum for siblings, for adoption-related expenses.

Religious support: Some families go to their house of worship for help, through outright financial assistance or fund-raising activities.

Loans and second mortgages: We've heard of some families who take out loans or get a second mortgage. If able to handle the extra payments, these loans offer the advantage of longer payback times and lower interest than short-term conventional or personal loans.

Corporate subsidies: Some businesses have adoption assistance programs and adoption/maternity time off. Check with the company personnel department about this. Corporate subsidies, where they exist, often range from $500 to $3,000.

A FINAL REMINDER: AFTER-ADOPTION CONSIDERATIONS

There are a few more things to do once the child's adoption is finalized in the foreign country. These include:

- A passport for the child.
- A foreign country exit visa for the child.
- A U.S. entrance visa (gives official permission to formally enter the United States through Immigration).
- Readopting the child in the United States (depending on the circumstances).
- Obtaining citizenship for your new child. Children adopted in a foreign country are eligible for what is called a "streamlined naturalization" in the United States.

For additional information on resources regarding the adoption and postadoption process, see the appendix.

> *Be sure you are right; then go ahead.*
>
> Davy Crockett

REFERENCES

1. International Concerns Committee for Children, Boulder, CO, 1995, 911 Cypress Dr., Boulder, CO 80303-2821.

2. Rumi Engineer, personal interview, Denver, CO, August 1995.

3. Ibid.

4. Ibid.

5. The "law" being referred to in an Orphan Petition is #8 C.F.R., 204.2-204.3, the Code of Federal Regulations, pp. 856–866.

6. "Vital Statistics," *Health*, January–February, 1994, p. 14.

7. KUSA-TV, Denver, CO., May 1, 1994.

8. Ibid.

9. Reuters News Service, 1994.

10. Anna Marie Merrill, International Concerns Committee for Children, Boulder, CO, November 1995.

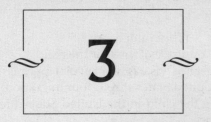

The Case of Romania

A Romanian child is born with a song and a poem in his mouth.

Anonymous, Romanian proverb

For many reasons, the Romanian experience is used as a model throughout the book. The intensity of exposure and interest in Romania's abandoned children from 1990 to the present has produced a wealth of information never before collected on a single population of adoptable or adopted children from a foreign country. Although they are unusually severe and complex, the problems and characteristics of Romanian children are consistent with those of adopted children from other foreign countries. In 1991, the introduction of Romania's adoption law set the first example and later became a predictive model for foreign adoption in other countries.

The tiny country of Romania (about the size of Arizona with a population of twenty-three million) was among the first to open its doors to international adoption when the Iron Curtain began to disintegrate. Discovered by the public media soon after the collapse of Communism in 1989, Romania's so-called orphans soon eclipsed the news of its revolution and new democracy. The plight of thousands of institutionalized children became the lead story in television programs and news publications throughout the Western world.

Images of Romania's lost children invaded every household and made indelible imprints upon the Western mind and soul. In morning papers, sad, pleading eyes stared through the rusty bars of cribs that were crammed together in seemingly endless rows. On evening programs, pale, solemn faces crawling with flies and the ghostly, silent rocking of children's small, frail bodies haunted television screens. Throughout the world, Romania's orphans provoked a global response that was unprecedented in modern history.[1] In the ensuing four years, more than 1,200 humanitarian relief and development agencies flooded into the country to provide services to children and help rebuild the health and human services systems.

Not all of the children were orphans. More than 90 percent of the 150,000 plus children found in Romania's state facilities in 1990 had at least one living parent and had been institutionalized for "social protection." Nearly all of the children had been admitted during early infancy, and most were transferred directly from maternity units. The two most common reasons for admission were poverty related: the birth family's inability to afford essential care for the child at home or a single parent with no means of support. Much less commonly, children were voluntarily admitted with untreatable conditions, birth defects, disabilities, or health conditions that required services not available in communities.[2]

As the country's economy crumbled during the last decade of Ceausescu's failing regime, dispirited Romanian families either relinquished or lost all hope of reuniting with their children. They were either too poor or sick to take care of their children, or they had lost all connections with them. Some Romanian parents couldn't find their children; they had not been notified when their child was moved to another facility.

Ironically, most of the children were abandoned to a failing institutional system where, by the mid-eighties, conditions had deteriorated as much as they had in the impoverished homes the children had come from in the first place. The social protection system, therefore, perpetuated the very condition it had been founded to prevent; it jeopardized rather than secured the futures of Romania's children.

The stated purpose of Romania's institutions was defeated long before the Ceausescu government fell. When institutional care was diverted from its child protection purpose and, instead, raised and groomed children to become future workers for the state, all semblance of care for disabled and high-risk children ceased. An environment purported to be protective often became more dangerous than that from which the child had been removed. The notion that children could realize their normal potential in institutions and become productive workers for the state was as unrealistic as the prospect of Ceausescu's "Industrial Utopia."

~

I (Bascom), like many others, was deeply moved by early newspaper stories about Romanian children who were trapped in institutions for the so-called irrecuperable. It was a February article in the *London Times* that first captured my attention and prompted me to respond to a request from Romania's minister of health. By early April 1990, I was aboard a TAROM airlines flight, headed for a country that I barely knew existed before reading the newspaper stories.

Coming from a professional background in physical therapy, child development, and program development for children with special needs, I was asked to evaluate the needs of Romania's institutionalized children and to assess the training needs of their professional staffs. When a six-week tour was completed, I was to make recommendations to the Health Ministry for reform and redevelopment projects.

My meandering career path seemed to straighten out as soon as I set foot in a Romanian orphanage. It was as if all the little roads I had traveled in my professional journey had suddenly converged. Every minute I had spent in lecture halls, wondering why I had signed on for a course, was useful. Every week I had sat on cold floors of church basements, trying to put together a program for disabled children and not getting enough support, suddenly made sense and was valuable. The realization that I was in the right place at the right time and was carrying the right baggage was a curse as well as a blessing. I knew what I was looking at when I toured the institutions and saw hall after hall of silent, rocking children. My knowledge made the whole experience more heart-wrenching than anything I could remember. My six-week tour turned into six years, and still hasn't stopped.

THE ORPHANAGES: LEAGANE DE COPII, ROMANIA'S CRADLES FOR CHILDREN

I visited more than thirty institutions in April 1990. Most were orphanages, but several were hospitals and clinics for children, and several others were institutions for older children, called *scoala*, the Romanian word for school. The orphanages were cold, cement buildings surrounded by walls and chain fences. There were guardhouses out front, where I had to show my official papers and wait for permission to enter. Inside the buildings (strangely called orphanages because there were very few orphans there), I found thousands of abandoned babies and children living in conditions so deplorable that it was unimaginable that any human being could survive. Certainly not a baby . . . or a fragile child or a sick one. Yet they did survive, thousands of them, and the miracle of that survival kept me going.

All the rooms were large and, except for Bucharest's showpiece Orphanage #1, devoid of playthings or any signs of childhood activities. Charitable donations that were just beginning to arrive in many of them never found their way beyond Bucharest. Others were often pilfered by black marketeers. Gradually, however, the market was flooded, and by the first of May every orphanage was stacked to the rafters with boxes of donated supplies, toys, and children's clothing.

In April, however, there was little evidence of the donation deluge to come. Some of the children had new blankets, but otherwise there was nothing. Toys, when they were present, were either lying in pieces on the floors or hanging limply on the walls, far from the grasp of children. When the children were given the toys, they didn't know how to play with them.

Most of the rooms were crammed with rusty cribs, placed side by side in rows to conserve space. Crib mattresses were old and saggy and were usually soaked with urine. There were no diapers, only thin muslin wraps that attendants briskly tied around the children in the morning and often did not return to change until the following day. Three times daily, older children were placed on plastic potty-seats in a bizarre ritual of attempted toilet training. There were no toilets or functional bathtubs.

In some orphanages, children were placed in large "play-pens" with wire-mesh sides for part of the day. There was no supervised play. In a few institutions, children over two years old were taken to a separate room downstairs where they sat, stone-faced, lined up on benches in front of young women who were called "educators." None of the educators I met had had one day of training or any formal education on how to be a teacher.

The same lack of formal training was true of the primary caregivers, called *infirmiere*. Supposedly the equivalent of Western nurses' aides, most infirmiere were women who had never completed secondary school. Their salaries were less than $20 a month. Most were very young and inexperienced. Some were illiterate. The ones who did well with the children were promoted to educator.

The orphanage nurseries were equally frightening. Coming into Romania as early as I did, most of the prerevolutionary routines were still in effect. I was often present in the mornings when new babies came literally rolling in the doors. On admission days, six to ten new babies would be brought in from maternity clinics on two-tiered rolling carts, wrapped stiffly from head to toe and capped, so that only their eyes were showing. Many babies, I learned later, spent the entire first two years of their lives wrapped up this way, lying flat on their backs, staring at distant ceilings.

All of the babies and young children were bottle-fed. Feedings were propped. When milk was in short supply, babies were given sweetened tea. The holes in the bottle nipples were enlarged to shorten feeding times. I was told this was done "to increase efficiency." No one talked to the babies. No one played with them, sang to them, rocked them (there was no such thing as rocking chairs in orphanages), cuddled them, or even touched them other than to change their bedding and "diapers" and prop up their bottles.

THE IRRECUPERABLES

When I got involved with the Camin Spitals in the summer of 1990, I fully understood, for the first time, what fate had in store for the children of the Cradles. I had been dealing with quality of survival issues, such as education, medical care, child development, and rehabilitation in designing programs for orphanages. But for what? Most of the children who had a disability (and at least 85 percent of them did, at that point in time), and unless they were totally cured would be labeled irrecuperable and sent to Camin Spitals. More than 50 percent of children who were admitted to Camins would die within twenty-four months of admission.

The sorting and labeling process took place at age three. Any child who was not deemed suitable for Romania's future workforce was considered "unsalvageable." Children with handicaps who had not been rehabilitated by their third birthday were classified as irrecuperable. Some children who had very minor problems, such as crossed eyes or difficult behavior, were also labeled irrecuperable. And there were many children in Camin Spitals in whom I could find no medical problems. Most of those youngsters were Gypsies.

Survival was the issue at the Camins, not quality of life, and certainly not rehabilitation. Time was up on rehabilitation when the children left the Cradles; this was usually at age three or four. In the Camin Spitals, there was little food, no medicine, often no indoor plumbing, and never any heat. Life support took on a new meaning. An extra crust of bread, a successful tug-of-war for a blanket, a bedmate to keep a child warm—those were the things that made the difference. When winter came, children who only got frostbite were called "the lucky ones."

~

During my first year in Romania, I was often interviewed by journalists or TV reporters; they usually asked, "What was your strongest impression, the thing that got to you most?" My answer was always the same: "It was the utter and awful silence of those places." I would walk into a facility and hear no sound other than the metallic chink of cribs knocking together as the children rocked themselves.

Never on that first tour of Romania's orphanages did I hear

children cry. Never did I hear a laugh, or song, or any language spoken by the children. The silence of Romania's children said more to me about the starkness of their existence and their total deprivation than any other factor. Nothing affected me as deeply.

It was inconceivable to me, as a doctor and a human being, that three hundred children under the age of four could be crowded into one building, and there would be no sound. Later, when our ROSES program began to work with children, our greatest sign of success was language—babbling, talking, children shouting in play or crying aloud when distressed. And singing! Astonishingly, when we brought music into the program, many children sang before they talked.

Laughter was the best of all. When children began to laugh, we knew that something of childhood had been returned to the children of the Cradles. When they laughed, we knew they had begun to heal.

Most of Romania's institutionalized children had never experienced childhood. The affection that a mother transfers to a young child through touch, care, and holding was unknown to all but the very few who had spent their early months in a home. The only loveliness, for most of them, had come from their fondness and attachments to each other. When all of our observations and studies were analyzed, years later, it was these attachments with each other that seemed to make the difference in the psychological development of children who spent their early childhood years without parents or loving adult caregivers.

My early days in Romania would have left me in emotional shreds were it not for the survivors of this so-called social protection system. Despite the deplorable conditions these children were forced to live in, and despite their early environments devoid of human touch, emotion, or any sensory experience, many of them not only survived but demonstrated a remarkable capacity for recovery as soon as someone, *anyone,* began to care for them. I felt deeply privileged to be that someone in seven of Romania's orphanages, where I developed my ROSES project. In the Camin Spitals, the survivors who not only stayed alive but thrived there were the most wonderful people I have ever known. They filled me with wonder and reaffirmed my belief in the human spirit.

LESSONS LEARNED IN PROJECT ROSES

My Romanian Orphans' Social, Educational and Services (ROSES) project was designed and approved by Romania's Ministry of Health in May 1990. Initial support was provided by the large humanitarian organization, World Vision, International. After January 1992, support was continued by The Brooke Foundation, a nonprofit organization founded by my husband and me to continue our work in eastern Europe.

Every good program needs a model. Mine was borrowed from the U.S. University Affiliated Programs in Child Development, UAPs, a system in which I had received all my training and early experience as an academician. With its dedication to provision of exemplary services in an interdisciplinary setting and conducting service-based training, the UAP model was particularly appropriate to Romania's needs. These I had summarized in my first report to the minister of health:

- The children are underserved and need a wide range of child development services.
- The institutions are understaffed.
- The staff are undertrained.

It is not my intent, nor is it within the scope of this book, to go into a lengthy description of the ROSES project and its accomplishments. Instead, I would like to share with the reader several of the many lessons learned that have a bearing on inter-country adoption. Although the media play in Romania was extensive in the early nineties, there was and still is a shortage of accurate information about adoptable children before they leave institutions. It is my belief that adopting parents should have as much information as possible about these children.

Information about Romania's institutionalized children came in three segments and has taken four years to evaluate:

- Lessons learned, in the early 1990s, from needs assessments and fact-finding activities of foreign-aid organizations and international adoption agencies.
- Lessons learned by humanitarian aid professionals as they established institution-based programs and observed children's responses to those programs.
- Lessons learned and still being learned by following the children after adoption.

FACT FINDING

During my first tour (in April 1990) I conducted random developmental screening evaluations in every orphanage I visited. After the first few institutional visits, it seemed almost pointless. Every child who had been institutionalized for more than six months was developmentally delayed, and the delays became more severe as the children got older. One had only to walk from room to room, observe, and ask a few questions to see clearly that children were falling farther and farther behind in growth and development as they grew older and spent more time in the orphanage environment.

But I continued the screening, partially for purposes of documentation with some reliable measures, and partially because so many children responded so quickly to the few minutes of stimulation and interaction. As soon as I would unzip my kit of screening toys and approach one crib, every child in the room would stop their rocking and watch the procedure with fascination.

It was remarkable how many children were able to learn a simple task after one or two demonstrations, given their total unfamiliarity with toys or supervised play. Only a small minority (10–15 percent) were so severely affected that they could not respond to screening. Most of those were untestable because they could not tolerate touch or handling. They would cringe, backing into the corner of their cribs, or they would crawl under them, if they were allowed out of bed.

Nearly all the children had self-stimulatory movements. Rocking was the most common. When I looked through the glass windows, I saw whole roomfuls of children rocking together, as if they were dancing to silent music. As soon as a stranger entered, however, most of the rocking would stop and the children would sit there, sizing me up (it seemed), until I started moving. Movement always triggered other habitual behaviors. When I approached a child in a crib or playpen, I was often greeted with a hand flung in front of a child's face in the defensive gesture called "face shielding." Face shielding was so pervasive in Romanian orphans as a response to invaders that I called it the "orphan salute."[3]

During my early months in Romania, I saw everything I had ever read about in a child development textbook and many things that weren't in any book. Piled on top of the epidemic of developmental disorders were a host of medical problems. The AIDS epidemic was heartbreaking. Romania has the largest pediatric AIDS problem in Europe. Almost all of the affected children were children of institutions, where transfusions with unscreened blood had been routinely given to babies and children who were not thriving.

My professional skills were stretched to their limits. The work was very hard because there was so much of it. For two years, I never slept in the same bed for more than five days running. The ongoing worldwide media circus, the chaos of program development, and the carnage I saw daily in many institutions demanded a great deal of me as a person. I developed great empathy for the hundreds of couples who came to the country to adopt Romania's abandoned children. Most of them had no information at all, and there was no regulation of Romania's adoption system at that time. We all had a common purpose, which was to give these children a chance at life. We helped each other.

Despite the fact that I felt very isolated (I was the only Western pediatrician in the country full-time), I had so much good help! Both technical and moral support came from ROSES staff and consultants who dropped everything in their home countries and came to Romania on very short notice. People dropped in (quite a feat) from all over the world with boxes of supplies for the children and Hershey bars for us. My husband and my colleagues in Romania were always there for me. That support made all the difference.

COUNTERPARTS

In Romania, my professional colleagues and the other health professionals I worked with were almost as deprived and neglected as the children they were trying to care for. It was hard to see how they had done as well as they had. They had no books, no journals, no specialty training programs, no labs, no backup facilities, and no communication with Western medicine. When I asked them what they wanted or needed, they told me they didn't know and wanted to know the possibilities.

The first and foremost need was for information.

Why? Eastern Europeans were totally deprived of the new body of knowledge about the relatively new field of child development and rehabilitation. Because it had only begun during the sixties in the West, this new branch of medicine as an interdisciplinary profession didn't reach pediatricians, physical therapists, or psychologists of Romania (or any eastern bloc country) because they had no access to information. The information blackout was especially profound in Romania and other eastern bloc countries that had recently been under Communist dictatorships. In Romania, the blackout had begun in the early seventies.

After programs were established and long-term development under way in the ROSES project, we soon discovered that information wasn't the only gap. When ROSES professional staff arrived, I required each of them to select a Romanian professional counterpart, a staff person whose job was a good match to theirs and with whom they could develop a working partnership. Although the concept was successful, we soon learned that most of our partners were not really counterparts:

- ◆ Except for the older ones, most pediatricians had had no specialty training since they left medical school.
- ◆ While many psychologists were university trained, most of their curricula were in political science. Speech and language therapists, called logopedists, belonged to logopedics and logopedics is a branch of psychology that was and still is a branch of political science.
- ◆ There were no higher education courses for nurses, physical

therapists, teachers, or social workers. Any specific training they had was obtained in secondary school.

♦ There was no such thing as occupational therapy.
♦ Most physical therapists were trained in "sport therapy," which is roughly equivalent to our physical education.

Higher education has now been established for most of these health professionals in Romania, but most of their students are still in university and won't graduate soon. Although the wreckage of Romania's health care system was particularly severe, adopting parents should know that this huge discrepancy between professional levels of training still exists in Romania, as well as many developing and redeveloping countries. This should be kept in mind when you are adopting a child and are having a talk with your waiting child's physical therapist. Or teacher, or pediatrician, or psychologist . . .

DISCOVERY

WHAT WERE THE CHILDREN LIKE?

One of our first tasks in the ROSES project was to screen and evaluate the children in the project. For some of the children, this was their first real comprehensive evaluation. For older children, rediagnosis was a major challenge because their problems had become so complex.

The following "top ten" lists summarize data from six hundred children who were enrolled in the ROSES project. Health[4] and developmental[5] problems are listed separately. Most of these clinical problems will be dealt with in greater detail in the chapters to follow.

Table 1

TOP TEN HEALTH PROBLEMS IN ROMANIAN ORPHANS

1. **Failure to thrive**—"dystrophic"
   Low birth weight—6–10% of dystrophics; continue to be dystrophic, never catch up

Deprivation—90% of infants institutionalized before age of 6 months show deceleration of growth that is progressive and results in abnormally small stature and low weight by age two; severity is related to time spent in institutions.

2. **Persistent small stature** +/− growth hormone deficiency
3. **Nutritional deficiencies:**
   Rickets—Calcium and vitamin D deficiency
   Anemia—Iron deficiency
   Protein/calorie deficiency—more severe in disabled and chronically ill children
4. **Communicable/infectious diseases:**
   HIV, hepatitis B
   Intestinal parasites, giardia most common; multiple infestations not unusual
   Tuberculosis (usually older children)
5. **Chronic/recurrent otitis media** (ear infections)
6. **Congenital malformations and deformations** ("birth defects"):
   Amniotic interruption syndromes (decreasing incidence since 1990); limb deficiency most common birth defect in orphanages
   Fetal alcohol syndrome and fetal alcohol effect
   Cleft palate/lip; probable + relationship to Cernobyl disaster
7. **Musculoskeletal disorders**
   Postpolio syndromes
   New syndrome (?) of fibrosis of quadriceps, genu recuvatum, dislocation of patella
   Congenital dislocation of hip (CDH), often not detected before adoption
8. **Strabismus +/− amblyopia** (crossed eyes, "lazy eye," with or without visual impairment)
9. **Environmental toxin-related illnesses:**
   Lead intoxication—paint and industrial sources
   Radiation—Cernobyl effect in children more than six years of age: leukemia and congenital malformations
   Multiple air, water, and soil pollutants
10. **Significant hearing impairment:** Significant relationship to number 5 (recurrent ear infections)

Table 2

TOP TEN DEVELOPMENTAL DISABILITIES COMMON TO ROMANIAN ORPHANS

1. **Global developmental delays of moderate severity** (<50%)
   85% of children institutionalized > six months: some demonstrable delay
   Severity is directly related to the length of time spent in orphanages and to age at time of admission
2. **Neuromotor deficits:**
   Hypotonia (poor muscle tone)
   Hyperextensibility of joints (loose jointed, unusually limber)
   "Pseudo-CP" (mimics cerebral palsy but has no neurological damage)
3. **Attachment disorders:** +/− autistic features
4. **Behavior disorders featuring stereotypes,** self-stimulating, and self-injurious behaviors
5. **Learning disabilities** (LD): language LD; ADHD (attention deficit with hyperactivity)
6. **Reactive behavior disorders**
7. **Profound, persistent retardation of language** and communication; elective mutism
8. **Post-traumatic stress disorder:** with night terrors, panic attacks, unusual fears or phobias (new-family attachment failures common in this group, seen most often with abuse)
9. **Sensorimotor and sensory integrative disorders:** previously called "perceptual problems"
10. **Persistent cognitive deficits:** permanently lowered IQ, mental deficiency

Although there are no detailed, parallel studies, the health and developmental problems of Romanian children summarized in these charts agree with those reported on other institutionalized children in other developing countries. While there are many published reports on communicable disorders, there is *very little* published data on foreign children's development, and almost none that addresses the institutionalized child specifically.

WHAT WERE ADOPTING PARENTS LIKE?

In the aftermath of the media blitz, and at the same time that humanitarian foreign-aid programs streamed into Romania's orphanages, couples from abroad began to arrive by the planeload to adopt the abandoned children. Although I was not directly involved in adoption per se, we often met each other in the orphanages. Most adopting parents were thirsty for information about the children they were adopting.

Their thirst and my desire to provide as much information as possible while they were there led to many after-hours meetings at the hotels where they were staying. One Bucharest hotel seemed to specialize in adopting families and was always filled with adopting parents from more than a dozen countries. The only telephone that worked for international calls was in the lobby. There were always lots of children waiting with their new parents for red tape to unravel and final court dates to be set. The scene was more than lively. In July 1990, I developmentally screened a Canadian adoptee in the hotel stairwell with the 20/20 crew perched on the stairs to film it all for "The Shame of a Nation."

Sometimes the children were sick and their parents were frantically worried. I remember rushing home one night to get my instruments so I could get back to the Hotel Triumph and look into the ear of a child who was leaving on the next morning's flight. Fortunately, the child's new mother had seen her pediatrician before leaving home and had brought along all sorts of liquid medicine, none of which was available in Romania. Mom had planned well and saved herself the anxiety of flying for fourteen hours with a child with an earache. The child had a bad infection. Her eardrum was ready to burst.

In talking and listening to adopting parents, I realized how damaging a lack of information can be. Without guidance or information, most adopting parents had built up unrealistic expectations and were headed for all the misery that is involved when a new child in the family doesn't meet those expectations and isn't getting the help he needs. We talked a lot about expectations, the misconceptions that accompanied them, and finally decided that the topic was important enough to do a survey and make the information we discovered available to professionals and other families.

With the help of nearly four hundred parents who were as frustrated as I was, a "top ten" list of expectations was designed. The survey[6] was conducted over a four-year time span (1990–1994) and was done in various locations, including church basements, hotel lobbies, orphanage salons, and on several baby flights from Romania—anyplace I could find parents congregated during the adoption rush in eastern Europe.

Table 3

TOP TEN EXPECTATIONS OF ADOPTING FAMILIES: FALSE EXPECTATIONS

1. **Developmental delays** imply normal potential and will resolve themselves with normal parental love and stimulation.
2. **Abnormal or unusual behaviors** associated with institutionalization (rocking, head tossing, etc.) will disappear in a home setting.
3. **The child will be glad to leave the institution.** Memories of orphanage life will provoke anxiety and fear and should be discouraged.
4. **Initial acceleration of growth and development** will be sustained until the child normalizes—usually expected within a year of adoption.
5. **Indiscriminate affection, smiling, and eye contact** are positive signs of normal attachment. Attachment is synonymous to bonding and should occur soon after adoption.
6. **Growth deficiency is always due to malnutrition.** When children are fed a normal diet for two years, growth should be "caught up."
7. **Language differences are significant barriers to development**—particularly learning abilities and speech "disorders."
8. **Emotional deprivation affects social and intellectual skills most severely.** Language and motor development are less affected.

9. **Adopted foreign children who pass developmental screening tests need no further assessment.**
10. **There is a national source of information** that adoptive families can access if problems arise regarding their adopted child.

Expectations are largely the product of the dream that any parent holds in their heart for the child they want to give birth to or adopt. When the plight of Romania's orphans was made public, many people came to Romania to adopt a child and get that child out of a brutal and destructive environment. Of the many parents I spoke to in 1990–91, this was the uppermost motive. Their expectations, therefore, were also based on what they thought they could accomplish with their children after adoption, how quickly they would recover, and how completely. Given the complexity and severity of problems in Romanian children and the fact that most adopting parents had no knowledge of the nature of their child's problem, it wasn't surprising that most of these expectations were unrealistic.

The purpose of this survey was not to demonstrate how many adopting parents were off on their expectations. The purpose was to find out what average, intelligent, committed parents expected in the first place. Once this was determined, professionals could start doing a better job of parent education and guidance. None of us knew what to expect. Romania's institutionalized children were boggling the minds of experts in child development around the globe.

Below is a comparison table[7] that corrects the false expectations and misconceptions. Except for the last one, all of the corrections require some in-depth knowledge of pediatrics, psychology, or early childhood development. This information is offered to adopting parents as a learning tool.

Table 4

CORRECTION OF MISCONCEPTIONS: EXPECTATIONS OF ADOPTING FAMILIES

1. **Developmental delays:** Despite normal potential at birth, many adoptees have moderate to severe delays that are not self-cor-

recting without intervention programs. A smaller percentage are never fully reversed and result in permanent developmental disability.

2. **Abnormal or unusual behaviors** are habitual and often persist long after the child has adjusted to a new family and home environment. Recurrences are common at times of stress.

3. **The child's feelings about leaving the institution:** Most children experience the sadness of separation and loss when they leave institutions; this occurs even when the environment was negative and/or traumatic.

4. **Initial acceleration of growth and development:** In most cases the initial growth spurt that occurs in the first 6+ months after adoption will level off and go slower thereafter. Children who fully catch up usually do so by two years postplacement.

5. **Indiscriminate affection, smiling, and eye contact** are signs of an attachment disorder in which the child is unable to select and make strong attachments. *Indiscriminate* affection is never a positive sign of attachment.

6. **Growth deficiency:** Growth deficiency is *not* always due to malnutrition. Well-nourished children who have been emotionally deprived can become growth deficient. In these cases, a deficiency of growth hormone, not calories, is the primary reason for their poor growth. Height is affected more than weight (with normal diets for two years, most children's weight does normalize). Love, not calories, is the best medicine for this condition. (See chapter 4.)

7. **Language differences are significant barriers to development:** Significant problems in language development *will not disappear* when the adopted child learns to speak English. Learning disabilities, developmental problems in language and communication, and speech "disorders" such as stuttering *are not caused* by lack of English-language skills.

8. **Emotional deprivation affects social and intellectual skills most severely:** *Language* and *motor* development are the most severely affected areas of development in severe maternal (emotional) deprivation. Measurable social *skills* usually refer to self-help skills (dressing, eating, learning rules, etc.) on general tests of early development and do not reflect personality development, which may be more severely affected. Although learning and school achievement may be lowered, most emotionally deprived children have normal IQs.

9. **Adopted foreign children who pass developmental screening tests need no further assessment:** Development should be monitored in any high-risk child, regardless of previous performances on screening tests. Screening is designed to identify significant problems at the time of testing and *cannot predict* problems that occur later in development. Screening, at any age, may overlook more subtle or milder problems.

10. **National source of information:** There is *no* national source of information that adoptive families can access if problems arise regarding their adopted child.

ADOPTION LAW IN ROMANIA

Although there was no legal process established until July 1992, and even though adoption was chaotic and riddled by corruption, thousands of couples completed successful adoptions via the wide-open, unregulated system in Romania. By December 1991, only two years post-revolution, more than ten thousand Romanian children had been adopted by citizens from multiple foreign countries.[8] More than twenty-six hundred of those children went to the United States. Of the 2,761 European children adopted to the United States in 1991, 2,552 came from Romania.[9]

Despite the impressive numbers of successful adoptions through the unregulated system, corrupt practices began to occur more frequently, and the need for an adoption law soon became pressing. Unscrupulous baby sellers invaded Romania's streets, and charlatan middlemen were positioned in every hotel lobby where foreigners were registered. Nearly every adopting couple had stories of encounters with would-be facilitators who offered their services for a price. It was difficult, if not impossible, for adopting families to differentiate sincere offers to help from the come-ons of unprincipled, greedy hustlers.

Finally, when the widespread corruption was exposed by Western media, all adoption was closed for a year while Romanian government agencies went to the drawing boards in an attempt to regulate the out-of-control system. Under tremendous pressure from both foreign and internal forces, a new law was finally enacted in 1992. With it, a new bureaucracy was born that has been both a source of protection and frustration for all.

ROMANIA'S ADOPTION BUREAUCRACY

In spite of the lofty principles Romania seemed to embrace when it ratified the UN Convention on the Rights of the Child and became an "emerging democracy," the process by which those principles were enacted remained mired in the old bureaucracy. More simply said, Romania embraced a new ideology, but found it difficult to change the way it did things.

Many officials of the Ceausescu regime remained in power after the revolution. They simply changed hats and kept going, using the same processes and management techniques. Persistent political processes and poor management practices were a deadly combination when it came to long-term development programs; intercountry adoption was no exception. When foreign assistance became established in Romania in 1991, it was widely agreed upon that the greatest barrier to real change was the pervasive lack of management skills.

Establishment of the new bureaucracy of international adoption was a classic example. The central government sought tightfisted control, but the Romania Adoption Committee (known as the RAC) and its new counterpart, the Committee for Social Protection of Children, were woefully understaffed and poorly supported by the government. District and local agencies, health departments, and social assistance agencies, for example, were given all of the responsibility and none of the authority to act on behalf of the children.

The RAC had no clerical support; its pediatricians were asked to translate and write letters. The simple selection of foreign agencies took more than a year and is still in progress. Cases backlogged. Pressure increased. RAC members were wooed by so many foreign governments and invited for so many out-of-country tours that their Bucharest offices went unmanned for weeks on end.

At the same time, competition became fierce among participating countries. It was equally intense among adoption agencies within individual countries. Everyone wanted a place on the approved list of agencies. More than two hundred agencies applied from the United States alone. (Only four were selected in the first go-round.) Criteria for selection were hazy. One American agency forged its authorization papers and was well into operations before the fraud was discovered.

There were also problems in the local districts. Most orphanage directors were soon overwhelmed by the administrative work involved in following the legal requirements, some of which represented powerful negative incentives for the adoption law's implementation at the local levels. Under the old regime, state support for the institutions depended upon quantities—"head counts" or "bed counts." This method of calculating state support did not change when the regime collapsed. Staff salaries, operational funds, and all financial support depended, and still depends, on keeping the beds full in the institutions.

Without children in cribs or lined up on benches in institutions, many Romanian professionals would be out of work if the law was fully implemented. Furthermore, the same orphanage directors who would lose their jobs and careers if orphanages were emptied *have been made responsible* for reporting abandoned children to the RAC. Therefore, a powerful disincentive threatens the new law's implementation. The prompt and responsible reporting of these children represents a nearly self-destructive act for these directors. Should orphanages and other institutions depopulate significantly, unemployment would number in the thousands.

When politics came into the picture, the performance of the RAC became tied to a number of political issues. By the end of the new bureaucracy's first operational year, the streets of Bucharest were filled with gossip of backroom deals, scandals, and a new, albeit more official corruption.

Every time a scandal occurred, or every time a loophole or deficiency in the new law was identified, the adoption process came to a halt. Months would then pass while the new bureaucracy amended the law and drafted new policies. Delays dragged on for months for adoptions in process. When the

backlogged system was reopened, the bureaucratic red tape
and cumbersome new policies seemed to put a stranglehold on
adoption rather than enhancing it. One only needed to review
the statistics to understand the negative impact that the bureaucracy had on U.S. adoption:

Years	Status of Adoption Law	Number of Adoptions
1990–1991	Before law was passed	2,673
1992–1994	After laws went into effect	431

Although the law was intended to protect children and
adopting parents, it seemed to be defeating its own purpose.
Part of the problem was traced to the frequent halt of all adoptions when the law needed revision. The bulk of the problem,
however, was that the newly created system was incapable of
functioning rapidly and efficiently enough to meet both the
needs of Romania's waiting children and the demands of international adoption agencies.

Romania's orphanages are as full as ever before with waiting
children. In America alone, there are ten qualified applicants
for each one of those children; qualified adopters wait in other
Western nations as well. By the end of 1993, more than a hundred thousand Romanian children were still "waiting." According to the unofficial report of one RAC official, more than sixty-
seven thousand of these children, between the ages of three and
seven years, were "known to be abandoned." Very few, if any,
of them had been reported to the RAC.

ROMANIA AS A PARADIGM

Described initially as innocent victims of an isolated, man-
made disaster, Romania's children turned out to be no exception to the thousands of children in orphanages in other countries. It was soon discovered that they were only the first of
many neglected child populations throughout the eastern bloc.
Reality became increasingly clear as governments collapsed,
and one border after another was opened to Westerners. In Al-
bania, Bulgaria, Poland, Ukraine, Moldavia, and Russia, hun-

dreds more institutions housing thousands more children were discovered by members of the international community. And in each of these countries, like Romania before them, Western journalists and media teams were often the first to report the discovery.

Once again, the Western world sat stunned before their television sets and wondered if this was a rerun. Once again, in shot after shot, country after country, children struggled to survive without food, warmth, medical care, or affection in overcrowded, crumbling, cement-block buildings. In one government ministry after another, officials and government leaders lived with the shame and embarrassment and desperately sought relief and assistance. Again, the Western world responded.

Although the type and intensity of humanitarian assistance varied from country to country, the welfare and protection of children became the priority of international funding agencies and foreign governments throughout the region. By early 1992, the plight of Romania's institutionalized and abandoned children had established a new prototype for international relief and development projects of the years ahead. By the end of 1992, virtually every one of Romania's 460 institutions had some kind of foreign assistance program under way. Some, like Bucharest's showpiece Orphanage #1, had so many foreign agencies involved that one had to be multilingual to communicate inside its walls.

Throughout the country, buildings were being renovated and light, heat, and plumbing were installed. Most of the programs involved specialized health and developmental services for children and some had training programs for the staff. Improvements began to show in children and their professional caregivers as well as the buildings.

As the model of Romania began to spread, we began to look at institutions that were outside eastern Europe, particularly orphanages, and found many similarities to what we had encountered in Romania. This was particularly true in Russia and the old USSR states. Although few countries had disasters the magnitude of Romania's, children were found languishing in institutions in every region of the globe. And most of the children who were over two years old were failing, both physically and developmentally.

THE IMMEDIATE FUTURE

With no functional child welfare system, with very few trained Romanian caseworkers, and with persistent disincentives at the local levels, the prospect for foreign adoption as a major solution for Romania's abandoned children remained and remains uncertain. The same is true in other countries. Throughout the developing nations of the world, children have become the chattel of whoever has authority over orphanages. In most of these countries, the children are the chattel of the state. Chattel unfortunately means that children can be viewed as commodities and will be considered, not in terms of human value, but in terms of tangible value to their owners.

It remains to be seen whether Romania's children are of more value in or out of Romania's institutions. But the tragic fact remains that thousands are being kept in orphanages who could find families and homes. Unless the situation changes, thousands more will fall through the cracks.

Only a small percentage of Americans on waiting lists for a Romanian child have been successful. The same is true in other eastern European countries and will continue to be true as other countries repeat Romanian history. That they have not learned from Romania's mistakes is costly. Hundreds of families are going through the same problems today in Russia that were experienced in Romania in 1992. Worldwide, this translates into thousands.

ROMANIA'S LOST TREASURES

In this chapter, too little has been said about the incredible capacity for recovery Romania's abandoned children demonstrated day after day, month after month, while we worked with them in the ROSES project. We didn't do anything fancy or extraordinary. Instead, we provided a basic early intervention program plus lots of mothering and love. We called it skilled loving care instead of TLC.

To reduce the appalling ratios of caregiver to child, we brought in community caregivers, assigned each of them four children, and taught them both routine child care and early education techniques. The therapists, educators, and psychologists did the highly technical remediation and rehabilitation.

The children responded so dramatically that we were grateful we had cameras. No one would have believed us otherwise. Without any change in diet, they grew so fast that every monthly review looked like time-lapse photography. One little girl, a dystrophic child, grew four inches in four months. Solid developmental achievements came more slowly than physical growth. But by the end of our first year, most of the previously crib-bound children were in our preschool program.

About 15 percent of the children were severely affected, and they required a lot of intensive work. The truly developmentally disabled children and physically challenged children broke our hearts because they had made so much improvement and were being bypassed by most of the families who came to adopt. They had no place to go in Romania after they left the Leaganes. Although we got permission to keep them until they were school age (six or seven), Romania couldn't catch up fast enough to provide the services disabled children need in the orphanage-*scoala*, the next step up in the institutional chain.

Most of these challenged children are still there. Somewhere.

The children with deep emotional wounds were our biggest challenge and required the highest intensity of services. There weren't enough skilled therapists in all of Europe to take care of so many damaged children. So we did what we could and selected some of them for one-on-one intervention and watched them respond one by one. They did respond. Although all of them are certain to have permanent injuries, it was in this group that we saw real miracles occurring. When they took me on rounds, the Romanian staff were full of words like "extraordinary" and "transformation."

The educators bore the brunt of this explosion in development that was occurring in the Leaganes. Once the problems of learning to walk, play, and talk were overcome, a lot of educational problems emerged. Many of the children who had been immobile before became hyperactive. Some got pretty aggressive. Behavior management became a big, big issue. The Romanians are very permissive with their children at home, and it was difficult for them to work on behavioral issues at work. So we worked hard on behavior modification using lots of praise and positive reinforcement.

Despite these issues, the preschoolers did very well. Our attempts to integrate them into the community, however, were less successful. The first class of preschoolers we sent to a community kindergarten bombed out on the first day. They refused to sit on their hands, a requirement of Romanian kindergarten teachers, and were described as "too eager" or "cheeky." We were finally able to convince the kindergarten to keep our children, but it took a lot of talking and maneuvering on our part. The school officials were right in one way. Most of these children were pretty proud of themselves and their accomplishments. Most of them *were* cheeky.

The common thread running through this story of ROSES and the universal miracle of childhood is that all of these children have the capacity for recovery, growth, and development. And it is wonderful to be part of the process. But most of these children will never fully realize that capacity or really thrive until they have a home and family. If this situation continues as it is going, a lot of potential parents will miss out on the supreme joy of loving and healing these children.

In December 1995, I returned to Romania for a monthlong stay. When I visited our ROSES orphanage during Christmas week, the children gave a little performance. Some visitors were also present—a man and woman from a local bank that had made a donation to the orphanage. I watched, delighted, as the children clung to the man and explored his pockets until the treats were distributed. Then, they lined up in costumes and sang for him.

Over the course of the past five years, I have made two observations about institutionalized children that stand apart from the developmental achievements I have measured. Although I never looked at them scientifically, and have been unable to find much written about them, adopting families may find them of value. They have to do with the response of these children to men and music:

◆ When my husband, Jim, visited orphanages, I often felt a little envious of the attention he received from children, many of whom had taken weeks to warm up to me or my staff. As soon as he sat down, they would be in his lap, exploring his shirt pockets and poking at his ears. His scratchy face fascinated them. They loved to hear him talk or make any kind of sound. (Jim is definitely a bass.) They liked to feel the rumble of his chest.

Jim likes and is good with kids. So he tolerated their explorations well. Once they had satisfied their curiosity, they would sit very still and become affectionate. And that was the wonder of it. They moved so quickly from investigation to reaching out for affection.

After watching this performance repeat itself a few times, I commented on it to a Romanian colleague. She responded quickly, saying, "Barbara, it's because he's a man. Many of these children have never seen a man, and none of them has been close to one emotionally. They are hungry for it."

I witnessed similar occurrences when other men came into the orphanage. My project manager, John Bratolaveanu, became the first *tata* (Romanian for papa) many of our children had ever known. They attached to him more rapidly than to female caregivers and they loved to hear him sing. (He did that very well.)

The hunger for a father is tremendous in children who have never had any exposure to men; they are children who cannot even imagine what it is like to have a father. There is no memory basis for that dream. When this hunger is coupled with long experience of neglecting or impersonal females, there are no clouds or obstacles for new fathers to overcome in establishing strong relationships with their children. Except for the novelty of maleness, which demands a little getting used to, the gate is open wide. Adopting dads might like to know this.

◆ The response of institutionalized children, even very severely damaged children, to music is almost spooky. It was such a consistent response and so reliable that we used it whenever we could. Emotionally withdrawn children would become quietly alert and attentive. They would often express feelings for the very first time. Developmentally delayed children progressed more rapidly when music was part of the program. One of our Romanian educators, Mariana, was gifted musically, and the children she worked with often sang before they talked and danced before they walked.

I have heard many comments that support this observation from American parents who have adopted Romanian children. One was particularly stirring. When I distributed the audiotapes of "Childsong" to Romanian adoptees so they could learn the words before the July 4 concert (Introduction), one little girl had a profound reaction. She had a severe language deficit because of her prior life in an institution. Her special education teacher had been teaching her sign-language to enhance her ability to communicate. Things were going slowly until the family received the tapes.

The little girl connected to the song. She understood its beautiful message. Soon she was expressing that message with her hands. She has subsequently opened up in ways that she never had before. Not only did a child who was silenced by her past find a way to communicate to others, she found a way to feel. You know the rest: She stood right up in front of hundreds of people and sang her heart out with her hands.

I am not proposing some new cure-all or magical answer to all the problems postinstitutionalized children suffer. Nor do I pretend to understand this response fully on an intellectual level. It is well known that most Romanian children, particularly Romanian *Gypsy* children, have a special gift for music; the response may not be as pronounced in other ethnic groups. But music, of all the things we do in intervention, is least likely to be harmful. When it helps, it helps tremendously. Adopting parents may want to know.

Men and music and their effects on children . . . Both were being replayed before me when I revisited the orphanage in December 1995. The last performance of the day was a group of three- to five-year-olds singing a song about frogs. Clad in green from head to toe and wearing green, fake glasses made from pipe cleaners, they were supposed to hop a bit and make gestures while they sang. One little boy, a dark-haired little

Gypsy child, couldn't quite get it together, and probably had some coordination problems. I could pinpoint the child because he had an exceptional, clear soprano voice that kept fading out when he tried to hop. *Be still,* I said to him silently. *Don't try to hop and move your arms at the same time. Just stand still and sing.* As if he heard my thoughts, the child suddenly gave up on the hopping, stood very still, and turned up the volume on one of the loveliest voices I have ever heard. "Do you hear that child singing?" I asked one of my Romanian friends. "Yes," she said. "He's a treasure."

And he is a treasure—one of many of Romania's lost treasures. He was born with a song and a poem in his mouth. We shouldn't be overconcerned about his hopping skills. We should be very concerned with finding him a home with a dad and a mom who are music lovers. What other qualifications should our fantasy family for this little boy have?

They should be good treasure hunters.

REFERENCES

1. ABC, 20/20, "The Shame of a Nation," Janice Tomlin, producer, Tom Jarriel, commentator; Barbara Bascom, guest. October 5, 1990.

2. Ministry of Health, Institute of Mother and Child Care, UNICEF, *Causes of Institutionalization of Romanian Children: Report of a Population Based Study with Recommendations.* Collaborative Study Report. December 1991.

3. J. K. Sweeney and B. B. Bascom, "Motor Development and Self-Stimulatory Movement in Institutionalized Romanian Children. *Pediatric Physical Therapy* (1995), pp. 124–132.

4. B. Bascom, ROSES Top Ten Survey #1: *Top Ten Health Problems in Romanian Orphans* (Denver: The Brooke Foundation, Inc. 1994).

5. B. Bascom, ROSES Top Ten Survey #2: *Top Ten Developmental Problems in Romanian Orphans* (Denver: The Brooke Foundation, 1994).

6. B. Bascom, ROSES Top Ten Survey #3: *Top Ten Expectations of Adopting Parents* (Denver: Brooke Foundation, Inc. 1994).

7. B. Bascom, ROSES Project Summary (The Brooke Foundation, December 1994).

8. Information made available by Ministry of Health, Division of Mother-Child Health. Bucharest, Romania. December 1991.

9. U.S. INS Report on Inter-country Adoptions, 1984–1994.

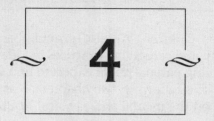

Children of Institutions

A simple child,
That lightly draws its breath,
And feels its life in every limb,
What should it know of death?

—William Wordsworth

Why include a chapter on institutionalized children in a book about international adoption? Prospective adopting parents who go abroad to adopt a child will, in the vast majority of cases, adopt the child from an institutional environment. To truly enlighten adoptive parents, we need to supply a full description of what children are like and what they have experienced before adoption and while in the institution. Adopting parents need to know how that experience has physically and mentally affected their children and what bearing that may have on their future development. This information is the most often missing piece of any adoption record. To select a child and to plan for that child's future, and to give that child the best chance in life, parents need to know everything possible about this missing piece.

This chapter deals with institutionalized children in general. It provides information about both the medical and developmental problems that occur as a result of deprivation in institutions and what is known about their causes and evolution. We take a backward glance at the history of institutionalization and introduce you to some of the pioneers in the field of study of institutionalized children. We also provide basic information about the health and caregiving practices in today's institutions and what adopting parents might expect to find when they visit an institution. The following two chapters, 5 and 6, will focus in more detail on the mental and physical health issues raised in this chapter.

FUTURE PARENTS' NEED TO KNOW

ANAMARIA

As a program director in Romania, I (Bascom) became aware of adopting parents' need to know very early in development of the ROSES project. I do not recall a single day in any of the project's seven orphanages that I didn't encounter at least two families who were either searching for a child to adopt or were in the process of adopting. In every orphanage, I saw the questions in the eyes of the parents who came to find or adopt the children. I saw the confusion on their faces when they were presented with a two-page medical summary that told them nothing they wanted to know about the child they were adopting. Not infrequently, when I made my rounds or was touring an orphanage ward, an adopting couple would approach me and ask, "Would you just take a peek at this child?" If I knew the child in question, I would know how complex his problems were and that a peek was not good enough. There had to be a better way to inform parents who would devote the rest of their lives to these children.

One opportunity for the "better way" was offered by the Western press and media who were so intensely involved in Romania in the early nineties. Although they usually focused on one aspect of the problem, they contributed heavily to mass dissemination of information and to raising public awareness about the problems of institutionalized children. The camera was so much a part of our everyday lives that Romanian colleagues accepted it as part of the program. "Are you bringing Cyclops today?" they would ask me when I called to schedule a clinical visit.

It was on such a day that we discovered Anamaria. "Cy-

clops," that day, was controlled by the assistant director of a
Hollywood-based company that made documentary films for
nonprofit organizations. It was their second trip to Romania,
and the film was to be an "update." The day was charged with
emotion because the director had been seriously injured the
night before when he was brutally attacked by a street gang in
the parking lot of his hotel. Uncertain as to whether the incident
was an isolated event or part of the angry backlash Romania
was exhibiting about all the negative publicity, we had debated
scrubbing the mission. Despite much advice to the contrary,
however, we decided to go ahead with the shoot, saying, "We
will do this one for Richard," our friend and director who lay,
critically injured, in a Romanian hospital a few blocks away.
Because it might be our last opportunity to make such a film,
we dedicated ourselves to finding and filming the child who
could most perfectly tell the story.

It is hard to say what led us to Anamaria. She was not yet
enrolled in the project and was kept in one of the orphanage's
back rooms where the most severely affected children were hidden from the view of outsiders and prospective adoptive parents. Most of my Romanian colleagues thought that her case
was hopeless and that she would never respond to treatment.
They said we couldn't "get through to her." The shell she had
built around herself was impenetrable.

The Romanian staff had many reasons for pessimism. Since
admission to the orphanage, two-year-old Anamaria had exhibited no sign of attachment to any of her caregivers. Nor was
she ever seen interacting with other children, even those who
crawled into her crib. She would not allow herself to be held or
touched. Her only attachment was to the physical aspects of her
environment, principally her crib, and if anyone attempted to
remove her from it, she would panic. She would not touch, handle, or play with toys or dolls. When we approached her and
tried to touch or hold her, she went into a frenzy and banged
her head so hard, I was afraid she would hurt herself. Even
routine caregiving tasks such as bathing and dressing were an
ordeal for both caregiver and Anamaria.

In essence, Anamaria had the classic signs of a severe attachment disorder with associated, profound delays in every area

of development. She was not only mute with respect to language, she was totally unable to express her feelings. No smiles, no laughter, things we would expect during the first months of life, not even crying when she was hurt.

Anamaria seemed immobile. She could not crawl or walk and never really moved much, except for the rocking. All day long, she either sat in her crib with her legs straight out in front of her, staring mutely at her environment, or she got onto her hands and knees and rocked back and forth, ramming her head into the nearest wall.

The decision to film Anamaria was largely intuitive. Despite the dismal picture painted by Romanian staff, she had something about her. There was something in the unwavering gaze of those huge blue eyes that told us someone was home inside that shell, someone who was hurt and wanted, desperately, to escape that inner prison but did not know how and was afraid to try.

"At least," I thought, "we can paint an accurate picture of the ravages of institutional life." Secretly, however, I wanted and probably expected to make a breakthrough. And if such a thing occurred, I wanted it to be documented by this film crew whose dedication and commitment to Romania's orphans were unequaled in my experience.

As the crew began their setup, I realized what an awful picture Anamaria's room depicted. More than thirty children sat disconsolately in cribs like little statues. Some sat, hunched over, on soiled mats that had been hastily thrown on the floor when the camera crew entered. The room stank of urine-soaked mattresses. There were very few toys and no organized play activities for the children on the mats, as there were in the other rooms where project activities were taking place, toys were in abundance, and bright murals adorned the walls. Two attendants sat listlessly, apathetic, on child-sized benches.

Because she was distracted and frightened by the sudden activity in the "playroom" adjoining the crib room, we turned Anamaria around, facing the window wall. The camera was inconspicuous. *Good,* I thought, as I threaded the microphone wires beneath my clothing. *The focus will be on the child and not the sordid environment.* I knew from personal experience how lost an observer could get in the peeling plaster, rusty cribs, and the stinking, sagging mattresses.

Before we started filming and while Melanie, the Romanian psychologist, gently began to introduce Anamaria to some toys, I was asked to give a short introduction and provide some background material:

> The first time I saw Anamaria, she was on a mat in the corner of this room. She was rocking herself on all fours, oblivious to her surroundings or others around her. As she usually does when she is away from her crib, she was banging her head into an iron pipe in the corner.
>
> At age two and a half, Anamaria is the size of a fifteen-month-old toddler. She is steadily falling away from the normal pattern of growth. Unable to walk or stand alone, she moves about only when she is rocking. She neither talks nor tries to communicate in any way with gestures, crying, or cooing. No one on the staff has ever seen her smile or heard her laugh. She rocks herself for most of her waking hours.
>
> When Anamaria is approached by an adult, she flings her hands in front of her face in the face-shielding posture I have labeled the "orphan salute," because it is such a pervasive response of children in these [Romanian] orphanages. She has other habitual or self-stimulating behaviors. For example, Anamaria keeps her tongue protruded most of the time; when stressed, she sucks it rhythmically. She constantly stares at whoever is in her line of vision Don't confuse this with meaningful eye contact. In technical jargon, this steady gaze is called "hypervigilant" and is part of the classic appearance of "frozen watchfulness" we see in neglected children.
>
> When I first looked at her chart and saw that she was classified as severely *dystrophic*, the word used for "failure to thrive" in Europe, the notes in her records alarmed me. She was going progressively downhill, falling farther and farther behind other children her age. In the last few months, her downhill course has accelerated. The attendants in her room have told me that she often "refuses to eat"; this will only make her worse and adds to my feelings of urgency regarding her situation. Unless we can gently break through the barriers

she has erected to protect herself from an environment she has found intolerable, Anamaria's chances of survival for another six to nine months are minimal.[1]

"Your gigantic blue eyes are beautiful," I said to Anamaria as I positioned myself on the mat beside her. "Unusually so, even in Romania where beautiful, big eyes are the rule rather than the exception."

She stared at me with incredible intensity, holding her small body rigidly erect and keeping both hands in front of her face. All of my energy was focused on trying to read that stare. Immediately but almost imperceptibly, she began to connect emotionally. I could feel it as well as see it. Her hands dropped slightly, and she became very still. She seemed to be waiting.

The session lasted nearly two hours and was like a dance. Sitting beside and slightly behind her, so as not to distract or upset her, I captured her attention with small toys from a developmental testing kit: a shiny bell, small colored blocks, a cup, a fuzzy yellow tennis ball. It wasn't hard to do. Although fascinated, she wouldn't touch anything and we didn't cross the first big barrier until Anamaria allowed us to place blocks in her hand. Once she started handling toys, the orphans' saluting disappeared. Using every technique I had ever learned, including some from physical and occupational therapy, I focused on breaking through her resistance to touch. I used support, positioning, facilitation, stroking for desensitization, and played little tricks on her nervous system to get her to grasp and release with her hands. Finally she broke through enough to engage in manipulation of the toys. As she became more absorbed, Anamaria began to relax emotionally and allowed more touch. She was opening doors so rapidly that I found myself holding my breath. Occasionally, when we moved too fast, she would fling up her hands again, but it didn't last too long. By the end of the first half-hour, she was piling blocks into a cup and allowing me to put my arm around her.

I wanted her to initiate some activities on her own, but she continued to hold back until I rang the bell and put it down in front of her. It worked like magic. Slowly and gracefully, she extended her little index finger and after hesitating for a few seconds, she touched the top of the bell. It was a beautiful moment, similar to the scene in *E.T.* when the alien and the child touched fingertips. From that moment on, Anamaria moved so rapidly through developmental stages that all who observed her were astounded. In quick succession, she picked up the silver bell, rang it, then turned it over to investigate what made it ring. Once satisfied with her own accomplishments, she turned to me with sparkling eyes, seeming to ask for praise. By that time, I had lost any semblance of objectivity. "Look, look, look at what she's doing," I exclaimed to the camera while I ruffled her hair and rubbed her back. At that moment, Anamaria broke through her emotional shell. I felt her relax and begin to lean into my touch. Her tension and resistance evaporated.

Anamaria just looked at me steadily and waited for more. "Let's see if you'll let me pick you up," I said to her while I moved her to my lap. Despite the fact that her little heart was racing, she came into my arms as willingly as any child I had ever held. I think I told her that it was nice out here in the world, and she must have agreed. As she nestled her curly head against my shoulder, I heard a little sound, guttural and hoarse at first, then stronger. It was the loveliest sound I had heard since I began my work in the Leaganes. Anamaria was laughing for the first time in her life.

We were all very moved by Anamaria's response. An eerie silence filled the room. All that could be heard was the quiet whir of the camera. I closed my eyes and held Anamaria until a crew member asked me to "please explain just exactly what had happened."

Explain? How could I explain such an experience? I could only know what I was feeling, respond emotionally and hold on to Anamaria. I had seen a tiny flickering light, deep within a wounded child, begin to burn brightly. A child who had never before trusted or allowed anyone to touch her had allowed me to hold her. I had heard her laugh. How did I feel? It's hard to describe. The words that came into my mind were lyrics to a song. Like Grizabella, the dying cat who was given a chance to live again, Anamaria had seemed to be saying . . . *touch me, and you will know what happiness is* . . . and given a moment of happiness. The choice was clearly hers. She had chosen to live again.

When I finally was able to speak coherently, I faced the camera and talked about Anamaria's vulnerability and how unprotected she was. "Now that this door is open," I said, "we must keep it that way. We must come back here every day, day after day, and do this all over. Once a child like Anamaria has emerged from her shell, we cannot let her return; we may not be able to reach her the second time around." My little speech was more appeal than explanation of an event that, at that time, defied explanation.

Several years later, I would come up with a lot of explanations and use the film as a teaching video in workshops for parents and social workers. Although I have thousands of slides, hundreds of videotapes, and reams of printed material to draw upon in giving instructional sessions and workshops, none of them is as effective as the film of Anamaria.

The feelings associated with the moments of her breakthrough are as powerful and promising today as they were in 1991 when Melanie Ciupurca, Anamaria, and I sat on that mat on the floor of the Leagane. Workshop participants, whether or not they learn anything about desensitization, facilitation, or how to respond to the cues of a child, always share that feeling and often ask for more. Sometimes, they ask to stay after the session and watch the film again. For most of them, especially the mothers, it is an intensely private experience. When I do get feedback, I am told that the film of Anamaria "fills me with hope."

LESSONS LEARNED FROM THE PAST

There are thousands, if not hundreds of thousands, of children like Anamaria abandoned to institutions in the developing nations of this world. Her clinical description is not only a classic example of the children found in eastern Europe's orphanages since the fall of the Iron Curtain, but it is also typical of children of institutions anywhere and at any time in history. Other than some changes in terminology and disease classification, the text of Anamaria's current medical summary could be interchanged with one from the literature of the 1940s.

Classic descriptions of institutional deprivation have been known to child development specialists and psychiatrists since the early decades of the twentieth century. Professional eyes were opened to new thinking when, in the 1930s, Dr. Rene Spitz described the often fatal "anaclitic depression" and progressive failure to thrive seen in children of institutions. Spitz's babies, a group of foundling-home infants who were separated from their mothers at birth, were compared with a group of French infants who were allowed regular contact with their mothers. Although all of the mothers were criminal offenders who were imprisoned in the French penal system, and although the penitentiary nursery lacked many of the physical attributes of the foundling home, the mother-child contact proved to be the critical factor in the well-being of the babies.

In contrast to the prison infants, the foundlings in Spitz's original report were provided adequate diets, warmth, clothing, and medical care. But they were unable to benefit from these physical advantages without the emotional nurturing of a parent. The foundlings not only failed to grow or develop, but developed apathy, "neurologic symptoms," including low muscle tone (hypotonia), abnormal, involuntary movements of their arms and legs, and various degrees of emotional withdrawal. This collection of symptoms was called "anaclitic depression." Almost without exception, the foundlings died before their second birthday.

In contrast, the prison babies in Spitz's case studies not only survived but did not suffer the emotional or developmental consequences seen in the foundling-home infants. Despite their disadvantaged physical environments, they had regular maternal contact and thrived, both physically and emotionally.[2]

During the years that followed Spitz's first case studies, health professionals confirmed the critical link between emotional nurturing and biological survival. Although revolutionary and controversial, the concept generated a furor of academic interest. Throughout the world, clinical investigators began to make systematic observations and conduct scientific research that verified the harmful effects of institutionalization upon infants and children and the cause-and-effect relationship between emotional nurturing and survival.

As a result of the research done during the ensuing decades, new scientific links between mind and body have been established. It has now been proven, beyond a scientific doubt, that human physiology can be profoundly altered by the emotions. Basic chemicals of the body can disappear when infants and children are not nurtured emotionally. Infants and children who are not emotionally nurtured, even though their physical needs are met, can indeed die from lack of love.

Disorders previously thought to be of unknown cause were linked to neglect rather than to vague biochemical diseases. Certain immune deficiencies were found to be rooted in neglect instead of in mysterious "congenital defects." Certain enzyme deficiencies causing intestinal malabsorption were linked to deprivation instead of "inborn errors of metabolism."[3] Neglect was established as the sole cause for some children's growth deficiency when it was shown that emotional deprivation alone could shut down the body's production of hormones that govern growth.[4] In severe cases, the growth centers of bones would close prematurely, long before adolescence, and the neglected child could be permanently affected—abnormally short, for example, or dwarfed.

If caught early enough, however, most cases of physical (organic) diseases caused by neglect did not result in permanent damage. After proper diagnosis was made (during which organic causes were ruled out) the provision of adequate emotional environments often resulted in either marked improvement or complete reversal (cure) of the physical disorder. This was particularly dramatic in growth-deficient children when, without change in diets, emotional nurturing resulted in phenomenal growth acceleration. "Love them and watch them grow," the doctors would say. The miraculous cure was soon dubbed "vitamin L."

Growth deficiency was not the only condition to miraculously respond to vitamin L. Most of the above physical conditions, once proven to be caused by deprivation, were treatable (if caught early enough) by reversing the cycle of physical and emotional neglect. Today, the cure is called nurturing.

Dr. Sally Provence, of Yale–New Haven's renowned Child Study Center, was among the first to investigate children in American institutions; her original studies featured children in orphanages. Provence's research not only confirmed the physical and psychological descriptions of Spitz's foundlings but also provided new details about the developmental problems seen in infants raised in institutions. First published in 1962 as the summation of her research, *Infants in Institutions* is still considered the classic description of maternal deprivation.[5] Although out of print, the book remains a key reference in child development literature and is often required reading for students of the discipline.

In the opening chapter of *Infants in Institutions*, Provence and Lipton introduce their research with the description of a thirteenth-century experiment in child care. Under the direction of Frederick II, "German King, King of Sicily and Emperor of the Holy Roman Empire," the project proved devastating to the children who were involved in the experiment.

> Frederick II wanted to find out what kind of speech and what manner of language children would have when they grew up if they spoke to no one beforehand. So he bade foster mothers and nurses to suckle the children, to bathe and wash them, but in no way to prattle with them or to speak to them, for he wanted to learn if they would speak the Hebrew language (which was the oldest), or Greek, or Latin, or Arabic—or perhaps the language of their (biologic) parents. . . . But he labored in vain because the children all died. They could not live without the petting and joyful faces and loving words of their foster mothers. And so, the songs are called swaddling songs which a woman sings while she is rocking the cradle to put the child to sleep and without them a child sleeps badly and has no rest.[6]

Today, *Infants in Institutions* is as accurate a description of the disastrous consequences of institutionalization as it was thirty years ago. Change the names, dates, and location, and Anamaria's case history could well have been included in Provence's first edition.

Have we learned much since the thirteenth century? The answer is both yes and no.

Yes, because we have made major advances in the technology surrounding the child-development disciplines. When standardized, reliable measures of growth and development became available in the mid-twentieth century, theoretical hypotheses of the past were gradually replaced by objective descriptions and new disease classifications were constructed. Real research in child development became possible. Old terminology, much of which was socially offensive, was discarded.

Yes, because we have been able to apply that new knowledge to child care, educational, and clinical settings and thus raise the standard of care in those settings. Yes, because we have developed reliable, standardized measurements and evaluations of children's growth and development. Yes, because we have translated the knowledge gained into social change. In the United States, particularly, social change has been reflected in new laws and social policy, the most important of which was deinstitutionalization and the change in our society's attitude when disabled persons were reintegrated into their communities.

The success of deinstitutionalization, initiated in the 1970s, was dependent upon the simultaneous development of community resources and protection of the rights of the disabled, which in turn gave the disabled unimpeded access, without discrimination, to all community resources. The technical and social advances in the West, however, have not been replicated in developing and third-world countries. As was discovered in eastern Europe, institutions and the collective attitude (called "mentality") that support them are still flourishing. For children who live and die in institutions, the clinical condition that results from deprivation is not being prevented; it exists in alarming proportions. Millions of the world's children continue to die or deteriorate in institutions.

WHY ARE THEY THERE?

Despite the shock we all experienced when Romania's borders opened, a great deal of objective information was collected when foreign-aid organizations rushed in from all over the globe. The complexity of the situation was immediately apparent:

- There were more than 440 institutional environments, including orphanages, residential schools, homes for the disabled, and the cruel homes for those classified "irrecuperable" scattered throughout the tiny country. All of them were damaging to children. Only eighty-seven of these institutions, the Leaganes (cradles), could be considered "orphanages," because they housed children up to age three and because most of their occupants were abandoned by living relatives who had left them to live their lives alone in the institutions.
- Children were institutionalized for a wide variety of reasons. The majority were there for "social protection," that is, they could not be cared for in their homes or communities. Most of the children under social protection were products of unwanted pregnancies that had been forced upon Romania's women through Caeusescu's diabolical plan to increase the population.
- Needy and abandoned children were combined with other "undesirable elements"[7] of society. Institutions, therefore, were being used as tools of the state to selectively and systematically remove disfavored minorities from society.

Gypsies, for example, made up 70 to 90 percent of the population of Romania's end-of-the-road institutions called "Camin Spitals for the unsalvageable." According to official census, however, the Gypsies represented less than 5 percent of the population of the country. Furthermore, many of the Gypsy children who were classified as unsalvageable had no discernible underlying handicaps. The use and abuse of institutional care to carry out discriminatory practices is by no means peculiar to Romania:

- Incarceration of Gypsies is common practice throughout the Balkans and Europe. Western Europe is not excluded!

- ◆ Gender discrimination against girls is flagrant in China's orphanages and institutions. Other countries, like India, dis-
  criminate against girls as well.
- ◆ Children of mixed racial background, particularly Eurasian
  children in countries like Vietnam and Korea, where non-
  Asian soldiers left offspring after the war, are outcasts of society and often end up in institutions.
- ◆ Disabled children are systematically institutionalized everywhere.

LESSONS LEARNED IN ROMANIA

What else did we learn through the fact-finding missions that
the West conducted as part of humanitarian aid to Romania?
In addition to the demographics, what did we learn about the
children that we had not been aware of before 1990? The cumulative experience of five years of foreign assistance in Romania's
institutions has provided a wealth of information.

The medical conditions and developmental disorders seen
commonly in Romanian orphans were extensively tracked and
documented. Foreign-aid experts in public health provided research and epidemiology on the AIDS epidemic in orphanages
and hospitals throughout the country. Reports on other communicable diseases soon followed. Teams of social scientists
tackled the social assistance system.[8] Consulting teams of virtually every kind of health care specialist invaded the orphanages
to complete needs assessment studies and make recommendations to the ministries.

In institutions where service programs existed, program staff
gathered information on children in orphanage-based remedial
programs and documented not only their problems and diagnoses, but also provided valuable information regarding the
children's responses to intervention.[9] Finally, when babies and
children left for intercountry adoptions, follow-up data, notably
from the United States[10] and Canada,[11] began to appear in the
scientific literature. Although the scene was chaotic and disorganized, and although the available information was fragmented, the reports of children's conditions and outcomes
(progress as a result of specific interventions) began to form a

continuum when in-country reports and follow-up data were put together. The natural history of the health and development of the institutionalized child began to emerge with increasing clarity.

Lessons learned in Romania are easily transferred to other countries from which children are being adopted. Although most of the studies reported in this book have involved Romanian children, parallel studies in other countries have confirmed Romania's findings. The medical risk-list for Romanian orphans (found in chapter 3), for example, concurs with follow-up data from a large, U.S.-based, international adoption clinic that reported on 293 children from fifteen countries.[12] In this report, infectious diseases made up the majority of medical conditions (73 percent). There are two major reasons for this:

1. Communicable diseases such as hepatitis and intestinal parasites are endemic (continuously present in epidemic proportions) in developing countries.
2. Institutionalized populations are more susceptible to any communicable disease because of crowding and poor hygienic practices in most institutions.

Although many of these infectious diseases seen in adopted children are serious and have long-term implications, most are treatable, and many are curable. Therefore, the rapid development of adequate screening procedures for adoptable children in foreign countries, before they come to America, has become a priority health issue in foreign adoption. Although medical screening and laboratory procedures are still not optimal, progress is being made. In addition to better screening and diagnosis of children leaving the country, improvements have been made in prevention and early detection of communicable diseases and the slowing of epidemics in institutional settings.

The impact of developmental and mental health problems on the future of children adopted from institutional settings, however, is less predictable. Although a significant amount of information is now available regarding institutionalized children while in the institution, there remains a great deal of uncertainty about how these children will do when they are placed in adoptive homes. The principle issues are both developmental and psychological. This much, however, has been learned from Romanian studies and agency follow-up material.

The child who is a product of institutional life is likely to fit into a characteristic developmental profile if he or she has been institutionalized long enough and if there is emotional deprivation. The infant's age at the time of admission is a significant factor, with vulnerability inversely related to age. Babies who were admitted directly from maternity units demonstrate the greatest risk for both developmental and growth failure. Although the time required (by most infants) to show the effects of institutionalization vary from child to child, a recent survey done in Romanian Cradles[13] (*Leagane*, commonly translated as "orphanages") housing children up to three years old, indicated that some degree of developmental delay was detectable in most children by the time they had spent six months in the institution. Furthermore, the longer the period of institutionalization, the more severe the developmental and emotional problems. Specifically:

◆ After six months in any depriving institution, 85 percent of infants and toddlers show *some* degree of growth deceleration and developmental delay.

◆ Virtually all three-year-olds who have lived all their lives in institutions will have demonstrable developmental disabilities of significance; screening and testing shows moderate to severe deficits (less than 50 percent of expected progress for age), instead of mild developmental delays.

◆ The pattern of disability is characteristic: delays and disabilities are more severe in language and gross motor skills and less severe in adaptive (intelligence) and social (self-help) areas.

ONE CHILD, TWO PROBLEMS: PUTTING THE PUZZLE TOGETHER

The mixed developmental and attachment disorder exhibited by Anamaria and hundreds of institutionalized children like her is a complex and multifaceted disorder. It is not only the most common problem seen in children of institutions, but it also represents the most serious threat to their future development. If and when these children are adopted into Western homes, it represents the biggest obstacle to their successful adaptation to their new homes and may interfere significantly with attachment to their new families.

Although it is difficult to comprehend, some form of attachment usually exists, even in children who come from grossly neglectful environments. This is particularly true in child-victims of neglect and abuse who have been adopted from foreign institutions. Rather than be surprised by it, adopting parents should expect their adopted children to express some anxiety or sadness when leaving the institution. When children have lost an attachment, they will suffer from that loss.

When attachment has not occurred, however (usually because there has been no opportunity to attach), the situation is analogous to a vacuum instead of the vacancy created by loss. There is no memory of an "attachment figure" for the child to reference when adoption takes place. Such a child may have substituted a crib, or some other aspect of his or her physical environment, for the human attachment. When diagnosed, these children are often referred to as "unattached children." This is not a milder form of attachment disorder. The unattached child suffers equally, perhaps more, than the child who has experienced loss. He or she usually exhibits a more pervasive developmental disorder of greater severity. In many of these children, neurophysiologic responses are primitive and development is arrested in very early stages. They look like Spitz's foundlings. Or Sally Provence's infants of institutions. Or Anamaria.

Post-institutionalized children suffer from profound sensory deprivation as well as lack of opportunity to attach emotionally to a mothering caregiver. This results in a mixed developmental and attachment disorder which we (authors) have named developmental attachment disorder. It's features are summarized in the following table:

Table 1

FEATURES OF DEVELOPMENTAL ATTACHMENT
DISORDER IN POSTINSTITUTIONALIZED
CHILDREN

- **Global Developmental Delays**
    Severity: Moderate to severe
    Pattern: Language and communication most affected
- **Stereotypic Behaviors**
    Self-stimulation: rocking
    Aversive: face shielding—"orphan's salute"
    Self-injurious behaviors.
- **Attachment Behaviors**
    Attached to physical environment—crib, room
    Object (toy, doll, blanket)—poor/absent
    Human—absent or abnormal (ambivalent, inconsistent); peers
      in older survivors
- **Hypervigilance of Gaze (Visual)**
- **General Physical/Behavioral**
    Disturbed sleep patterns
    Feeding problems, unrelated to dietary practice
    Generalized failure to thrive
    Short stature
- **Sensory and Sensori-Motor**
    Avoidance behaviors—"tactile defensiveness"
    Severe sensory processing deficits—most severe in tactile and
      vestibular
    Sensori-integrative disorders when older
- **Neuromotor**
    Severe gross motor delays
    Poor muscle tone—hypotonia
- **Cognitive/Learning**
    Persistent delays—language most affected
    Learning disabilities; most frequent—"language LD"
    Attention deficit disorder/hyperactivity in older, treated child
- **Miscellaneous**
    Unique response to music
    Underlying sadness or depression
    Better response to intervention in most cases

It is impossible to separate the various components of the combined developmental and attachment disorder seen in post-institutionalized children. They are enmeshed and in continuous interplay with one another. It is common, however, for one problem to dominate the picture, thus obscuring or eclipsing others that need attention. Hyperactivity, for example, can so command the attention of parents and teachers that underlying problems that also need intervention are unintentionally ignored.

Adopting parents should know that there are significant differences between the attachment disorders seen in troubled children of Western inner cities and those seen in foreign adoptees who have spent their infancies and early childhoods in institutions (see chapter 5). Despite these differences, however, the same diagnostic classification, that of "reactive attachment disorder,"[14] is often applied to both groups of children in the United States.

Developmental attachment disorder in foreign, post-institutionalized children and the reactive attachment disorder seen in U.S. foster-home children differ in several ways. The most noticeable difference is that communication and language deficits of post-institutionalized children are usually more profound. The following associated developmental problems are more common in post-institutionalized children:

- *Sensory integrative deficits*[15]—commonly called perceptual problems; in the post-institutionalized, most often caused by the severe sensory deprivation (lack of touch, holding, rocking, visual and auditory input, for example) during infancy and early childhood.
- *Motor delays*—delay in the rate of acquisition of motor milestones (crawling, walking, for example); often referred to as "behind" or "slow" development.
- *Stereotypic or self-stimulatory behaviors*[16]—repetitive, nonvolitional (no purpose) movements such as rocking, head banging, shaking of hands, face shielding, that become habitual in institutionalized children who have been deprived and neglected. Called "stereotypic" because they label the child. Although purposeless in terms of activity, the unconscious

purpose is usually interpreted as self-stimulation, or seeking to replace a sensory experience (rocking, for example) that the child was deprived of while institutionalized. Usually persistent for a long time after institutionalization; may seem to disappear, but reappear at time of stress or separation.

◆ *Cognitive delays*[17]—delays in mental or intellectual skills; often referred to as "problem-solving skills" in infants and younger children. In post-institutionalized children, cognitive delays are most often due to lack of stimulation and/or lack of learning opportunity.

◆ *Severe learning disabilities*—often associated with short attention span, with or without hyperactivity. Many types described. Very common in post-institutionalized children; often severe and require long-term special education. May be generalized or specific to one area of learning, as with dyslexia (reading disability) or "language LD."

Parents should be aware of this "package plan" their adopted children may present. Awareness allows a parent to detect problems in early stages and to plan for intervention in a holistic, enlightened way.

COMMUNICATION

When the professional West met East after the collapse of Communism, doctors and other health scientists couldn't talk to each other. The problem was not a simple language barrier. There were often no words for them to learn. The foreign language, Romanian, for example, contained no translation for terms like "developmental delay." Because the terms for their correct diagnosis did not even exist, hundreds of thousands of children, abandoned to institutions, were not only mislabeled, they were misdiagnosed. Nowhere was this more evident than in the medical records of children in institutions.

This summary, typical for any child "exiting" Romania, is so filled with mis- and disinformation that it was only slightly useful. In addition to mistakes, a significant amount of vital information is omitted or missing entirely. There is no information on the growth or development of the child. Beginning with the

Table 2

SAMPLE DISCHARGE SUMMARY

XXXXXX COUNTY, CITY OF XXXXXX ORPHAN'S HOUSE
DATE: 1991, 7.18
EXIT NG NOTE FROM THE HOSPITAL

The patient: XXXX (family name) Iuliana (first name)
Sex: M/F, of age : 3 years, 2 months
Residing in XXXXXX County, City of XXXX, Xxxxxx village
Health Center Xxxxxx
Was hospitalized in the Section I with the diagnosis: Social sheltering
From: June 8, 1988; till July 18, 1991.
Exits: healthy. She is/is not the bearer of the following germs:
HAV (Hepatitis-acute, viral) August 25, 1991, with HBs antibody; April 10, 1991, Ag HBs negative
Hepatitesvir., June 6, 1990—negative

Summary of the observation file:
The child hospitalized in our unit since June 8, 1988 till July 18, 1991. During the hospitalization, she presented the following infections:
BDA, acute rhynopharingitis; she was treated with: Penicillin V, Erythromycin, Amoxicillin
She was given Calcium and Vitamin D2, according to Ministry of Health Requirements.
German measles January 8, 1990   Rubeole—January 30, 1990

Vacinums:

BCG (antituberculosis)		06/03/88	cic. BCG = 5mm		
Antipolio	d1	12/02/88			
	d1	03/24/89			
	d2	06/02/89		r1	12/01/89
Trivacinum	d1	08/09/88		r1	07/11/89
	d2	09/15/88		r2	01/15/91
	d3	12/02/88			
Antirubeolic		01/30/89	Antidiptheric		05/08/90
AD (?)		05/14/91	05/17/91		05/20/91
		05/20-23-26/1991			

Recommendations:
    Will inform the local health center.
    Will be given proper food according to her age.
    The rahitism—treated with calcium and Vitamin D2
                Doctor, seal, signature, undecipherable

absent birth date, and progressing throughout the record, there is not one comment, one measurement, not even one estimate about the most important long-term risk shared by all Romanian orphans: growth and development.

Nor is there any mention of behavior. The nearest eastern Europe physicians could come to including an emotional component in 1991 was to assign the label *hospitalitis* to the pervasive developmental and psychological problems the institutionalized children displayed. Even that term was missing from this record.

What is "hospitalitis"?

Hospitalism was the term used by Spitz to refer to the failure to thrive, developmental, and psychological disorders that chronically ill infants suffered when subjected to prolonged hospitalizations.[18] By 1990, the terminology had long been replaced by new nomenclature. More than fifty conditions had been defined to describe the psychological and physical effects of neglect, abuse, and deprivation.

In 1990 Romania, however, neither the new terminology nor disease classification nomenclature existed in the professional vocabulary. By the end of 1991, more than 2,500 U.S. families had adopted Romanian children. Most of them had been given medical summaries using terms like "encephalopathy" or "oligophrenia" to describe the developmental problems.

Table 3

COMMONLY USED/CONFUSED TERMS IN FOREIGN MEDICAL SUMMARIES

Term	Literal Meaning	Application
Oligophrenia	Pathological: A shortage of brain white matter. Not a clinical condition.	Mental deficiency
Encephalopathy, or neonatal encephalopathy	General term for abnormal brain function. Needs specifiers.	Brain damage: "Neonatal" implies brain injury at birth.

Little's disease	Old name for spastic form of cerebral palsy.	Any form of increased muscle tone or tightness.
Dystrophic	From *dystrophy-weakening, degeneration,* or *faulty development*	Failure to thrive.
Hospitalitis	From *hospitalism,* the term coined by Spitz to describe chronically ill, hospitalized children. (See text.)	FTT with self-stimulatory and/or other stereotypic behaviors (rocking, head banging, etc.)

During 1991, however, substantial progress was made in the introduction of modern terminology into the eastern European vocabulary. By the end of 1991, Anamaria, the child with whom this chapter began, had a thick clinical record that could be read and understood anyplace in the world.

Despite the strides that have been made in the training and continuing education of foreign professionals, accurate, clinical diagnosis of both physical and developmental disorders still has a long way to go. Internationally adopted children continue to arrive with clinical records that have mislabeled them due to incorrect diagnoses. Many medical and psychological conditions have gone undetected, only to be discovered after the children arrive in their new homes. In addition to incorrect diagnoses, therefore, many are missed entirely. According to one Romanian survey of outgoing records, the following missed and misdiagnoses were seen frequently:

Table 4

TOP ELEVEN MISSED AND MISDIAGNOSES IN
ROMANIAN ORPHANS

Misdiagnoses	Missed Diagnoses
Spasticity	Normal
Mental retardation (oligophrenia)	Attachment disorders
	Developmental delay
Developmental delay (since 1993)	Congenital hip dysplasia
	Behavior disorders of childhood
Organic brain syndromes (encephalopathy)	Hearing loss before age seven
	Cerebral palsy
Prematurity	Congenital malformation
Schizophrenia	syndromes (FAS)
Tuberculosis	Child abuse
"Hospitalitis"	Mild MR and/or learning
Malabsorption disorders (intestinal)	disability
	ADHD
Hepatitis	Progressive active hepatitis

NO PLACE TO GO BUT HOME

Soon after the film featuring Anamaria was released, she was enrolled in a full-time intervention program. Treatment for her developmental problems was provided through one of the orphanage-based humanitarian programs that had been established in response to 1990's widely publicized disaster in Romania.

Despite the severity of her problems, Anamaria—and many others like her—made astonishing progress in a newly established developmental program. She overcame her major developmental delays and growth problems by mid-1992. By late summer 1993, she had stopped most of the self-stimulation and was able to leave her room to attend preschool and playground activities. Most astonishingly, and in contradiction to expert predictions, she showed every indication of the desire and ability to form strong relationships with both peers and the maternal adults in her environment. When a group of benefactors visited the orphanage in the late summer of 1994, one of the families, a Colorado couple, fell in love with Anamaria and decided to adopt her.

The couple took immediate action, and the adoption proceeded well until April 1995 when it became bogged down with bureaucratic delays. To facilitate matters at that point, the following summary was included in a medical statement provided to the adoption agency:

PROGRESS: Anamaria's response to treatment was rapid and positive... After two years in program, Anamaria has overcome nearly all of her initial symptoms. She functions normally in a pre-school environment, and socializes well with both peers and adults. There is very little residual sign of fear unless she is in a strange environment. She rocks herself only occasionally, and has lost all other involuntary, stereotypical behaviors. Her growth has caught up, and measurements now fall within normal range for height, weight and head circumference. Although still slightly delayed, her language is near normal.

Most impressive is her intellectual performance: both formal testing and observation place her in the normal range, if not higher. Her learning continues to accelerate. She even sings songs, loves music, does some gymnastics and knows a few words in French and English in addition to her new Romanian vocabulary.

CURRENT STATUS: / IMPRESSION (of Anamaria):
1. Growth and nutritional status: Normal.
2. Developmental delays: Minimal residual delay in language, if any.
3. Neuromotor deficits: No residual. Mile perceptual motor and sensory motor deficits that are often associated with learning disabilities cannot be ruled out at this age. Anamaria is at risk for mild learning disabilities.
4. Psychological and behavioral: Anamaria remains very emotionally vulnerable, but it has been demonstrated that with treatment and a nurturing environment she can make strong attachments. She remains at risk for residual attachment-related problems as she matures.

> *RECOMMENDATION:* Anamaria is at a critical period in her psychological development regarding formation of attachments. It is imperative she receive continuity of services to avoid serious regression and recurrence of her emotional reaction. Because she has "outgrown" the comprehensive services now available at Leaganes, every effort should be made to facilitate the current adoption. Otherwise, she is at serious risk for recurrence of her problems.[19]

Prior to 1992, most experts in child development would have agreed upon a very pessimistic outlook for Anamaria. However, the results of humanitarian efforts initiated in eastern Europe in the early nineties have renewed hope for the world's Anamarias. Doors have opened, not only for individual children, but for whole populations of children in those countries. Many international relief and development projects have included the "healthy development of children" as part of their loftier and more complex mission of democratization and nation building. The results are heartening. Children like Anamaria everywhere are demonstrating that these two missions—the democratization of societies and the healthy development of their children—are not mutually exclusive.

Anamaria's response to a child-development program is typical of the gains being made by institutionalized children wherever there are programs like the ROSES project in which she was enrolled. In these programs, the highly professional collaboration of international relief and development teams and their counterpart foreign colleagues has opened the door. Time, however, is growing short for the abandoned children of eastern Europe. Highly professional foreign aid is not enough for them. It is time for them to go home.

They are outgrowing the early intervention programs that international aid programs have brought into their countries. They are fast approaching new and so-called critical stages of development, and further progress and recovery will depend upon continuation of special services that may not yet exist in their countries of origin. Because training courses have just begun in many of the clinical specialties required to provide these services, highly specialized therapies will not be available in developing countries for years to come.

Children who are still struggling to overcome the problems of years of institutionalization cannot get the therapy they need. Thousands of sensory deprived children, who would benefit from occupational therapy (OT) to treat their sensory handicaps, have no opportunity for that therapy except for services provided by professional volunteers from the West. Occupational therapists are not in place in what was once the land beyond the Iron Curtain. Many countries in eastern Europe—Bulgaria, Romania, and Ukraine, for example—do not have OT at all.

Many of the children are ready to move on to special education programs, and none are available to them. Many surviving children have shown great resilience and have the capacity to learn and to love. They have opened up emotionally and are in critical need of secure and loving homes where they can form attachments to parents while they are still able to make those attachments. Most of these children are still waiting.

Abused and abandoned children who have developed strong defenses in order to survive often must break down those defenses in order to continue to improve. Until they can develop healthier defenses, they are extremely fragile and sensitive. If they are moved to new institutions, for example, and separated from the only adults with whom they have ever formed attachments, their secure base is gone.

Unless children find homes at this very critical juncture in their development, they are in danger of regressing developmentally and reverting to their former, less healthy behavior. Retrieving a child from an emotional shell the second time around is often more difficult than it was when they first broke through that shell. Some of these children cannot make it. Although their physical health is stronger, their ability to trust any relationship is very, very frail.

For thousands of developing country orphans who have been in programs since the early nineties, time is running out. Defenseless, and rapidly losing the support of special programs they have come to depend upon, they are excruciatingly vulnerable.

NEGLECT AND ABUSE

Neglect is the sine qua non of institutional life. All physical, developmental, and mental health problems that occur in children as a result of institutionalization represent some form of neglect. Physical, medical, and emotional neglect occur simultaneously in any one child in an institution. Each has its distinct effect and each plays off of the other to the detriment of the child's growth and development.

Any form of deprivation may dominate the picture or even occur in isolation. A baby may be medically neglected, for example, but be well loved and adequately stimulated. The result may be chronic illness or even life-threatening disease such as hepatitis, tuberculosis, or polio. An infant may be cared for physically but emotionally deprived like Spitz's foundlings; the result may be attachment disorders, behavior problems, growth deficiency, or inability to survive. The severity of response is related to a child's innate, constitutional factors, the length of time the child experiences neglect, and the age at which the neglect began. The problem with institutional care, however, is that there is usually a combination of all forms of deprivation and most children are institutionalized very early in life. The result, therefore, is a composite and cannot be separated into neat little categories. Any caregiver must consider the whole picture the child presents.

The most damaging aspect of physical neglect in young children is sensory deprivation. Without touching, holding, rocking, or hearing the voice of a caregiver, little children are deprived, not only of emotional nurturing but also of any opportunity to learn from their sensory experiences. In the infant and young child, this occurs at the very time that their nervous systems are ideally set up to respond to and learn from hearing and seeing, feeling (tactile), and experiencing handling and movement. If the stimulus is not provided, learning is not possible, and the next step in development cannot be taken.

Sensory deprivation has many forms, but the two most damaging are tactile (touch) and vestibular (sensing movement). If the child is deprived of sensory experience, he will often try to replace it by a set of stereotypic behaviors called "self-stimulation." Because the child can never replace the stimulus that comes from another human, self-stimulation often becomes habitual, and in some children, insatiably driven. The rocking behaviors that are characteristic of so many deprived children from institutions are the most frequently seen self-stimulatory movements. Hence, the term "stereotypic" is often applied.

Rocking and its relationship to vestibular stimulation is a good example of how sensory deprivation leads to both failures in future development and social interaction. The sensory organ or physical receiver for vestibular sense lies in the inner ear. Deep in the innermost chamber of the ear are a set of fluid-filled loops. Suspended in these canals are tiny granules that shift in position when the child is rocked or moved and send signals to the nervous system telling the child if he's upside up or upside down. During the first year of life, the baby has a set of automatic, reflexive reactions that respond to these signals and allow him to correct his position: a baby is tilted and changes his head position automatically; a baby is lifted suddenly or loses his balance and stretches out his arms to catch himself. When the baby "learns" how to adjust his posture or protect himself, the reflexes disappear. He doesn't need them anymore. He has learned and is now able to learn to walk, run, and move around through his environment.

When our baby has spent most of his time swaddled in a crib, lying flat on his back, when he is never rocked or tumbled or bounced on a knee, he will not only be unable to walk or move smoothly, he will not have had any experience that teaches him about position in space and spatial relationships. This not only leads to poor motor skills, it also can lead to perceptual problems and learning disabilities. If someone comes into his institutional environment and provides a "stimulation" program, he may be slow to respond because his lovely reflexes are gone now; nothing comes naturally, and he has to consciously learn what other toddlers do automatically. Furthermore, with no stimulation in the past, he does not know how to process the things he is feeling and may be terrified by the new experience.

Many areas of sensorimotor development have what are called critical periods during which skills must be acquired or they can never develop properly, no matter how much stimulation is provided. The eye that is patched or blindfolded long enough will eventually go blind. The child with a constant middle ear infection may never be able speak with normal pronunciation, even when hearing is restored to normal. Not all the stimulation in the world will make up for the deprivation.

The interplay between sensory and emotional deprivation is obvious. The baby who is never rocked by a parent also never has that opportunity for closeness that is part of being rocked to sleep and held close to a parent. The baby who is not touched will never feel the tenderness that is always communicated by the touch from a loving caregiver. Both the social and physical interaction routinely experienced every time a baby's diaper is changed—the talking or tickling or making a game of it—never occurs. Instead, he experiences cold, impersonal hands and stinging skin. Babies, being human, will eventually begin to avoid the experience that is uncomfortable, strange, or frightening. They will, like Anamaria, develop all kinds of behaviors that are designed to avoid the experience.

Imagine such a child on his first night in an adoptive home. Imagine the scene when he meets his father. The new father picks him up and joyfully lifts him over his head, or tumbles him in play on a bed. Our baby cannot respond normally due to his deprivation and does what one might expect. He grabs for anything he can find (usually, a handful of hair) to cling to and holds on for dear life. A tiny misunderstanding enters into a fragile, beginning relationship.

Early intervention programs can go a long way in reversing the damage done by sensory deprivation. Almost every American community offers a number of these programs for children and parents. Although most children, with help, can respond to programs such as "infant stimulation" or "early intervention," other more severely involved children may need formal therapy. Occupational therapists are often highly skilled in helping the sensory deprived child in these circumstances. When a post-institutionalized child gets the help needed, more serious developmental and learning deficits are often prevented.

Although all of them stem from a single cause, there is a tremendous variation of expression of the effects of neglect upon the neglected or abuse upon the abused. In addition to this variety of responses, any single child can show a number of additional problems. A child with reactive attachment disorder can also have growth deficiency, or attention deficit disorder with hyperactivity (ADHD). If the child has experienced or witnessed abuse in addition to having been neglected, he may exhibit the delayed anxiety reaction known as post-traumatic stress disorder (PTSD) in addition to attachment problems.

ABUSE

Abuse, when it accompanies neglect, compounds all other problems. Furthermore, abuse often causes problems that are not seen in children who are simply neglected. Abuse is more common in institutions than in families, however, and often takes a different and more vicious form. There is no underlying attachment between child and abusive caregiver. The occurrence is arbitrary and indifferent, robbing the child of any opportunity to manipulate, modify, or control the situation. Tragically, there are increasing numbers of cases of child abuse being reported in children adopted from foreign institutions in the 1990s.

Neglectful patterns of caregivers can—and often do—overlap with abusive patterns. A rejecting caregiver can, under stress, become abusive. When personal stress is lessened, an abusive caregiver can revert to simple neglect, or even to more loving caregiving. It should not be forgotten that abusive caregivers can, and often do love the children they abuse. When this is the case, the caregiver often has a history of abuse herself when she was a child. (While this is the case of most children who are abused in homes, the more insidious and indifferent pattern of abuse is characteristic of institutional environments.)

Although it is centuries old, child abuse, its causes and effects, was reintroduced to health professionals in the 1960s when Dr. C. Henry Kempe in his original book, *The Battered*

Child,[20] defined the disorder as a syndrome. His classical description of the medical and social pathology of child abuse and neglect is now part of every Western professional's fund of knowledge and has provided the clinical basis for both diagnosis and treatment of abused and neglected children. Like sensory deprivation, the consequences of abuse and neglect are now treatable conditions. Help is available to the abusive caregiver as well.

When adopting parents visit foreign orphanages, it is extremely rare to see actual abuse taking place. They may be tipped off if a child has some physical signs of abuse, such as bruises, scars of cigarette burns, crooked arms or legs (often evidence of past, poorly healed fractures), or signs of having been tied up or otherwise physically restrained, such as rope burns. Occasionally, there is obvious, harsh behavior on the part of the caregiver. Adopting parents should know, however, that the fact that there is evidence of affection between caregiver and child does not rule out that the caregiver may be the abuser.

COMBINING THE PICTURE

There is a tremendous variation of expression of the effects of neglect upon the neglected or abuse upon the abused. In addition to this variety of responses, any single child can show a number of additional problems, all of which stem from the same deprivational circumstances. A child with reactive attachment disorder can also have growth deficiency, or attention deficit disorder with hyperactivity (ADHD). If the child has experienced or witnessed abuse in addition to having been neglected, he may exhibit the delayed anxiety reaction known as post-traumatic stress disorder (PTSD) in addition to attachment problems.

When the unattached child has also experienced abuse from caregivers, the abuse is usually the determining factor in the recovery potential of the child. Such was the case in many of the three- to seven-year-old children of institutions now being reported. These children were sexually abused in arbitrary, ritualistic fashion. There are now more than a hundred documented cases of this macabre practice. The fact that reports are coming from multiple countries, that children are talking to their teachers, therapists, and parents and telling precisely the same stories, lend credibility to otherwise "unbelievable" stories.

Most of the child victims of these abusive situations suffer some degree of post-traumatic stress syndrome (PTSD). However, symptoms of this disorder may not be expressed until after children have arrived in their new home. Most often, these symptoms include recurrent nightmares, phobias, and unprovoked "spells," during which the child may relive the abusive episode. Because of the distress associated with symptoms of this nature, parents invariably seek professional attention early.

As tragic as these case histories are, they do not provide much help to adopting parents before or during the adoption process. There is no way to "prediagnose" their condition. Although centers that specialize in child abuse and neglect may have some information available to assist in the identification of abused children, this information is rarely part of adopting parents' preadoptive counseling.

There is no way, without prior knowledge, to recognize the offending institution. When visited by agencies or adopting parents, the offending institutions often look just like any other institution. The staff looks the same. Abusive activities never take place when foreign visitors are present. The children look, if anything, precocious and unusually "sociable."

PTSD cannot be diagnosed during the child's stay in the institution. In both children and adults, it is a delayed reaction disorder. The original syndrome was described in American veterans of the Vietnam war. Of the hundreds of thousands of American soldiers who fought in that war, it was impossible to recognize the thousands who would suffer PTSD until they returned home and began to relive the nightmare. The same is true of "orphans" who have begun, often more than a year postadoption, to tell their stories.

Like sensory deprivation and its resulting problems with development and learning, abuse and its attendant psychological problems can be treated. Early psychotherapeutic intervention can help many of these children lead more secure, happy lives and many are able to reverse the deadly effects of abuse that are seen when they first enter their new homes.

MAKING PREDICTIONS

The future prognoses or outcomes of adopted children who have experienced absence of affection and sensory input rather than loss is unknown. The problems they pose are similar to the age-old question, "Is it better to have loved and lost than never to have loved at all?"

Despite the encouraging experience Western professionals have had with children while they are still in institutions, experts are less certain about long-term prognoses in children after adoption. Although we have reestablished, with some degree of academic certainty, most of the immediate effects of institutionalization—what kind, how severe, commonly associated findings and complications, for example—the permanent effects of institutionalization have not been adequately studied in light of today's technology. To fully understand the long-term effects of early deprivation, years of follow-up investigation of post-institutionalized children is required.

Therefore, it is not yet known what percent of the foreign adoptees of the nineties will fully recover, what percent will have residual problems, or what kind of difficulty may crop up later in the life of the child. Furthermore, it has not yet been determined what kind of interventions are most effective in reversing the disabilities seen after discharge from an institution. The many human variations in response to treatment are unpredictable. The role of genetics and temperament in resilience and intact survival is not yet fully known.

"It's a mystery to me," said an adoptive mother of one Romanian boy, "how my adopted child is now in a gifted program while the child from the next room of the same orphanage cannot even talk yet and still rocks himself to sleep every night. Some of these kids just came with a built-in immunity." That built in immunity, which we call resilience, remains a partial mystery to professionals as well.

It is difficult to recognize beforehand the child who has inborn strengths and resiliency and who will recover fully to become a loving, productive adult. Despite the history of neglect, rejection, and abuse, some children from institutions have not only survived but seem to be thriving. Even in more severe cases, including those that involve abuse, children are responding to treatment and intervention programs. Experts can only speculate that somewhere in that past of brutality and deprivation was a caregiver who connected with the child. In his memoir of life in an Irish institution, author Paddy Doyle lends credence to this speculation:

> Many people familiar with the effects of institutional care will say that I have gone too easy on them. Lives have been ruined by the tyrannical rule and lack of love in such places. People have been scarred for life. . . .
>
> It is important to point out that interspersed with this trauma were moments of great love and affection. From the gentle kiss of a young nurse to the soft hand of a caring nun, it may well be the case that these were the moments that preserved my sanity and gave me something to live for.[21]

THE NEED TO KNOW

Throughout the world, parents are crying out their need for honest and accurate information about the children they are adopting. This desperate need to know is frustrated by the paucity and inaccuracy of information available.

"Everything I know about these kids I learned from television programs," commented a Texas father, "and that's not near enough."

There is no current, updated encyclopedia of adoption that would contain enough for today's parents seeking information about children of institutions. There is, however, a wealth of information from the past, and lessons may be learned by reviewing the written accounts of professional pioneers such as Spitz (on foundlings), Provence (on infants in institutions), Bowlby (on attachment), Kempe (on child abuse and neglect), and others who have been quoted in this chapter. The writings of authors like Paddy Doyle, who was a child of the institution, are particularly valuable, because they offer the child's perspective.

More recently, eastern Europe's orphans have provided us a fresh look at children of institutions. The information just now becoming available about these children while they are in institutions and the firsthand accounts of adopting parents and professionals who have lived with these children should be invaluable in enlightening today's adopting parents.

Enlightened adoption is the best opportunity for institutionalized children, anywhere on the globe, to realize their own potential for growth, development, and emotional security. For those children institutionalized in third-world or developing countries, it may be the only opportunity.

Destruction of a child's potential for healthy growth and development while in institutional care is a very old problem and a tragic one. If Romania's children have served any larger purpose, then it may be that society has been given a second chance to solve these problems.

This chapter is dedicated to Anamaria, and to the Colorado family who have, after two years of waiting, adopted her, and to the many children of institutions like her who harbor, deep inside, the luminitsa *(little light) that wants so badly to shine.*

REFERENCES

1. B. Bascom, *Romania Update* (a documentary video production). R. B. Davies, Inc., Hollywood, CA. R. B. Davies, executive director; Robin Groth, producer. Filmed in Iasi, Romania, February 1991.

2. R. A. Spitz and K. M. Wolf, "Anaclitic Depression: An Inquiry into the Genesis of Psychiatric Conditions in Early Childhood," *The Psychoanalytic Study of the Child* 3, no. 4 (1946), pp. 85–120.

3. L. A. Barness, *Nelson Textbook of Pediatrics: Nutritional Disorder*, 14th ed. (W. B. Saunders, 1992), pp. 130–47.

4. J. Money, "The Syndrome of Abuse (Psychosocial) Dwarfism," *Am I Dis Child* 131 (1977), p. 508.

5. S. Provence and S. E. Lipton, *Infants in Institutions* (New York: International Universities Press, 1962).

6. Salimbene, quoted in Provence and Lipton, p. 3.

7. Nicolai Caeusescu, ex-dictator of Romania, in a 1978 speech.

8. A. K. Johnson, R. L. Edwards, and H. Puwak, "Foster Care and

Adoption Policy in Romania: Suggestions for International Intervention," *Child Welfare* 63, no. 5 (September–October 1993), pp. 489–506.

9. B. Bascom et al., "Prevention of Developmental Delays in Young Children in a Romanian Orphanage," *East European Medical Journal* 1, no. 2 (1992), pp. 7–19.

10. D. E. Johnson et al., "The Health of Children Adopted from Romania," *Journal of the American Medical Association* 268 (1992), pp. 3446–3451.

11. E. W. Ames and M. C. Carter, "A Study of Romanian Orphanage Children in Canada: Symposium on Development of Romanian Orphanage Children Adopted to Canada," Canadian Psychological Association. Quebec City, Canada, June 13, 1992. Published by Simon Fraser University, 1992.

12. M. K. Hostetter et al., "Medical Evaluation of Internationally Adopted Children," *The New England Journal of Medicine* 325, no. 7 (August 15, 1991), pp. 479–485.

13. B. Bascom, *The ROSES Project: Facts, Figures and Outcomes* (Washington, D. C.: The Brooke Foundation, Inc., 1993).

14. "Reactive Attachment Disorder of Infancy or Early Childhood," *Diagnostic and Statistical Manual IV* (Washington, D. C.: American Psychiatric Association, 1994), pp. 116–18.

15. G. L. Haradon and B. Bascom, "Sensory Functions of Institutionalized Romanian Orphans: A Pilot Study," *Occupational Therapy International* 1, no. 4 (1994), pp. 164–201.

16. J. K. Sweeney and B. Bascom, "Motor Development and Self-Stimulatory Movement in Institutionalized Romanian Children," *Pediatric Physical Therapy* 7, no. 3 (fall 1995), pp. 124–33.

17. S. J. Kaler and B. J. Freeman, "Analysis of Environmental Deprivation: Cognitive and Social Development in Romanian Orphans," *Journal of Child Psychology and Psychiatry* 35, no. 4 (1994), pp. 769–78. A ROSES project study conducted in Timisoara, Romania, 1991–93.

18. R. A. Spitz, "Hospitalism: An Inquiry into the Genesis of Psychiatric Conditions in Early Childhood," *The Psychoanalytic Study of the Child* 1 (1945), pp. 53–74.

19. B. Bascom, *ROSES Case Files* (Denver, CO: The Brooke Foundation, 1995).

20. R. E. Helfer and C. H. Kempe, *The Battered Child* (University of Chicago Press, 1968).

21. P. Doyle, *The God Squad* (Corgi Books Ltd., 1985).

Special Children,
Special Issues

Someday, maybe, there will exist a well-informed,
well-considered, and yet fervent public conviction
that the most deadly of all possible sins
is the mutilation of the child's spirit. . . .

Erik Erikson
Journal of the American Medical Association, 1975

Adoption, whether it be international or domestic, involves a complex, sometimes mysterious, and often frustrating process. Whatever its motives, the ultimate goal is the establishment of a relationship between parent and child. Every obstacle, problem, frustration, or delay creates a little more distance between the would-be parent and the waiting child. Every success, solved problem, and lesson learned brings them closer together.

The process of foreign adoption is rarely smooth. More often than not, parents encounter obstacles, some of which are harbingers of real and more serious problems, but most of which are just irritating and time-consuming. The challenge to overcome both large and small obstacles usually rests with the adopting parents. To hurdle the barriers and solve the problems, the would-be parent needs to know what they are and how to deal with them. The risks of not knowing are threefold: The would-be parent remains would-be, the waiting child continues to wait, or, saddest of all, the relationship cannot form.

The cases presented in this chapter are intended to illustrate major issues about the health and mental health risks embedded in international adoption. These are not easy stories to read. We present them to inform—not to inflame or frighten. Having promised to tell the whole truth of adoption, we feel it would be dishonest to do otherwise. The experiences of parents who have adopted children with very special needs should give potential parents a new perspective on the complex choices ahead of them and arm them with information upon which they can base many of those choices. We feel that the issues they illustrate are critically important. Three issues are explored:

1. *Information:* the importance of informed adoptive parents; knowledge and recognition of both the special needs and strengths of children who have survived early neglect and abuse.
2. *Expectations:* common expectations and misconceptions of adopting parents. Outcomes, best- and worst-case scenarios.
3. *The healing process:* healing the wounds of children; the healing process for parents and children.

Parents who have adopted special-needs children are often people who have already started a family and seek to enrich their experience as parents by bringing another, less fortunate child into their families. When a child has special needs, his parents are given the unique opportunity to experience the fulfillment of becoming part of the process of healing for that child. Some of these parents, like Gene Goldberg (chapter 1), express this desire as a need: "We have two gorgeous, perfectly normal children," he said. "But I thought, we need to get this kid!"

If parents are not well informed about the injuries that abandoned and neglected children may have sustained before adoption, they cannot be well prepared for the challenges ahead of them. Uninformed or ill informed, they are robbed of the unique joy and fulfillment that comes with parenting when it is combined with healing. Serge's parents (Introduction) "did everything right and jumped through all the hoops" but, with no information, suppressed their intuition that something was wrong. When confronted with a terribly injured child, they found themselves saying, "Well, he is very small, the food is bad, his boots are too small, and he has difficulty walking outside because of that." Overriding strong misgivings about Serge's problems, their compassion for him prevailed. Hoping against hope that once he was out of this environment, he would be fine, they brought a terribly wounded child into their home.

The children in these stories are survivors. The very fact of their survival signals a strength of spirit and constitution that is hard to imagine and impossible to fully explain scientifically. The scars that wounded children bear give testimony not only to the terrible damage they have suffered but also to that strength.

The parents in these stories have courageously taken on challenges and made sacrifices that most people would never consider. Despite the fact that most of them were not well informed about the road ahead, their level of commitment and willingness to make those sacrifices has been both extraordinary and inspirational to others who may choose to follow their footsteps.

In these stories, neither the children nor the parents are ordinary people. They are, instead, people like Lori Eisinger. . . .

DI DI EISINGER

Di Di Eisinger is a child who screamed nonstop from the minute her new mother left the eastern European orphanage with her until she arrived home in the United States.

Desperate and confused about the decision she had made, Lori Eisinger of Montana said she began to doubt herself, even as she flew home from Frankfort to New York with the two-and-a-half-year-old child.

"I really felt like I was having a nervous breakdown. I'd been cooped up alone for so long with this baby who wouldn't let me feed her or hold her. She was so inconsolable, so anxious, and screaming so loudly, I finally resorted to giving her Benadryl [an antihistamine with sedative properties] to put her to sleep. I actually thought, 'Dear God, I hope I don't kill her with this medicine.'

"As she lay there, asleep in my lap, I looked at her and panicked. I thought to myself, 'What have I done?' Something other than hepatitis is wrong with her; something else is terribly wrong with her. Our lives will never be the same. Let me die now, with this child in my arms."

Lori Eisinger's initial feelings of doubt have never gone away, even though she has grown to love little Di Di immensely since the horror of that mid-1991 flight from Romania. This child, originally diagnosed as having hepatitis B (she just tested positive for the antibodies and doesn't have the disease), has turned out, instead, to have a deadly combination of severe developmental and mental health disorders. The combination was deadly because each disorder made the other worse.

Now five years old, Di Di is severely developmentally delayed; she has been diagnosed as "borderline autistic." Her severe delays in talking are only part of a larger, severe language and communication disorder, and stem, at least partially, from a condition known as "elective mutism" (a condition in which a child has no spoken language, even though physically able; the cause is usually psychological).

Di Di has symptoms of recurring phobias. During a phobic attack, she will not go outside or allow her feet to touch the ground. In addition to the phobic episodes, Di Di has what Lori refers to as spells. Lori describes them as follows:

Without any warning or provocation, Di Di flies into uncontrollable rages that far exceed even the severest temper tantrums (which she also has). Screaming and writhing on the floor, Di Di bites her hands and pounds herself with her fists to the point of self-injury. Inconsolable once she is into one of these spells, Di Di lashes out at anyone who tries to stop her or comfort her. When picked up, she arches her back and pushes away. Her mother, Lori, bears the brunt of her anger.

"They just have to run their course," says Lori with resignation.

Di Di seems unable to love her new parents. Only once in the four years the Eisingers have had her in their home has Di Di called Lori "Mama." She never reaches out, Lori says, except when she wants something.

Di Di and her family have suffered enormously because of

her neglect in the institution. The lack of love and touch she had as a baby has affected the entire family. Her two older brothers are embarrassed to be with her, and neither Lori or her husband take her out when they leave the house. If one parent has to go to a boy's baseball game, for example, the other must stay home with Di Di. Baby-sitters, even those with some special training, are unable to cope. The family, therefore, has no opportunity for relief or respite and has lost any semblance of normal family activity. They feel like virtual prisoners in their home, never able to leave Di Di alone for a second. They fear for her and they fear for themselves.

The adoption of this very difficult child has caused the Eisingers to see a marriage counselor. "I wonder how many of these children cause divorces," Lori muses. "I'm sure it's a lot."[1]

Like many others, the Eisingers, who have older children at home, chose to adopt in Romania because of media pictures of waiflike children in sterile metal cribs. "I just had to go and get a child out of there," Lori says.

Like so many other children who aren't true "orphans," Di Di was born out of wedlock and had been abandoned to an orphanage soon after birth. When Di Di was born, there was no law that allowed a single mother to relinquish the child she could not care for. Giving the child up for adoption was not an option for Di Di's mother. She could only abandon her to the state system of social protection. Furthermore, there was no law that rendered Di Di adoptable by virtue of her abandonment. In Romania, abandonment was not legally defined until 1993.

Although Di Di was illegitimate, unwanted, and abandoned, and although her birth mother had never taken any responsibility for her care, the birth mother had to be present for all court hearings. The process involved long hours waiting for court appearances. The adopting family had to make multiple trips to the birth mother's home to obtain permission to adopt and then provide transportation for the again pregnant woman to get her back and forth to the courts.

Lori notes with irony a woman who traveled to Romania with her to bring back a son, a child about Di Di's age who was in the same orphanage. "He's doing so well. I don't know how you can tell what is going to happen. He's adjusting just fine," says Lori.

"I was very ill informed and had no idea what I was doing," says Lori, who went to Romania at a time when no one had adequate information about the children in institutions there. Even those who had some information were thrown into a chaotic situation in the spring of 1991. Thousands of adopting parents from multiple countries were searching the halls of every institution to find their child before the old adoption system shut down. The word was out that when Romania went to the drawing boards to develop an adoption law, the entire system would shut down for months. Although everyone knew that the event was imminent, no official date was released to the public.

Lori Eisinger was among the last adopting parents who made it through the old adoption system. A short time after she and Di Di boarded the plane for Frankfort, all adoption was halted and Romania began to write its law.

Although Di Di was found in a relatively good orphanage, Lori had been unfortunate. The day she arrived to select her child was the same day Di Di had been transferred in from another facility. No one knew the beautiful little girl with the somber eyes who sat so still in her crib. None of the professional staff had time to evaluate her, and none had the skills or training to recognize complex problems like Di Di's. The records that came with Di Di were inadequate. Other than indicating that Di Di was "small for her age" (dystrophic), and had tested positive on a hepatitis screen, the handwritten file gave no hint of Di Di's other problems. "Otherwise," the record read, "she is normal."

Every day, Lori Eisinger and her husband pray to find a cure for Di Di. "I hope someone can help us," says Lori. "We so want to love her."

Because of her past, Di Di's ability to accept and give love are hidden deep inside her, locked far away from the family who wants to desperately to love her. The search for the key to Di Di's heart is never-ending.

"Sometimes I look at this tiny little girl and wonder how on earth she can inflict so much pain."[2]

Lori Eisinger agreed to talk about her adoption of Di Di in the hope that she might help other parents and, if possible, spare them some of the pain that she and her family have experienced. She stresses how difficult it is, "when you're in the emotion and rush of an international adoption," to make judgments. With no guidance or information, before or during adoption, those judgments are impossible.

Lori might have been spared much of the pain she experienced had there been a regulated system of adoption in Romania. As it was, she had nothing to protect her. In 1991, there was no adoption law. There was no policy, no list of approved agencies, and no social work. There were no trained Romanian social workers. Most adopting families, like Lori, did independent adoptions, without an agency. Other than what she could glean from other, equally desperate adopting families, Lori had no guidance at all.

Both Lori and Di Di might have been spared the agony of that plane ride had there been any system of identification of the child's problems before she left the country. In 1991, however, there was no trained professional in Di Di's orphanage to provide an evaluation. Basic developmental screening was not started until months after Di Di's departure.

Although both Di Di and Lori would have benefited from a guided transition program before Di Di left the orphanage, none existed. Had Di Di been adopted in the United States, transition to a new home and family might have been gradual and supervised. Nothing would have been finalized until both child and family were ready. There is still not, in 1995, a formal program of transition for intercountry adoptions in Romania.

The Eisinger family might have been spared much of what they have gone through had there been an adequate support system in place in the United States when they came home. There was not. Information about the children was scanty and none of Lori's friends who had adopted were having problems. Evaluation of Di Di's problems took months and took its toll on the family budget. Their insurance health plan paid only a tiny fraction of the costs. After evaluation, Di Di's new parents needed access to the services they and their newly adopted child required. They did not get it and had to fight for every service that Di Di was entitled to.

Although it is unusually severe, the Eisinger story poignantly illustrates what can and often does happen in ill informed foreign adoptions of children with very special needs:

- ◆ Thousands of children of foreign adoption have been deeply wounded by their past environments of neglect, abuse, deprivation, and abandonment. Although all wounds can heal, some will leave scars that can never be erased and are often difficult to detect.

- ◆ Thousands of adopting parents become victims themselves in the process—or of the process. They have responded to a child by believing that their basic human instincts to nurture and love a child will also heal that child. They have acted upon those instincts without benefit of accurate information or guidance. With no anticipatory guidance before leaving home, they are too often misled by false information when they arrive in a foreign country. They have found inadequate support when they return home.

FOREIGN ADOPTION'S INFORMATION GAP

Lack of information is the first obstacle to enlightened adoption of foreign children with special needs. After leaving home without information or guidance, families don't know what they are looking for when they travel to the sending country. Once they arrive, they often accept whatever they are given.

Many children's medical forms say that the child is "healthy" or "well," and any psychological difficulties the child may have acquired are either glossed over or completely missed. In most cases, institutional personnel simply do not know the child well enough or haven't the expertise or knowledge to recognize the difficulty. Adoption agencies often do not employ therapists or clinical social workers with the training to spot these difficulties.

Despite the improvements that have been made in intercountry adoption since 1991 when Lori Eisinger adopted Di Di, the information gap persists. Due to their backgrounds of deprivation, neglect, and abuse, foreign children with special needs still come to adoptive homes with a host of unidentified problems. The problem lists grow in direct proportion to the length of time children have had to wait for a home and loving family. This combination of no information and misinformation that many adopting parents bring to special-needs foreign adoption tends to reinforce any unrealistic or false expectations adopting parents may harbor.

The following three are additional examples offered to specifically illustrate some of the problems that can befall a well-intended family when they adopt a foreign child and are given no information about the risks that child may come with. Adopting parents should have some basic knowledge of the serious clinical challenges these children demonstrate and it is best to be informed before leaving home. It is very unlikely that information will be available in a developing country.

The nature and complexity of the medical and mental health problems the following adopted children suffered is extreme and severe, making it all the more ludicrous that none of their conditions were recognized before they were released for adoption. In telling these stories, it is not our purpose to engage in long, erudite discussions regarding diagnosis or treatment methods. Whole books have been written about most of these disorders. But recognizing the great need for information about the most common clinical problems adopting parents will encounter, we have included thumbnail clinical explanations throughout the chapter. References are provided at the end of the chapter.

A Brother and a Sister

In mid-1993, a delighted California couple (who wish to remain anonymous) returned from Russia with two children. Their joy was short-lived, however. The younger child, a six-month-old baby boy, was diagnosed as having fetal alcohol syndrome (FAS) soon after their arrival. The little girl, Sandy, age four, showed signs of severe emotional disturbance and was unable to attach to her new family.

After evaluation, the couple was led to suspect that Sandy had been abused, probably sexually, at the Moscow orphanage. Sandy was unresponsive to therapy. No one seemed to be able to offer solutions.

The agency made it clear that this adoptive couple was on their own. Running low on resources and feeling they had only enough energy to deal with one challenged child, they were forced to disrupt, or interrupt, the U.S. adoption of Sandy and return her to an adoption agency to find another family.

"We never expected this. We never dreamed this would happen. No one—at the embassy, at INS [Immigration and Naturalization Service], at the adoption agency—no one, simply no one, told us this was a possibility. We never dreamed that our children would end up so disabled."[3]

~

Jason

Fourteen-year-old Jason (not his real name) was the second Korean-born child this midwestern family adopted. The other child, sixteen, had adjusted well and was a joy to the family. But Jason was different. Although a severe form of hepatitis B and "functional illiteracy" were two of the differences (between him and his adopted sister), it was neither his progressive liver disease nor his learning disability that finally ended the adoption.

The last few weeks the couple had their adopted son, they actually tied bells to their bedroom door when they went to bed. They feared for their own safety and that of their daughter. Their fears were justifiable.

Within the first eighteen months of placement, Jason had told his adopted sister he wanted her dead. He had physically attacked his mother and eight children at school. He brutalized animals, tore things to shreds just for spite, had never done *anything* his parents told him to do. He was caught drawing pictures of the devil while sitting in church.

Realizing the magnitude of Jason's problems, the family consulted experts. They were advised to "get the boy out of the house as soon as they could," that he was dangerous to them and to himself. After what was described as an agonizing decision, they ended the adoption (dissolution, or legal termination) and Jason was returned to the original placement agency, which agreed to take him back and attempt to place him in a long-term-care facility.[4]

José's Survival Story

When his adoptive parents first saw José (not his real name), he was comatose, suffering from hypothermia (lowered body temperature), severe malnutrition, and the consequences of long-term neglect. Not wanting another child, the baby's mother was hoping he would die, so she left him alone and unattended on a concrete floor, without food, water, or blankets, for days. By the time she brought José to the doctor, the child showed few signs of life.

Working in central Mexico, José's new parents had hoped to adopt one of the dark-haired children they had felt so drawn to for several months. When they heard about the sick baby who would be up for adoption, should he live, they decided to consider little José for their own and went to the doctor's office. Looking over his nearly lifeless form, they could "see no hint of the child he could be." When the doctor indicated the child could be saved, however, the couple decided they could adopt José.

The child that could have been, however, was not to be. The ravages of profound neglect, abuse, and total rejection had destroyed any possibility José had for living a normal life, or even for learning to give and receive affection. As José grew older, a severe and violent emotional disorder emerged. He was diagnosed as having a reactive attachment disorder, a mental health disorder of children caused by severe neglect and abuse in early childhood. It seemed José would never be able to form a loving attachment to his adoptive parents.

José's new parents took him to a treatment facility that provided specialized care for such children. But José was so severely damaged he was unable to respond to the therapy he and his family received. Before the therapeutic intervention could be completed, José ran away. Painfully disappointed and exhausted from their efforts to parent the abusive child, his parents just couldn't continue. The adoption was ended. When social services deemed him too dangerous and emotionally disturbed for any family, José was placed in a residential treatment center where he would receive long-term mental health care and educational services.[5]

It is impossible to say what might have occurred had the parents in these stories been armed with enough information and guidance beforehand and gone into these adoptions enlightened and prepared. Some or all of them might have been able to continue their role as parents even though their adopted children required long-term psychiatric treatment out of the home. For those who had no choice but to disrupt the adoptions (discontinue the U.S. adoption proceedings and return the child to the agency for alternate placement), the experience would not have been as shattering and the decisions they made not as painful for their families. All of them, however, would have had the knowledge they needed to make the appropriate decisions and choices before going into the adoption.

In addition to illustrating the dangers of inadequate information, these cases raise many issues about the medical and mental health risks involved in adoption of abandoned and severely deprived children. Although the diseases these children suffered were unusually severe, none of these disorders are uncommon. Adopting parents may find it useful to know more about the serious health and psychiatric problems illustrated by these cases.

HEALTH PROBLEMS

- *Failure to thrive*—a mixed condition of growth and development characterized by failure to maintain normal growth (primarily weight gain) and development at a normal rate; cause(s): nonorganic (psychosocial, deprivation) and organic (malnutrition and a wide range of chronic medical conditions and congenital anomalies). Treatment: appropriate to cause.
- *Hepatitis B*—an infectious disease of the liver caused by hepatitis B virus and transmitted through blood and body fluids.

Causes a wide spectrum of clinical manifestations ranging from asymptomatic seroconversion (positive blood test, an indication of exposure and development of immunity) to active disease and progressive liver failure. Treatment: supportive (secondary problems only). There is no definitive treatment for the primary disease. Several experimental drug programs are promising (alpha-interferon, particularly) in older children and adults; organ transplant for liver failure. Endemic (always present in epidemic proportions) in many developing countries. Institutional environments at particular risk.

◆ *Fetal alcohol syndrome (FAS)*—a specific pattern of malformations caused by high levels of alcohol ingestion during pregnancy. Occurs (worldwide) in one to two infants per 1,000 live births. Characteristics:

1. Prenatal onset, persistent growth deficiency in height, weight, and head circumference.
2. Facial characteristics: thin upper lip, small maxilla (cheek bone) and mandible (jawbone), short palpebral fissure (eye opening), epicanthal folds (folds of tissue in the inner corner/angle of the eye).
3. Minor (nondisabling) abnormalities of the joints and limbs. May restrict movement.
4. Cardiac abnormalities; primarily septal defects.
5. Delayed development and mental deficiency, ranging from borderline to severe.

◆ *Fetal alcohol effect (FAE)*—a term applied to children with some but not all characteristics of FAS. Facial features and developmental deficits (albeit milder) are commonly described.

Fetal alcohol syndrome is common in those developing countries where alcoholism is prevalent. Its incidence is particularly high in Russia, but it is seen throughout eastern Europe. The diagnosis is rarely made in-country (preadoptive). Pamphlets with photographs are available and can be obtained by inquiring at most health care facilities or at drug and alcohol prevention and treatment centers. If adopting parents see characteristics in a child they are considering that make them suspicious after they have arrived in a foreign country, they may want to consult a pediatric specialist or photograph the child and send photos to the United States for an expert opinion. If the latter route is chosen, try to obtain copies of any X rays that have been done in the past.

MENTAL HEALTH PROBLEMS

As previously noted, the most common diagnostic label assigned to children of international adoption who have mental health problems is that of reactive attachment disorder (RAD). This condition is described in the American Psychiatric Association's manual, the *Diagnostic and Statistical Manual of Mental Disorders* (DSM-IV). (DSM, widely used by mental health field workers, is the official guide for all current disease classifications and definitions for mental disorders.) In DSM, the essential features of reactive attachment disorder are described as follows:

> The essential feature of Reactive Attachment Disorder is markedly disturbed and developmentally inappropriate social relatedness in most contexts that begins before age five years and is associated with grossly pathological care.[6]

Table 1

REACTIVE ATTACHMENT DISORDER

Features of Pathogenic Care
- Persistent disregard of the child's basic **emotional needs** for comfort, stimulation, and affection.
- Persistent disregard of the child's basic **physical needs**.
- Repeated changes of primary caregiver that prevent formation of stable attachments.

Clinical Features of Reactive Attachment Disorder
Markedly disturbed and developmentally inappropriate social relatedness, beginning before age five years:
- **Inhibited type:**
  Persistent failure to initiate or socially respond in a developmentally appropriate fashion as manifest by excessively inhibited or highly ambivalent and contradictory responses.
  Examples: The child has an *inconsistent response* to caregivers

with a mixture of approach. Child aviods and resists comforting. The child may exhibit an attitude of *frozen watchfulness*.

◆ **Disinhibited type:**
Diffuse attachments: manifest by indiscriminate sociability; inability to exhibit appropriate, selective attachments.
Examples: excessive familiarity with strangers; lack of selectivity in choice of "attachments."

Table 2

REACTIVE ATTACHMENT DISORDER: COMPARISON OF POST-INSTITUTION AND COMMUNITY-BASED CHILDREN

Associated Deficits	Post-institution (Foreign Adoptees)	Community-based (American foster homes)
Growth	+ + +	+
Language delays	+ + + +	Rare; often loquacious, glib
Motor delays	+ + +	*
Learning disability	+ + +	Poor achievment; LD**
Stereotypic behavior	+ + +	Not characteristic
Sensory integrative deficits	+ + + +	+ +
PTSD (post-traumatic stress syndrome)	+ + +	+ + (abuse history)
MR (mental retardation)	+ +	Equals general incidence
Conduct disorder	Rare	+ + +
Antisocial psychopathologies	Rare; seen with sexual abuse	+ + + +

ADHD (attention deficit hyperactive disorder)—approximately equal in both groups; incidence is slightly greater than in general population.

*Seen, but no more frequently than in general population.
**Seen more often than in general population.

Although their medical problems and countries of origin differ, there is a common thread winding through the children's histories featured earlier in this chapter. It is also the thread that caused their adoptions either to terminate or to fail in the sense that no relationship could be formed. All of these children—Di Di, Jason, José, and Sandy—have severe emotional problems that stem from their lack of attachment. Even with expert attention, none of them were able to develop (or recover) the capacity to attach.

Although most children who come from environments of neglect and deprivation have some form of attachment problem, many do not have the component of rage and violence illustrated by these cases. The addition of conduct and character disorders make these cases very difficult to treat successfully. When attachment disorders are severe enough to cause violent, destructive behavior, raising safety issues for both child and other family members, there is often little choice left to adoptive parents but to find a qualified, experienced therapist familiar with attachment disorder and seek therapy, or to end the adoption and/or seek residential care for the child.

Fortunately, these cases are extreme examples—worst-case scenarios—and represent a small (but loud) minority of all foreign adoptions. The exact percentage of foreign adoptees who have attachment disorders is not known. Available information indicates, however, that attachment is an issue in the majority of children who are adopted after age two and that children who have less severe forms of attachment disorder are usually responsive to treatment. Through therapy programs for children and guidance programs for families, there is now hope for the families who suffer the turmoil and grief these problems involve.

In reviewing the case files and reports in the professional literature available on postinstitutionalized children, the following mental health disorders were most commonly reported:

♦ *Post-traumatic stress disorder (PTSD):* An anxiety disorder seen in children who have experienced extremely traumatic events involving death, injury, or mutilation. Characteristic symptoms:

- ◆ Episodes of fear, helplessness or horror; in children—may be expressed as disorganized or agitated behavior.
- ◆ Recurrent, distressing recollections; in children may be acted out in play.
- ◆ Recurrent nightmares of the event; in children, frightening dreams may not have recognizable content.
- ◆ Recurrent episodes of reliving the traumatic events, such as flashbacks, etc.; children may act out the event during such episodes. Intense reactions when cues occur that symbolize or resemble some aspect of the trauma; may have physical reaction, such as sweating, heart racing, stomach aches, headaches, etc.
- ◆ Loss of interest in activities. Restricted ability to interact with others. Children have a sense of "foreshortened future," cannot see themselves as grown-ups.
- ◆ Children with PTSD who have "escaped" their traumatic environments often have a profound sense of betrayal or desertion of others left behind.

Treatment is psychotherapeutic. Reports indicate that 50 percent of children with PTSD recover.

- ◆ *Autism and pervasive developmental disorder (PDD):*
  - ◆ Autism is a severe developmental disorder with marked impairment of
    1. Reciprocal social/interpersonal interaction.
    2. Communication skills, both spoken language and comprehension, inability to use language to communicate with others.
    3. Repetitive, sterotyped behaviors, including motor mannerisms ("finger games"), rigidity, nonfunctional rituals and routines, preoccupation with detail and/or parts of objects.
  - ◆ Symptoms appear before age three. 75 percent of autistic children have mild to moderate mental deficiency. Outcome (prognosis) is related to mental ability. Treatment is psychotherapeutic and educational.
- ◆ *Attachment disorders, reactive attachment disorder:*

A disorder of infancy or early childhood (see Table 1) characterized by:

- Impaired or lack of ability to bond or form personal attachments to others.
- Always related to grossly pathological caregiving.
- Treatment is psychotherapeutic, including family therapy or guidance.
- *Childhood psychoses and conduct disorders:*
- Childhood psychoses, including schizophrenia.
- Conduct disorder (childhood or adolescence): "repetitive or persistent pattern of behavior in which the basic rights of others or major age-appropriate societal norms or rules are violated.[7]

EARLY RECOGNITION

The cases presented in this chapter raise significant questions for parents who adopt children from institutions and wish to recognize any serious mental health problems before they finalize their decision to adopt. There may be little evidence of a mental health problem, even one of magnitude, before the child is adopted. This is particularly true if there is a serious, overlying medical problem, as there were in several of the cases described. When not well, the adopted child doesn't manifest any symptoms until he or she is healthier. As a result, the adopting family discovers the condition after the fact, and the insidious, more dangerous, underlying mental illness is unmasked only after physical health is improved. Often a family is months into an adoption before that occurs.

There are, however, some clues that may be of help to adopting families and agency personnel in identifying the child who may be at risk for mental health problems while in the institution.

Environmental Factors

1. Any signs of any form of abuse—physical, sexual, or emotional.
2. Signs of *active rejection* of the child by caregivers (pushing away, prolonged placement in quarantine or isolation, shunning) *in addition to* passive neglect of the child.
3. Physical or chemical restraints: The child is tied up or other-

wise physically bound to the bed. Or the child has been sedated or given "tranquilizers" to control behavior.

Child Factors

1. Abnormal eye contact (two types):
   Children with reactive attachment disorder often have what is called "hypervigilance of gaze." Maintaining a steady gaze, their eyes follow you (or any intruder in their environment) everywhere, never leaving their target.
   Children with autism and other severe emotional problems usually avoid eye contact, "avert" their gaze, and won't "look you straight in the eye"; in order to establish eye contact, these children often have to be moved physically into the observer's line of vision.

2. Self-injurious or self-abusive behaviors, such as biting, forceful, repetitive hitting, violent head banging that causes bumps on the head, picking at skin and causing open sores, eye gouging, or inserting foreign objects into body orifices.

3. Autistic features: Autistic children often play "finger games" that are distinctly different from repetitive finger flicking and wrist flapping that are self-stimulations rather than sterotypic of autism. "Delayed ecoholalia," repetitive chanting or mechanical recitals of words, often in a singsong fashion, not related to anything that is going on at that time but may relate to (or echo) a past event, sometimes months before. (There are many other features of autism, but these are two that may be easily detected by a casual observer.

4. Physical signs of past abuse: poorly healed fractures where lack of attention has caused abnormal bends or obvious deformity of arms or legs; cigarette burn scars; or telltale signs that a child has been restrained, such as rope burns or scars around wrists and ankles.

5. Profound isolation, often self-imposed, no evidence of friends or playmates or social interaction with other children in the institution.

Not all children who come from grossly pathological caregiving situations develop mental health problems. Experience has taught us that it is possible for those coming from even the worst circumstances to survive the experience seemingly unscathed. Some children miraculously survive the same early deprivation that has wounded their companions. Some who are injured can make astonishing progress in intervention programs while others don't respond. For example, what factors make a child such as Michael Vasile Goldberg (from chapter 1) able to recover and respond when a child like Di Di Eisinger, who came from the same Romanian orphanage system, seems unable to bounce back? What made Susan Goldberg say "as much as we've claimed him, he's claimed us," as testimony to Michael's ability to attach?

The research work of Stella Chess and Alexander Thomas[8] revealed that some children are helped to overcome adverse situations because of inborn strengths and personality factors, some of which are genetic in origin. Present in newborn babies and demonstrable by evaluations, this infant personality is called *temperament*. Further studies of these constitutional personality factors enabled professionals to not only categorize infants' behavior but also predict how they would react to their environments and interact with their mothers. Subsequent longitudinal studies (studies done over a long period of time) showed how temperament contributed to a hardiness in some babies when their environments were harsh while other infants were more sensitive and vulnerable.

Some children are able to bounce back when subjected to the same harsh, abusive environments that bring other children down. The ability to bounce back is called *resilience*. (In Romania, we called it the "R factor.") Temperament is only one of many important factors in resilience. It is a complex subject with many facets. It will continue to mystify and astonish both parents and research scientists for years to come.

Additional work of Chess[9] and others has established that the critical environmental factor in helping a child survive dire circumstances is an adult person—perhaps a teacher, caregiver, godparent, grandparent, or even an orphanage caretaker—who is *consistently available to support the child*. It is this consistency that establishes a *secure base* that enables the child not only to survive but to form healthy attachments with other human beings.

Michael Vasile had a loving physical therapist. Anamaria (chapter 4) was able to attach to Melanie, the orphanage psychologist. Paddy Doyle knew the loving touch of a caring nun. In the following story, a little Filipino girl named Wendi had Sister Marietta. . . .

The Dewey Family

Some special families take pride in the fact they have developed a multicultural family. Fred and Karleen Dewey of Lakewood, Colorado, are such a family. Over the years they have added four adopted children to their six birth children.

The Deweys' adopted children come from a variety of ethnic backgrounds. After surviving the 1975 plane crash that was part of the baby lift following the Vietnam War, five-month-old Shane, now twenty-one, was the first. Jon came next, from the Philippines. Following the two boys were Christine and Wendi. Christine was a domestic adoption and is part American Indian and part Hispanic; Wendi, along with Jon, is from the Philippines.

Karleen, who runs the Mothering Center in Denver (a center associated with Mercy Ministries that helps young mothers learn how to bond with their babies), said she and her husband have always loved children and felt strongly they could give a loving home to foreign children. "Our kids were always excited about the adoptions; we always discussed it as a family. We are interested in other cultures and countries. And we saw a need for good families. Ours is a family of faith and it is within our faith that we saw this to be something God would give us the strength to do."[10]

Fred Dewey, a professor at Metropolitan State College of Denver, said that when the couple first started adoptions of children from different cultures, they were not well informed about what might be involved. "With cross-cultural adoption of children with unknown backgrounds, we didn't know what could arise." Even a background with a B.A. in early childhood development did not prepare the couple for the attachment and bonding problems of children adopted cross-culturally.

"When you are adopting a foreign child cross-culturally and have no background on the child you need to be better informed and you must be prepared to use resources. You need to be open," says Karleen. "While a birth child would never come into the kitchen and say some other mother can cook better than you, an adopted child can come in and say, 'I'll bet an Asian mother can cook rice better than you.' "

It is during the preteen years, she says, that some of the differences between birth children and adopted children become apparent. Reactive attachment disorder (RAD) is often something parents of children adopted cross-culturally must face, she notes. Karleen says adoptive parents would be wise to read the book *Primal Wound* by Nancy Verrier.

"Adopted children may question that you love them and some of them just need to be reaffirmed all the time. I would die for any of them." There is a nuance to the parenting of an internationally adopted child that can be different, she notes.

Their daughter Wendi, now fourteen, was adopted in the Philippines while the Deweys lived there. Fred was on a Fulbright grant. Knowing they might adopt again, the couple had already completed a home study in the States.

The Deweys still had connections to adoption in the Philippines because of Jon's adoption. After four or five months in the country, they began to explore adoption, seeking a three-year-old girl to add to their growing family. At first they were told no girls were available, so the couple decided to stay calm and continue looking. Within three weeks a little girl had been found for them.

Karleen says she thinks the history they had in adoption and their family values—so close to those of the Philippines—helped them secure Wendi.

An orphanage in Manila showed the family picture to a child who had a choice of several families. "She chose us," Karleen says. "She was the pet of the orphanage and was very close to Sister Marietta, who had given her the mothering she needed at an early age. Sister Marietta had a great love for Wendi. Allowing her to pick out a family and then giving her up to us showed how much she wanted the best for Wendi."

After a series of meetings with the nun who headed the orphanage, and after two short meetings with Wendi, the Deweys drove to the orphanage to bring Wendi home. Before leaving, they spent some time with the little girl and played a bit. "Then it was time to go, even though Sister Marietta was nowhere to be found. We didn't know any better way than cold turkey, so that was the way we did it. One of the sisters handed Wendi to me and she began screaming hysterically. All the way to the car she was screaming about being taken. She was grabbing at the nun and trying to get away."

Fred Dewey climbed into the driver's side and the little girl grabbed him and hung on, still sobbing. He drove away like that, fearing she would jump out of the car. The couple said it was lucky a Filipino social worker was with them, or passersby might have thought they were kidnapping the child.

After arriving home, Wendi went through about six weeks in a state of depression. Karleen and Fred had to sing to her until she fell asleep at night. Unable to speak English, Wendi clung to the domestic help because they spoke her language.

Karleen says she knew enough about attachment to know that she and Wendi needed time alone together. "When the other kids went to school in the daytime, I did all kinds of things one-on-one with her. In the muggy, Philippine heat of the afternoon, we would go to my bedroom with the air conditioning and rest and read books. We did a lot of things in the next few weeks that prepared her to go home to the States with us. She began to understand that this was permanent."

Wendi hasn't shown any signs of attachment problems during the ensuing years and appears to be a happy, well-adjusted child who is naturally good at sports. Her brother Jon has been able to respond to treatment for his attachment problems. Now, as a self-reliant young adult, he has healed many of his wounds.[11]

The body of knowledge referred to as attachment theory has been derived from the research in child psychiatry initiated in the 1930s and 1940s. Before going to a foreign country armed with a "list of danger signals," adopting parents may find some additional knowledge about normal attachment and attachment problems useful.

Child psychiatrist Dr. John Bowlby (1907–1990) was the father of attachment theory. His prolific writings on the subject are recognized as the theoretical backbone of the field.[12] In his books and lectures on attachment, Bowlby describes the caregiver-child relationship that is essential for any child to develop and maintain normal attachments. Bowlby's contemporary, Mary Ainsworth, made major contributions to the field when she introduced the concept of the "secure base"—the mothering caregiver as a haven from which the child can safely explore his environment and subsequently learn and grow.

Once normal attachment was understood, the nature of abnormal patterns of attachment came to light. Applying Bowlby's original theory, Ainsworth developed an assessment tool to help determine the nature of the attachment of babies and toddlers to their mothers. Children were found to fall into two groups—those with secure (normal) attachments and those with insecure attachments. Children with insecure attachments were further described as either "ambivalent" or "anxious."[13]

Applications of the pioneering work of Bowlby and Ainsworth have given rise to a host of clinical approaches to the child who has attachment problems. Adopting parents who are interested in learning more about this critical topic will find Bowlby's book, *The Making and Breaking of Affectional Bonds*,[14] informative reading. Additional Bowlby writings can be found listed in the reference section of the Appendix.

THE HEALING PROCESS: A FAMILY MATTER

The challenges facing parents who have adopted children with very special needs do not end with completion of adoption procedures. Looming ahead, like a mountain to climb, is the tremendous task of helping the child heal the wounds of abandonment and neglect. Before any parent takes on this task, he or she must be certain to fortify the base she hopes to establish as a secure base for the child.

SAFETY FIRST

Although it may not be necessary, it is helpful to discuss and make plans of action if the safety of either the child or any family member becomes an issue. Like Di Di Eisinger, whose story opened this chapter, children who are severely affected by their backgrounds of abuse and neglect often cannot control their own behavior. Leaving the orphanage may be traumatic. Hotels and airplanes may be terrifying. Wounded children are inconsolable in their reactions because they do not yet have an attachment. They have lost their secure base, which was in and of itself pathological.

Guided transition programs are of tremendous value to parents in these situations. Unfortunately, such transition programs are rarely available in foreign adoption. Despite all the delays that are experienced in finalizing the in-country procedures, the child's final day in the orphanage often comes suddenly and neither parent nor child feels adequately prepared for such momentous changes in their lives. (See chapter 9 for more on transition.)

With special-needs children who are at risk for mental health problems, it is best to be prepared to deal with an agitated child on an airplane. Even without a mental health problem, something as simple as an earache can make for a miserable fourteen hours. Anticipatory guidance from a physician can be very helpful.

A baby flight experience is only the beginning. Once home, there are adjustment periods and long-term plans to be dealt with. Behaviors that once were protective or adaptive resurface, but are often unacceptable or maladaptive in a new environment. Behaviors that were never protective can become dangerous. If a child has self-injurious behaviors, for example, professional treatment is needed, not only to keep the child from seriously injuring himself but also to keep the condition from getting worse. If a disturbed child becomes aggressive or abuses other children, the family often needs to remove the child from the environment where he represents a danger to himself or other household members. This may be a skilled respite care facility or short-term in-patient psychiatric care. Early treatment for the aggressive child may enhance his chances for reversal of the behavior before it becomes ingrained or a serious, chronic problem.

PREVENTION

Living with a child with a mental health problem puts enormous stress on entire families. Other children may feel left out or embarrassed, as did Di Di's siblings. Martial strain is very common. It is important for adoptive families to continue family routines and activities and to avoid isolation to the point that, as Lori Eisinger said, they "feel like prisoners in their own home." Respite care should be sought on a regular basis and before you think you need it. Respite care is often provided through state social services agencies; another source is parent organizations where mothers form a buddy system and provide respite for each other on a rotating basis. Both family and adopted child are given a little vacation from the stress that is part of their everyday lives.

DEALING WITH DISAPPOINTMENT

Parenting a child with severe handicaps or chronic illnesses is not unlike going through a continuous grief and mourning process. All of the same features are there—denial, anger, sadness, acceptance—except that they don't resolve as they do with total loss of a family member. And they do not proceed in an orderly sequence of stages. It is important to be aware that these emotional stages are normal in families who have chronically ill or disabled children. Support groups and religious affiliations are often helpful to families as they go through this process.

FINDING AND GETTING HELP

Karleen Dewey said "you must be prepared to use resources," and she was correct. When parents begin to plan treatment and intervention they are in a constant state of decision making. Medical problems are typically much easier to accept and deal with by both parents and helping professionals. Professional help for physical (organic) problems is more standardized and unified in both diagnosis and case management. Parents are not as confused by conflicting opinions and recommendations.

In mental health problems, however, experts may not be in agreement about diagnosis and recommendations for therapy. Second opinions often lead to third and fourth opinions. Once decisions are made, parents of special needs children often need to become an advocate for their child in the system. Again, parent organizations are a good source of information about entitlements and resource identification. Magazines such as *Exceptional Parent* provide valuable, current information to parents of special-needs children and also provide opportunity for networking.

HEALING THE WOUNDED CHILD

In her eleven-volume audio series, Jungian psychoanalyst/author, Dr. Clarissa Pinkola Estés has created an original tape entitled "Warming the Stone Child, Myths and Stories about Abandonment and the Unmothered Child."[15] Providing hope and inspiration for any parent of postinstitutionalized children, Dr. Estés opens her stories by telling about the "curiously special gifts and powers" of unmothered children, the strengths and inner spirit they bring with them to the healing process.

Before any parent embarks upon the healing process with a child, it is essential to know and believe in the strengths children harbor deep inside. Effective therapy always takes those strengths, like grains of sand, and builds upon them, bit by bit. When abandonment and a lack (or loss) of maternal love is the root of the problem, the new mother becomes the healer. Therapists, teachers, and psychologists may be involved, but it is the parent who is the key. For children to begin to thrive instead of just surviving, they must establish and learn to trust the consistent, never wavering securing of a mother. Once they do that, and gain a little confidence, they can venture out into the world and learn and grow. For children who already have a secure base and healthy maternal attachment, this process of venturing is very safe. For children whose secure base and attachment are under construction, venturing becomes a dangerous adventure.

All of the children you have met (and will meet) in this book are survivors. All of the children who were once unmothered and abandoned but are now adopted are survivors. The fact of their survival is how we know they have strength. Armed by temperaments and resilience that give them what is best described as a fighting spirit, they have fought, really fought, and won a battle with death. But this is just the battle. When they come home to a family, they are at a point in their lives that survival is not enough. They must learn to thrive.

So far, they have failed to thrive—physically, psychologically, and emotionally. Even their medical records say so. *Failure to thrive.* Overcoming that failure requires a lot of courage and energy. The world of abandonment is very dark and sad and lonely. But it is a familiar world and the child who survives it has adapted to it. Coming out of that world can be frightening, particularly if every effort to come out in the past has been ignored or invalidated. Children need guides when they are wandering through those tunnels. The mother becomes that guide.

Strength, resilience, and a fighting spirit are only part of a special child's power. The other special gift that abandoned children have is their incredible sensitivity and intuition. They have sat very still for months or years, like little sentries guarding their castles and cribs. They have watched so intently that they scarcely blink their eyes. They have been good little soldiers, extremely vigilant. We call their appearance "frozen watchfulness" and their watching "hypervigilance." Whether their intuition is a product of all that vigilant surveillance or whether they were born with it, we don't know. But what we do know is that they are so intuitive that some think they are psychic. They hear a great deal more than is said to them and see much more than is shown them. They know everything that is going on and seem to know what will happen next.

Every step along the way toward healing is a small victory for wounded children and their parents. Special children must learn to do everything that seems to occur and flow automatically in other children. Special children must learn to trust, learn to love, learn to control themselves, consciously learn to do everything. Something as simple as sitting still for five minutes on a father's lap takes effort and concentration. This has a good side. Because achievement requires so much conscious effort, every success is a building block of self-esteem in the child because he is consciously aware of it. And beginning to feel good about themselves is an important first step in healing. No human being can form healthy attachments if he does not first feel good about himself.

These are abandoned children's gifts and powers—strength of spirit to fight to survive, a strong will to live, and an inner directedness that drives them forward, aided by intuition. Guiding these children and helping them learn to thrive is not easy. Unless we were wounded children ourselves, we may not have these unique gifts and powers. But children help us and send us cues and drop a lot of clues. To respond to these cues appropriately, however, we often need guidance ourselves.

In the "Warming the Stone Child" tape, Clarissa Estés puts a very bright candle in a very dark window. She tells us a truth that is very important about abandoned and unloved children. She tells us that in every one of them, there is always an internal light, a tiny, flickering flame, that will never go out. And she assures all of us who care deeply for these children that the internal light, like an ember within a charred piece of wood, can always be fanned to life, even by the smallest wind, and not only has the potential to ignite, but to really catch fire and burn brightly.

REFERENCES

1. Lori Eisinger, personal interview, Wyoming, June 1994.

2. Ibid.

3. Anonymous personal interview, California, 1994.

4. C. A. McKelvey and J. E. Stevens, *Adoption Crisis: The Truth About Adoption and Foster Care* (Golden, CO: Fulcrum Publishing, 1994).

5. Anonymous personal interview, Denver, CO, 1994.

6. *Diagnostic and Statistical Manual of Mental Disorders,* 4th ed. (Washington, DC: American Psychiatric Association, 1994).

7. Ibid.

8. A. Thomas and S. Chess, "Genesis and Evolution of Behavioral Disorders from Infancy to Early Adult Life," *American Journal of Psychiatry* 141 (1984), p. 1.

9. S. Chess, "The Plasticity of Human Development," *Journal of the American Academy of Child Adolescent Psychiatry* 17 (1978), p. 80.

10. Karleen and Fred Dewey, personal interview, Mercy Ministries, The Mothering Center, 1530 Maricn St., Denver, CO 80203, December 1995.

11. The authors gratefully acknowledge Fred and Karleen Dewey for consenting to be interviewed about their family, and Wendi for allowing us to tell her story.

12. J. Bowlby, *Attachment and Loss*, vols. 1 and 2 (New York: Basic Books, 1969 and 1973).

13. M. S. Ainsworth and S. M. Bell, "Attachment, Exploration and Separation," *Child Development* 41 (1970), pp. 49–67.

14. (London: Routledge, 1994).

15. Clarissa Pinkola Estés, *Warming the Stone Child: Myths and Stories About Abandonment and the Unmothered Child*, Tape A104 (Boulder, CO: Sounds True, 1990), audio series.

6

The Challenged Child

"God bless us, everyone!"

Tiny Tim, a challenged child
from Dickens's *A Christmas Carol*

"**W**hy go halfway around the world if you are going to adopt a child with special needs? There are plenty of *those* children in America."

The question is no easier to answer than why you fell in love or why you wanted to be a doctor. Answers don't come easily, and when they come, they are varied:

- "We have two gorgeous, normal children," said Eugene Goldberg, "but I thought 'We need to get this kid.'" When he and Susan decided to adopt Vasile, they did so because of his disability, not in spite of it. "You don't get a chance to do something like this very often in life," he said later. "I had to grab it."[1]

- "The first time I saw her face in *People* magazine," said Greti Dorr of Adriana (Ana), "I just knew she belonged to our family. Her handicaps just made her more precious."[2]

The question *Why go halfway round the world?* is being asked more and more frequently in America today. Today's answers, however, sound much the same as those of 1990 when hundreds of couples, like the Goldbergs and the Dorrs, responded, almost reflexively, to the graphic horror of Romania's disabled orphans seen on their TV sets. "We could do this," couples said throughout the land. "We could adopt that child." They simply dropped everything to board the international flight that would take them to the children.

The persistence of such a massive response to needy children, like the answer to the question why go halfway round the world for a child, is difficult to analyze objectively. The instinctive, humanitarian response in society's reaction when confronted with tragic disasters, particularly those involving children, has been described variously as a human *nature, instinct,* or a *calling.* Whatever its origin, the response is universal. In the current decade of depersonalization and objective-evaluation criteria for every human event, it tells us that humanism is still alive.

"It is a fantastic mess," said one relief worker from the French organization *Medicin du Monde* (Doctors of the World) in Romania. "Everyone has come to save the children."

Not all of the couples who came flooding into eastern Europe were childless. Not all came to adopt young infants who were not readily available through the domestic route. Instead, many who opened their arms and their homes had children of their own, but responded to the plight of older or more obviously disabled children who had no chance at life unless they got them out of there. Some who came had watched television or seen a picture in a newspaper or magazine and had seen the face of one particular child who seemed to belong to their family. A few had the specific desire to take a seriously disabled child into their homes.

The motivations of professionals drawn to the disaster were equally humanitarian. Jobs were dropped, secure positions abandoned, and switchboards jammed at nonprofit organizations that were recruiting volunteer professionals.

"For most of us, this was a knee-jerk response," said one American orthopedist in 1991 after viewing one of the television programs about Romanian orphans. "As soon as the show ended, I called my travel agent."

Professionals and adopting parents were not the only ones who offered assistance. College students with backpacks and Eurail passes showed up on the doorsteps of orphanages and offered their assistance. A California woman arrived in Bucharest with the cargo hold of her jet filled with disposable diapers. A planeload of women from Texas arrived in Romania to give affection to the babies. They named their organization "Operation Hug."

Almost without exception, a TV show or written article had triggered the decision to drop everything and go to eastern Europe. People from every walk of life wanted to help the children they had seen in *USA Today* or the *London Times* or in *People* magazine, or on one of the *20/20* shows. It was one of the largest, most passionate rescue operations the world has ever seen.

ADRIANA

I (Bascom) first met Adriana in the fall of 1990. In preparation for setting up the ROSES project sites, I was screening children in Bucharest's Orphanage #1. Bucharest had nine orphanages, but we went to #1 because it had a long history of affiliation with the medical university. Although several NGOs (nongovernmental organizations) were involved in setting up programs at #1, ROSES had its focus on children with special needs.

Most of these children were housed in the Emily Warner Pavilion, a wing of the orphanage named after a grateful European parent who had endowed the wing soon after she adopted her child. Warner, a philanthropist, had renovated the pavilion with the intent to provide a special place for children who were not considered adoptable. They were children like Adriana, who later became Ana Dorr.

I was finishing rounds with the Romanian pediatrician in charge of the pavilion when I spotted Adriana. The child was supposed to be sleeping. One of the four-hour nap times that were customary in the Leaganes was just beginning. As we tiptoed through the salon, this curly head popped up from beneath the covers of one of the cribs. Beneath the curls were these beautiful bright eyes and a smile as wide as a canyon. When she realized she had captured my interest, she giggled.

"This is one of our special cases," the pediatrician began to explain in whispers. She pulled the covers back to point out Adriana's special properties: one missing hand, malformed, scissorlike pincers on the other arm for fingers, and two club feet. She giggled again when I touched her feet. I remember thinking *she is ticklish!* She was adorable. Special case? Indeed. She was very special. At that time in Romania, I hadn't heard many children giggle.

Adriana had more than her share of special needs, not the least of which was a need for a family. A family that not only would see the shining eyes and hear the giggles and respond to them but one who lived in a community that could provide the special care she needed. Ana would never have her needs met totally, unless she could find:

- ◆ A family who lived in a country that would consider her "challenged" instead of *deficient.*
- ◆ A family who belonged to a society that would never label her *unsalvageable* or *irrecuperable* and send her away at age three to live out her life in a chamber of horrors known as a home for the irrecuperables.

Ranking sixth among all birth defects, Adriana's problem was one of the most common in the world. It was particularly common in Romania. The cause of "limb deficiency" was "amniotic interruption," or rupturing or tearing of the amniotic sac (commonly referred to as the "bag of waters") early in pregnancy. It was common because many Romanian women had attempted illegal, backstreet abortions during Ceausescu's time. When the abortion attempt failed, but resulted in the rupture of the sac, the internal injury caused abnormal development of the fetus's arms and/or legs. The resulting birth defect is similar to that seen in Thalidomide babies.

Most children with this birth defect have no other significant problems; given prostheses and proper care, they can lead normal, productive lives. But in Romania in 1990, there was no proper care available for children like Adriana. Prosthetic devices were limited in supply, crudely made, and not available to children. The pediatric orthopedic care she would need for correction of her foot deformity was available only in the West. There was no appropriate physical therapy, no possibility of rehabilitation. None of her special needs could be met.

Disabled children, or children with birth defects (congenital malformations), were sent to institutions to live and die, not for "recuperation" (rehabilitation). If children like Adriana survived until age three, and most of them didn't, they were labeled irrecuperable and sent to Camin Spitals. Literally translated, Camin Spital means "hospital home." Originally designed to be nursing homes for the disabled, they had deteriorated and been diverted from their original purpose. Under Ceausescu, when health care was given the lowest priority because it was considered the most nonproductive industry, the Camin Spitals received almost no support from the government. As a result, admission there was tantamount to a death sentence.

Adriana was two and a half. Soon after her third birthday, she could be labeled irrecuperable and sent to a Camin Spital. By the time Romania could rebuild its health care system and provide rehabilitation for challenged children, it would be too late for Adriana and thousands of others like her.

When I saw the impact that 20/20's "The Shame of a Nation" had made on the life of Vasile Goldberg, I understood why it was so important to identify children like Adriana to the media. I knew what would happen if the media told her story. I knew how strong their voice was in comparison to mine alone. When a child like Adriana had her story told to tens of millions of viewers and readers, one of those readers would see that face and come to Romania to adopt her.

Opportunity presented itself when *People* magazine contacted me to do a story. I not only encouraged *People*'s compassionate writer, Cathy Nolan, to feature Adriana in the story, but when photographer Taro Yamasaki told me he was looking for a cover girl, I took him straight to her crib.

Adriana was the lead story in the article, but she didn't make the cover—Cher did. And that was good because, as the magazine editors rightly said, "Cher will sell more magazines" and increase the numbers of readers who would also read about Adriana.

The Dorrs of Cincinnati first saw a picture of Adriana in an article in that January 1991 *People* magazine. They knew instantly she was the one for them. Says her mother, Greti, "We didn't have to think about it. When I first saw the *People* magazine, Ana's picture just leaped off the page. Her picture and expression portrayed a child who, despite her living conditions, had a spirit about her. I just knew she was a child for our family."[3]

Despite husband Rick's gentle warning—"Just what makes you think we'll be the ones to get her?"—Greti headed for Romania in May 1991. She went to adopt the child with "a spirit about her" who seemed to belong to her family. The fact that Adriana was born without a hand and with club feet "only made her more precious."

At first, she was told that Adriana was "spoken for." Refusing to take that kind of "no" for an answer, Greti pulled out a copy of *People*. A conference of officials from the adoption committee immediately went into session behind closed doors. When the officials returned to the room where Greti waited, they suggested that perhaps they were mistaken, perhaps Adriana had not been spoken for. There were many children that would answer Greti's description of Adriana, they explained, but when they saw her picture in the magazine article, the mistake had been corrected. Greti could adopt Adriana.

Soon, Greti Dorr was on her way to find Adriana's birth mother and obtain the signed permission to adopt the child. The visit was rewarding in many ways. Greti learned that Adriana's birth defects were not due to a failed or attempted abortion, as was true of most cases of limb deficiency. The mother had been a victim of spouse abuse, and was brutally kicked and beaten during pregnancy. This had resulted in the same kind of problem that occurs when the amniotic sac is ruptured in a crude abortion attempt. Although she loved her little girl, she had to give her up because of the problems at home.

"Keeping her home with me," said the birth mother, "was not an option. But it has always been my dream that someone would take care of her for me. I have prayed every night that someone would come from another country and take her away."

"The first time I saw Ana in person," said Greti in an interview, "was the day I went to take her away from the orphanage. An orphanage worker told me to wait in a room while she went for Ana. When she put her in my arms, all I could do was hold her and cry."[4]

After six weeks of red tape, Greti was able to bring Ana out of Romania and take the journey home where her new father, Rick, and siblings Elizabeth and Ben waited to greet her. Greti Dorr had accomplished her mission to adopt Adriana; a birth mother's prayer had been answered. A curly-haired moppet had lost her label of *irrecuperable* and was about to join the legion of American youngsters known as "challenged children."

On her first night home, Rick Dorr was nearly overwhelmed by the challenge before him as he surveyed his tiny new daughter and "could only see those turned-in feet and missing hands." Adriana, by then named Ana, soon overcame any parental anxiety by demonstrating that she did indeed "have a spirit about her." Within weeks, she demonstrated a resilience so remarkable that even the medical experts were astonished. Winning the hearts of everyone around her, and adapting instantly to her new home, Ana was soon as firmly attached to her new family as they were to her.

"I used to live in Romania," she said, sitting on my lap and talking to her old friend, Taro Yamasaki, who was photographing her for *People*. "Then I came to live with these other guys, my family."

The Dorrs did learn, however, that families adopting challenged children have a few challenges of their own. Gaining access to the highly specialized health care system that complex problems like Ana Dorr's required was not easy. Finding a way to pay for the care was even more difficult. Unable to afford the enormous medical costs required to rehabilitate Ana, the Dorrs turned to Shriners Hospital. They were grateful and delighted when Shriners committed to providing a prosthesis for Ana's missing hand and the braces needed for her legs until age eighteen.

Ana has had surgery to correct her feet. Following additional surgery, she has one usable hand and a prosthesis on the other that allows her to do just about anything another child of her age can do. "I was born without a hand," said five-year-old Ana when *People* visited her in Indiana.[5] "Now I have a new one. I feel better."

The Dorrs are an exception to the usual Romania postadoption story. Unlike so many of her contemporaries, Ana has shown no sign of severe developmental or attachment disorders. The glow in her face that took Greti to Romania on a mission really did reflect "the spirit within her." Her handicaps, once labeled *deficiencies*, were indeed only challenges. She had a resilience within her that allowed her to meet those challenges. And she had that mysterious, sixth-sense gift that is intuitive in children who have histories of deprivation. In 1994, when we sat on a couch with Ana and we looked at old copies of *People* together, she said, "I don't know if I remember or not, but I know."

Ana's challenges, and those her family faces every week, have only begun. Today, the Dorrs are faced with the tough decisions about her education. Is she ready for full-time public school? Or should she be held back for one more year so that she can mature and become more secure? How sensitive and vulnerable will she be about her physical problems when she gets into the sometimes cruel environment of playgrounds and classrooms? Will she, due to her early deprivation, have learning problems that are not evident now, but will surface in an educational setting?

Ana and her family approach all these challenges with an optimism born out of an experience that has been extraordinary. Both Ana and her family are profoundly grateful for the blessings they have been given and the joy they have brought each other. "It's not just what we've done for her," said Greti Dorr to CBS when they shot "Where Are They Now?" and filmed Ana riding her horse and using her new prosthesis to make a goal in field hockey. "It's what she's done for our family."

THE DOUBLE CHALLENGE

Whether by circumstances of birth or adoption, the particular rewards of parenting *special-needs* or challenged children have been known for decades. Challenged children, adopted from foreign countries, come with a double set of challenges, however. They are challenged not only by a birth defect like Vasile's club foot or Ana Dorr's limb deficiencies. They are also challenged by the environments of deprivation they come from—the streets and institutions of developing countries.

The two sets of disabilities compound one another. One always makes the other worse. The challenges, therefore, are greater, both for child and adopting family.

UNDERSTANDING THE ENVIRONMENTS ADOPTED CHILDREN COME FROM

Visitors to foreign countries, including many health professionals, are often shocked and deeply disturbed by the specter of grotesque deformities and severe, complex handicaps seen in children in institutions. "It's worse than walking into Dachau," one adopting mother commented after visiting a Camin Spital in Romania. Some visitors witness the death of a child for the first time in their lives.

Adoptive parents are often thrown into these repugnant situations without any preparation when they arrive to adopt their child. Not only do they see, firsthand, children who have received no treatment, they see their chosen child housed in an environment that precludes any human dignity and seems to be designed specifically to destroy the child's chances of survival.

While nothing can adequately prepare you for a first visit to a Camin Spital, or any institution like it, a basic knowledge of the system and some of the cultural attitudes that reinforce it should help you understand how it got that way. Knowledge and understanding may help you roll up your sleeves and go to work on the successful completion of your adoption without being overwhelmed. We offer the following discussion of the health care system in redeveloping countries in the hope that it lends some insight to future adopting parents. It is helpful to know, in addition, about the attitudes and common beliefs that foreign professionals often have with regard to disabled children.

We would like to see you better protected and better armed to cope with the circumstances you are likely to encounter when you adopt a child like Ana Dorr or Michael Vasile Gold-berg.

~

When my husband and I (Bascom) went to Romania, we were stunned by the extent to which health care had been damaged throughout the country. The deeper we dug, the more rotten the infrastructure seemed to be. The entire health care system and the education programs (that should have been the hope for the future) had been systematically dismantled by the Communist dictatorships that had ruled the country since the Second World War. There were no adequate support facilities anywhere. Medical libraries, laboratories, operating rooms, even medical schools, had either been totally destroyed or were frozen in time somewhere around the mid-fifties. Our medical colleagues were so isolated and deprived of information that they broke down in tears when we offered them something as simple as a current textbook of pediatrics. They broke our hearts and became our best friends when we joined forces to start the rebuilding process.

This was the tragedy behind the tragedy of Romania's children. Understanding it and being able to help do something about it enabled us to overcome the outrage we often felt. Through our work in medical schools and orphanages, our travels to other countries that were having similar problems, and through our research on the topic, this is some of the knowledge we gained.

HEALTH SCIENCES AND MEDICAL EDUCATION

In most developing countries the educational background of professionals is far below Western standards. Although most doctors are well versed in theory, there is no access to current information for either professors or students. There is no continuing medical education to keep a practitioner current in his skills. To subscribe to a single, prestigious medical journal, a third-world practitioner would have to spend more than his total annual salary.

In most developing countries, the health sciences are dominated by medical doctors. In many countries there is an over-abundance of doctors, with ratios in some cities as low as one practitioner for every four hundred people. In contrast, there are few, if any, allied health practitioners, such as nurses, physical therapists, and clinical psychologists. Medical schools have not yet become health science centers, where nurses, doctors, and physical therapists all go to school together. Health care in general is usually considered a nonproductive industry; there is no government support for opening of new schools or training programs for either doctors or allied health practitioners.

The whole society feels the impact of deficient professional caregiving, but children, the elderly, and the disabled are the most affected. Disabled children receive no physical therapy, no speech therapy, and no special education. There are no child psychologists to evaluate or treat them. There is no such thing as occupational therapy, as the West knows it, in many developing countries. The highly technical infrastructure that is required to practice modern medicine as we know it in the West is absent. Basic hospital services like pharmacies, labs, and radiology (X ray) are undersupplied, underequipped, and understaffed. If they exist at all, they are only in major city hospitals and are therefore only able to provide services to a very small percentage of the population.

In eastern European orphanages, for example, technicians did simple blood counts to diagnose anemia using ancient microscopes. Labs could not run the hemoglobin test needed to determine the type of anemia and follow a child's response to treatment. When foreign aid brought in screening kits for diseases like hepatitis B, the labs were unable to determine if liver disease was active because the chemicals and equipment to make that determination were not yet available.

Even when laboratories were better equipped after foreign aid arrived, there were no lasting supplies of chemicals to run the tests they were equipped to run. When visiting surgical teams arrived, surgical equipment was so outmoded that complex procedures could not be done. There was no modern anesthetic equipment, and even when that was made available, a shortage of trained anesthetists prevented its usage. No modern antibiotics were available to treat the simplest wound infection.

In many hospitals, as late as 1993, scrub sinks with antiseptic soap and running water, where a surgeon could wash his hands, were absent from many surgical suites. Doctors and nurses were forced to dip their hands into basins of cold water mixed with iodine solution. In one central Asian country, there was no oxygen in the hospitals as late as 1995.

FOREIGN AID AND TECHNICAL ASSISTANCE

When foreign aid is offered to a needy country, technology always tops the want lists of proposed beneficiaries. These want lists are quickly translated into needs by the foreign-aid establishment. Unless the donated equipment is part of long-term development instead of emergency relief, however, its usefulness is often short-lived. Most developing countries lack the infrastructure to maintain highly technical equipment. Spare parts are not available for repairs. Calibration and maintenance are impossible in many circumstances; often there are no trained bioengineers, native to the country, to look after the equipment and keep it in working condition after the initial relief effort has subsided.

Problems with distribution of donated equipment further complicate the picture. When equipment pours into a disaster area, it often arrives in pieces. Vital pieces, like connecting tubes or electrical connections, are often missing. These mysterious disappearances are very common, suggestive of black-market pilfering or thefts that probably take place before equipment ever arrives at its destination. When the donated equipment does arrive intact, it rarely comes with a training package for the health professionals who will be using it. With the equipment must come the knowledge of how to use and apply it, and there is an agonizing frustration in seeing one or the other arrive en masse, rendered almost useless without its counterpart.

THE INFLUENCE OF CULTURAL BELIEFS AND ATTITUDES

In redeveloping countries, health practitioners in medicine are centrally directed by government policy makers. Both practice and policy are heavily influenced by ingrained beliefs and cultural attitudes that may be centuries old. In the prior eastern bloc countries, for example, nationalism and pervasive attitudes about ethnic purity resurfaced when those nations emerged from the Iron Curtain. The mix of persistent nationalistic policy and deeply ingrained cultural beliefs results in a collective mind-set, best described as the "mentality" of the people.

(There is no adequate substitute for the word *mentality*. Every adopting couple who went to Russia or any other eastern European country during the early nineties was exposed to it, sometimes angered or frustrated by it, and knows exactly what it means.)

Long before deterioration began in their economies, the practice of putting away the disabled was the societal norm in most developing countries. Although Western countries have also had deplorable histories in this regard, most of them have undergone significant changes in both practice and attitudes during the past three decades. The discoveries made by Western professionals of the deleterious effects of institutionalization on developing children (chapter 4) prompted many of those changes.

Third-world and developing countries have not undergone similar social change. Old attitudes persist in many of them. In China, for example, unwanted infant girls are placed in institutions where many of those who are not adopted die from intentional starvation and neglect; this reflects not only the centuries-old attitude about the value of women in society, but also the habitual practice of institutionalization of unwanted members of society.

The stresses of poverty, war, and disaster have increased rather than diminished the institutional populations in most countries of the developing (or redeveloping) world. Whether they descended into the so called third-world through failed economies, or failed to become industrialized in the first place, or fell under tyrannical leadership, the pattern is the same in underdeveloped countries. Attitudes and ingrained cultural practices work together and continue to force children into institutional care. Foreign aid and reform movements will probably do little to change this pattern unless the mentality changes.

In many developing countries, disabled people are not seen on the streets of their communities. Nor are they seen in the workplace. When disabled children do appear in public, they are often being exploited. In India, for example (although India is not alone in this practice), physically deformed children are known to be the most successful beggars. The younger the person and the more grotesque the deformity, the more potential income for the impoverished family. There have been documented cases of intentional maiming to enhance a child's income potential.

Offers to adopt such a child may be greeted with blunt refusal, not gratitude, because such offers threaten the family's meager income. The child is not an orphan. In most instances, there is no child welfare system that will remove the child from the family. Although international human rights organizations are fighting these deplorable practices, the problems are far from solved. Institutionalization, however, is no solution to the larger issue. Adopting parents should be aware that they are likely to encounter such children on the streets of many cities. Most of them are not adoptable.

This cultural practice to institutionalize disabled children, therefore, is more than social protection or economic necessity. In most countries, it is rooted in a cultural mentality that promotes removal of the disabled along with other "undesirables" from society with no regard for their human rights. Before the human rights issues inherent in these tragic situations can be addressed, however, the mentality must change.

ATTITUDES ABOUT ADOPTION

What happens to children unfortunate enough to have been born in a country where they hide and incarcerate the disabled in institutions? Once institutionalized, a disabled child can disappear from public view forever. Institutions housing the disabled are often hidden, far away from the public view. No one knows about them until a Romania or a China happens. No one remembers that institutionalization for the disabled has long been the mentality of the culture. When a group of foreigners invade such a scene and wish to reach out to disabled children, they are greeted with astonishment.

When countries are exposed to global scrutiny (of their child care practices in institutions), as was eastern Europe, for example, their citizens are often perplexed by the outrage expressed by outsiders when they come in to assist or adopt abandoned children. Most in-country professionals see their plight as predominantly socioeconomic and feel no shame regarding their handling of disadvantaged or disabled people. They seek to reestablish pride in a system that was once a source of esteem in their communities. They wish to restore their institutions, and to pay for the needed restoration with foreign-aid dollars. They often dream of five-star institutions.

The major shifts in attitude that occurred in America during the last three decades and resulted in deinstitutionalization and integration of the disabled population into society will not occur overnight in developing countries, regardless of how much foreign aid or technical assistance comes in. The incentives to fix up the system and keep it going are too powerful. The mentality is too ingrained and pervasive.

Indigenous professionals usually view the carnage of their institutions as tragedies of fate and consider it history. Still, they often continue to pursue their careers in the same institutions, applying many of the old standards of care. Medical knowledge and case management skill levels advance much more quickly than changes in attitudes regarding the disabled. Terms like unadoptable and irrecuperable tend to remain in their vocabulary.

Given those circumstances, it is not surprising that when families arrive offering homes for disabled children, they are often greeted with utter disbelief that anyone would want to adopt a child with a disability. Driving the habitual practice of putting away the disabled is the pervasive attitude that they are "damaged goods" (a term I heard frequently in reference to special needs adoptions in Romania between 1990 and 1993).

Experience in special-needs adoption has not differed markedly in countries outside of eastern Europe. Disabled children are often institutionalized in Asia, the Philippines, and South America. Noninstitutionalized children may find no services in their communities, and will likely make their way into institutions at older ages when their care becomes too much of a burden at home. When orphaned (or relinquished), these children are not likely to be taken in by extended families. They are even less likely to be adopted by in-country nationals.

PEDIATRIC REHABILITATION

Professional resources in pediatric rehabilitation are woefully deficient at the community level in virtually all developing countries. Outside of the industrialized democracies, there is a global shortage of physical therapists. Even in countries where physical therapists (PTs) exist, those who are trained with speciality skills in pediatric or neurodevelopmental therapy are scarce to nonexistent. The shortage of trained therapists is much more pervasive than that of orthopedic surgeons, yet orthopedists are often dependent upon good physical therapy for their patients to benefit from the surgery they have done. A good PT program can, in many instances, prevent the necessity of surgery in the first place.

The knife is no substitute for a skilled pair of therapeutic hands anyplace on the globe. In developing countries, however, it is not unusual to see a child with a physical deformity who has had a series of operations, but never a day of therapy. That same child would most probably have never required any surgery at all had the child received physical therapy. The operations, therefore, are rarely successful in achieving any functional improvement. Improvement, if it occurs, is often temporary. The child is often left with a permanent deformity that is more disabling than the original, albeit untreated, condition.

These tragic situations often contribute to already bad public relations. The poor surgical results, if done by surgeons from the child's country of origin, are often misinterpreted as "botched" or "bungled" by the media and by private volunteer organizations who use the material in fund-raising promotions. These programs are tremendously valuable in raising public consciousness. But the damaged pride and offended sensibility that occur in the foreign country are a poor basis for international cooperation.

Thousands of dollars are spent to fly in visiting orthopedists from the outside. In medical foreign assistance programs, very little is spent to fly in pediatric therapists. Therapists in the foreign country, therefore, are not given much opportunity to learn from their colleagues in the West. The resulting lack of high-standard, current therapeutic services in institutions and communities has a serious impact on challenged children of developing nations. It places them in double jeopardy:

- ◆ Without rehabilitation they fail to improve and fall farther behind their peers in all areas of development. As a result they develop complications and fixed deformities that are often more severe and compromising than their original disability.
- ◆ When surgical assistance is brought in from the outside, surgery is often done as an isolated event rather than as part of an overall treatment plan. Children are often brought to a capital city where they have their operations, then return to institutions where there is no follow-up rehabilitation. Eventually, the benefits of the surgery are lost to the child.

RISK FACTORS

Children who are merely "at risk," such as premature babies who had birth injury, move directly from insult (potentially damaging events) to serious disability. They have no opportunity to be "challenged," unless they are removed from their neglectful circumstances.

Medical neglect makes everything worse in the child who has a known disability. Conversely, the underlying disability makes the child more vulnerable to neglect of any kind. Furthermore, neglect multiples the risk factors for other diseases and maltreatment, and it does so exponentially. An immobile child, for example, is much more prone to respiratory infections and any communicable disease; a developmentally disabled child is at higher risk of being severely neglected or even abused than his nondisabled counterpart. For many of these at-risk children, foreign adoption represents the best and sometimes the only opportunity.

A special group of children deserves some mention in this context. Many of today's street children are older children and youth who have run away from some form of institutional care.

A significant number of them have some form of disability. Efforts to identify and provide permanent shelters have met with mixed success, although many good programs have begun to take effect. In developing countries, glue sniffing and child exploitation are major problems in this growing population. Although it is believed that a large percentage of these children are abandoned, very few have made their way into the intercountry adoption process.

ADOPTION'S ROLE IN CHANGING ATTITUDES

Despite the many negative attitudes about special-needs adoption that prevail in redeveloping countries, the situation is changing. Adoptive parents have contributed significantly to the changes that were seen in eastern Europe between 1991 and 1993, for example. Walls of directors' offices were often adorned with the visible proof of an adopted child's rehabilitation potential. Sometimes the pictures are displayed beneath the glass tops of conference tables.

In a Transylvanian orphanage, for example, a small black-and-white photo of a pale, dystrophic child lying disconsolately in his crib is displayed next to the color enlargement of this husky toddler now pedaling a tricycle across a Minnesota lawn. In one director's office in Moldova (Romania's neediest district), a large press photo of a child named Hope portrays a mischievous toddler in a swimming pool, a tiny pair of stylish sunglasses perched on her little nose. It lies beneath the glass of the table for all visitors to see and make comment. Adjacent is a small color photo of Petronella before she left the orphanage (before her name was Hope) with her face aglow and standing in a walker with tiny stubs of arms reaching out to the camera.

The truth portrayed by the pictures was not so important as the impact that illustrated follow-up material had upon Romanian professionals. It has helped restore their pride. With the knowledge that they had contributed as much as they could, given the circumstance, and not been personally at "fault" in the child's disability, many of them were relieved of the terrible guilt they had harbored. They were doubly exonerated when they realized that the services required were so highly technical and specialized. It wasn't a case of incompetence but instead a lack of resources and equipment to do the job.

Furthermore, the correspondence and pictures helped change a negative attitude about disabled children. The term "challenged," previously meaningless, began to make sense in eastern Europe. Children who were previously perceived as unsalvageable or irrecuperable were suddenly candidates for treatment programs. If rehabilitation wasn't available to them, they began to receive priority for intercountry adoption.

Expectations began to change regarding the potential for intercountry adoption of children with special needs. Professionals at the local levels began to cooperate with adopting parents. Medical knowledge, however, had advanced much more quickly than changes in attitude regarding the disabled. It is still difficult for most developing country doctors to understand and accept that anyone would go halfway round the world to adopt a "damaged" child.

WHAT ARE THE CHALLENGES?

Although many conditions will challenge a child, there are a number of medical conditions for which there is no adequate treatment available in foreign countries. These conditions are usually treatable, and appropriate treatment often results in the health condition remaining a challenge to the child rather than becoming a disability. Even in older children who have developed secondary problems, much of their lost function can be restored.

Children who suffer these conditions are often institutionalized. Once in institutions, they are further removed from any opportunity for medical care. If abandoned or relinquished willingly by their parents, all of these children are adoptable.

When adopting a challenged child from a developing country's institutions, parents will be better prepared to meet their "special needs" if they have some knowledge about the most common problems. The following health problems are examples of potentially handicapping conditions often seen in foreign institutional populations. In each of these conditions, foreign adoption can prevent real handicap and ensure the permanent classification of "challenge" rather than disability.

CEREBRAL PALSY (CP)

Cerebral palsy is a general term referring to motor (locomotion and movement) control abnormalities seen in individuals with central nervous system injury. CP is categorized into subclassifications depending on the type of abnormal movement. The two most common forms are spastic (muscles are rigid or tight, inhibiting normal movement) and athetoid (control of movement is disordered, resulting in extraneous movements and inability to perform simple motor tasks. The main character in the film *My Left Foot* was athetoid). Either form of CP can be mild or severe. Although mental deficiency may be an associated feature, many cerebral palsied children have normal intelligence.

In America, most CP children have had physical therapy or a specialized form of PT called neurodevelopmental therapy (NDT) since infancy. If mildly affected, they have no or minimally discernible disability by the time they reach the classroom. In a needy country, that same child is likely to be cribbound and totally unable to function independently by the time he or she is of school age. This is almost entirely due to secondary deformity that has become fixed and sometimes untreatable and to the low priority given any handicapped child for educational opportunity in many foreign countries.

Children with cerebral palsy are much more vulnerable to neglect than their nondisabled counterparts. Many of them do not survive childhood in institutions. Very many are never diagnosed correctly. Some may be missed—athetoids more often than spastics, because the early signs may be subtle. Early diagnosis is difficult in any country, except in the severely involved infant. When misdiagnosed, the most common misapplied label is "psychomotor retardation."

Parents looking for special-needs children to adopt should know this: Of all the joys and rewards of providing a home for a special-needs child, few have the potential that adopting a cerebral-palsied child has. If adopted at an early age, the capacity of the child to reach his potential is excellent. Furthermore, the young age is important because:

- Crippling "fixed deformities" can be prevented by provision of good physical therapy and orthopedic care available in the West. These secondary disabilities, such as contractures (solidification of muscles), joint dislocations, and skeletal changes—often more disabling than the CP itself—are either totally prevented or minimized, allowing mobility and maximal functioning.

- Cognitive function is protected by provision of early, consistent educational programs and the "early intervention" and special education available (and required by law) to all children in the West. Many cerebral-palsied children have normal intelligence and are intellectually compromised only by lack of educational opportunity.

- Associated disabilities, even very severe ones, are often treatable through the sophisticated technologies available only in the West. Inability to speak fluently, for example, can be ameliorated by use of computer-assisted communication. Battery-operated, motorized wheelchairs give mobility to children unable to control wheelchairs manually. Highly technical surgical procedures can be done, ensuring optimal results at lower risk.

CP is more common in underdeveloped countries because of the lower standard of prenatal and neonatal care. Children with cerebral palsy who are institutionalized in environments of medical neglect and deprivation *are truly saved by adoption*.

HEARING IMPAIRMENT OR DEAFNESS

In most foreign countries that have adoptable children, hearing impairment and deafness go undetected until school age. This often results in permanent speech, communication, and educational problems. The technical equipment necessary to detect hearing problems in very young children is not available in most underdeveloped foreign countries. Neither are trained speech and language therapists and special education. In institutions, untreated, recurrent, or chronic ear infections are a major cause of hearing impairment. When hearing-impaired children are adopted from institutions, the hearing abnormalities are often missed diagnoses. If hearing deficits are detected, most foreign children in these circumstances have received no intervention (hearing aids, etc.); most of these children have very little, if any, speech. Secondary emotional problems are common.

Gianina is an example. This adopted child was hearing impaired. Medical neglect of her recurring middle ear infections eventually converted her impairment to total deafness. Adopted at eighteen months of age, the child's lack of responsiveness was interpreted as the result of general deprivation.

In her country of origin, there were neither diagnostic nor treatment facilities for hearing-impaired children until the age of seven. By age seven most deaf children, if they have not received augmentation (hearing aids) and speech/language therapy, have already passed the critical periods for developing oral communication skills (speech). Either they derive no benefit from hearing aids, or that benefit is markedly lessened.

In the overcrowded, understaffed orphanage from which Gianina came, unresponsive babies received even less attention than their noisier, more demanding counterparts. As she plummeted into a permanent world of silence, tiny Gianina's life became increasingly devoid of touch, movement, or nurturing. She withdrew emotionally more rapidly than hearing babies did in the same facility. She failed to progress and decelerated in her development. By the time she was adopted, self-stimulation and withdrawal into her own inner world had become her only response.

Because they were well prepared to deal with the consequences of neglect, Gianina's adoptive parents were able to help her through many of her developmental problems. The totality of her deafness, however, came as a total shock and was much more difficult to accept for that reason.

CHILDREN AT RISK FOR VISUAL IMPAIRMENT

Crossed eyes: Thousands of institutionalized children have *crossed eyes* (strabismus). Many do not receive treatment with corrective lenses or surgery. The most affected eye (one is nearly always more affected) is usually subconsciously suppressed by the child who cannot tolerate seeing double. The unused eye becomes deficient in functioning, just as leg muscles will weaken and shrink when kept too long in a cast. This preventable form of visual impairment is very common in institutional settings. If untreated, the condition can lead to total blindness in the affected eye(s) and is called amblyopia. Amblyopia is preventable by giving proper medical care.

Cataracts are any opacity or cloudiness of the lens of the eye. Often associated with other conditions (such as congenital malformations, certain metabolic diseases, etc.) cataract is another condition that, if treated soon enough, will not result in blindness. In babies and young children, cataracts are often tiny specks at the beginning. The young child can see around them. But the cataracts usually grow, and as the cloudy film grows and gets denser, it blots out more and more of the young child's vision. Finally, when light and objects are blocked entirely, the eye gives up. If the cataract is removed too late, vision does not return. The seeing part of the eye is permanently damaged.

Hundreds of children in institutions have cataracts that are not being treated. These children are gradually losing vision, and will be blind if someone doesn't provide them the medical care they need. Many of these children have otherwise normal potential.

A visually impaired child in a bad institution has a decreased chance of survival. He or she has lost one of his best defenses against the cruelty of institutions and often becomes bedridden because of inability to move around and learn to care for himself. Institutionalized children who have survived often have teamed up with a friend or buddy who has vision. The relationship with a sighted companion often restores the blind child to normal daily function; these friendships can become very close and difficult separations can occur if one of the partners leaves the institution.

PHYSICALLY INJURED CHILDREN

Amputation is one of the most common injuries in orphaned children of war, due to traumatic amputation from battlefield

injury itself or, more commonly, explosion injuries from playing in mindfields afterward.

Congenital amputation is a term that is applied to infants born
with amputation due to physical injury or structural abnormalities within the uterus that constrict or cut off circulation to developing limbs. Congenital amputation is seen more often in
countries where abortion is illegal; in such cases, loss of limb
was caused by either direct injury of crude instruments or con-
striction by scar tissue inside the womb.

Whether amputation is caused by birth deformation or is
traumatically acquired later in childhood, it represents a significant threat to the future development of any institutionalized child. In institutions, a child with no hands cannot hold a
bottle or retrieve a propped one that has become dislodged. He
cannot use a spoon, play with a toy, explore his environment
tactually. If feet or legs are affected, he is less likely to become
mobile; mobility has been found to be a significant factor in
survival of disabled individuals in institutions. In a war-torn
country, an amputated child who has also lost his family has no
place to go after he leaves the hospital. Many stay in hospitals,
another form of institution, for long-term care. Some go to the
streets. It is difficult to compete on the streets when a limb is
missing. Exploitation is common.

Child amputees in underdeveloped nations don't have access
to the Western world of therapy, prosthetics, orthotics, and
classrooms that give full access to learning opportunity. Unless
a child is provided that opportunity, the child will not only
remain physically disabled, "challenged," but will also acquire
a host of other developmental and psychological disabilities.

In the redeveloping countries that have limited fuel supplies
(eastern Europe particularly), *burns* were the most common ac-
cidental injuries. All over the eastern bloc, cottages caught fire
due to frantic attempts to heat them with open fires. Dozens of
children were caught in burning cottages. Cases were reported
in Romania where childred had been placed in ovens to get
them warm.

Many burn injuries were caused by hot water. Babies and
young children were bathed on stovetops in cold countries
where the state controlled the meager supply of fuel (usually

gas) and the supply of hot water was limited. When children were left unattended, or when temperature control was not monitored, children were often seriously burned.

Developing countries do not have "burn units" at their hospitals. Or, if they exist, they are usually in military hospitals with restricted admisison policies. The tremendously sophisticated treatment needed for burns in children is not available. There are no antibiotics to treat the complicated infections that usually occur. Second-degree burns are converted to third degree by severe infection. Third-degree burns leave lifelong scars and deformity. There is no physical therapy or reconstructive surgery to reduce the secondary complications of those scars.

Children who survive are often more disabled by the burn complications than the injury itself. Deformed and disfigured by thick scars, unable to move well, and cosmetically marred for life, child victims of burns are often institutionalized. Once institutionalized, the cycle of superimposed neglect begins its vicious work. Plastic surgery, skin grafts, physical therapy, or cosmetic surgery are beyond any possibility.

A significant number of institutionalized burn-injured children are legally adoptable. Unless other injuries were sustained or subsequent, severe neglect caused additional damage, these children often have normal potential. Because of the disfiguring cosmetic appearance of untreated burn scars, these children are often passed over for adoption.

After adoption, children who have suffered burn injuries often need extensive medical care; this may include prolonged hospitalization for serialized reconstructive and plastic surgery. The results of these surgical procedures, however, are often miraculous.

TREATABLE CONGENITAL MALFORMATIONS (BIRTH DEFECTS)

Cleft lip and palate is one of the commonest birth defects in the world. Arising from a failure of closure of the palate (roof of the mouth) during early fetal life, the malformation causes a persistent opening between the mouth and nasal cavities. Cleft palate is commonly associated with cleft lip ("hare lip") and has multiple causes and associations, including a large number of congenital malformation syndromes and several genetic (inheritable) defects.

An increased incidence of cleft palate has been associated with intrauterine radiation exposure and was seen in all the eastern European countries in the path of the Chernobyl disaster's fallout.

Because of the sophisticated technology required to correct the cleft palate and the relatively simple process of lip closure, it is not unusual to find an institutionalized child who has had cosmetic closure of the lip but no repair of the palate. If adoptive parents notice a surgical scar on any adoptive candidate's upper lip, it is advisable to inquire about the palate or to ask the child to open his mouth and look.[6]

Children whose cleft palates remain unrepaired, or whose repairs are long delayed, are at significant risk for persistent problems related to functional deficit of the palate; these may include feeding and swallowing problems, severe speech defects, and major dental problems. When treatment is delayed, the likelihood of developing normal speech is markedly decreased.

Because of their appearance and the stigma often attached to this birth defect, many cleft palate children from developing countries are placed in institutions soon after birth. Adopting parents should know that:

◆ Despite satisfactory surgical procedures, children with cleft palate may have residual problems with palate function and speech.
◆ Cleft palate is frequently associated with other syndromes and congenital abnormalities that may not be obvious to either parents or inexperienced professionals.
◆ Any child with cleft palate is at some increased risk for learning disorders and/or hearing problems (latter related to chronic congestion).

HYDROCEPHALIC CHILDREN

Hydrocephalus is the medical term for an abnormal collection of fluid within the brain. Although commonly associated with spinal defects, the condition does occur in isolation. In untreated hydrocephalus, the fluid collection progresses, causing increasing pressure and damage to surrounding brain tissue. Hydrocephalus may arrest (stop, self-correct) spontaneously during childhood or adolescence.

In developed countries, most hydrocephalic babies are surgically treated with a procedure called "shunting." The shunt apparatus, usually a plastic valve or tube, is placed under the skin so that the extra fluid can be diverted away from the brain cavity, relieving the pressure and sparing the brain further damage. Given appropriate and early medical care and follow-up, many hydrocephalic babies can lead normal lives.

Hydrocephalus is not treated in many developing countries due to lack of needed medical services. Hydrocephalic babies are invariably institutionalized soon after birth. In institutions, they are given little more than custodial care. This discussion of hydrocephalus is included because of the tremendous empathy these babies and children provoked in parents seeking adoption in Romania. I heard offers to adopt these children many times and know of several cases in which parents adopted both a lower-risk normal child and one with hydrocephalus or spina bifida.

In underdeveloped countries, even when neurosurgeons are available, there are no sophisticated follow-up facilities, such as advanced X ray and special antibiotics to treat the tough infections that invariably occur in these patients. *It is this follow-up care that is most often deficient in these countries.* Therefore, an abundance of neurosurgeons will not solve the problem in developing or redeveloping countries. There must also be sufficient infrastructure with the technical capability to provide a decent level of follow-up care for shunted, hydrocephalic children. One can predict, therefore, that these babies will be available to adoptive parents for many years to come.

The few adopting parents who are interested in this type of special-needs adoption should know that many complex ethical and medical decisions must be made regarding the treatability of hydrocephalic children. To make enlightened decisions in these instances, parents often need access to sophisticated diagnostic facilities and may find it hard to locate them in the child's

country of origin. Long-distance consultation and advice is recommended before final decisions are made to adopt.

POLIO

Despite the discovery of vaccines and their worldwide distribution, polio remains a significant problem in developing
countries. In eastern Europe, the available vaccines (often manufactured in inferior plants in-country) were not effective. In
Southern Hemisphere countries with hot climates, vaccines lost
their potency because of lack of refrigeration. In many countries, distribution was a major problem.

Adopting parents should know: Many medical records will
indicate that a child was fully immunized for polio. When a
skilled examination reveals that the child has classical findings
of polio, however, the most likely diagnosis is polio. The most
likely explanation for the missed diagnosis is that the vaccine,
if actually given, was not potent.

Whatever the cause, there are hundreds of abandoned, physically disabled children living in institutions with residual effects of polio. These children are excellent adoptive candidates
for parents who are interested in adopting a physically challenged child but who do not feel able to parent a child with an
associated mental challenge. Polio attacks the spinal cord, not
the brain, and does not cause mental retardation or any other
kind of brain damage.

These children are in desperate need of homes. Once institutionalized, they often begin deteriorating because of both medical and psychological neglect. Neither rehabilitation nor education is a viable option for most of them, in or out of institutions.

Adoption of children who have had polio can be a very rewarding experience. If given loving homes and medical attention, education, and rehabilitation, most of them can live
fruitful lives with their challenges.

CONGENITAL DISLOCATION OF THE HIP (CDH)

More recently this has been named "developmental dislocation
of the hip, or DDH," but it is still most widely called CDH,
despite the new, more accurate descriptive wording.

Congenital dislocation of the hip is just what it says: dislocation of the hip joint, present at birth. The condition is most often caused by a shallow hip socket from which the bone easily slips into a dislocated position. Babies are either born with the hip already dislocated or, more often, with an unstable joint from which the bone slips easily. Both conditions are diagnosable in the newborn period.

A description of DDH (or CDH) is included in this section not because its presence provides a rationale for adoption but because it is so common and may be overlooked in the foreign adoptee until the child begins walking and develops symptoms of deterioration of the hip.

Early detection and treatment can prevent this condition from ever becoming either a challenge or permanent disability. Although physicians routinely check for this condition in newborn examinations and well-baby checkups, this examination may be overlooked when the newly adopted child first sees an American doctor. (You don't want that to happen, of course, and it won't be offensive if you make the request for a hip check for DDH, or CDH.)

If DDH is not detected and treated early, the child can become permanently disabled. Occurring more often in females, this easily remedied condition is detected early in most Western countries. When detected in early infancy, simple splinting or application of several extra layers of diapers can prevent the crippling effects of the disorder in many cases. Others, more severe, will usually respond to orthopedic care, casting, and/or surgery without significant permanent disability.

If undetected, untreated, or if treatment is delayed significantly, CDH will lead to limping, pain from dislocation, and eventual destruction of the bones of the hip joint. Once bone is damaged, permanent disability follows. This is the case in many institutions in developing countries.

The common practice of leaving small babies tightly wrapped or swaddled all day adds to the risk of developing dislocation from DDH. Swaddling alone is not the problem; many cultures swaddle infants. However, not many cultures leave their babies swaddled and unattended for hours on end, handling them only twice a day to prop their bottles and change their swaddles. It is this neglect that converts a "shallow hip socket," a CDH in early stages, to a crippling disability.

Adoptive parents should know that foreign adoptees, particularly those who were neglected in institutions, are at increased risk for this condition. Adopting parents should be on special alert for this problem in any country that traditionally swaddles infants, such as China and some South American countries. Furthermore, early detection after arriving home with an adopted baby can prevent an otherwise normal baby from becoming a physically challenged child.

ADVANCED, COMPLEX, OR "LATE-STAGE" DISORDERS

In nonindustrialized and redeveloping countries that have been depleted of both human and material resources, health problems occur that are virtually unknown to industrialized, more affluent societies. Many medical problems progress to advanced stages that we do not see in our own countries. The general public is often made aware of the extent and severity of these problems when disaster strikes or substandard care is exposed by the press or media.

Foreign adoption usually comes into the picture when children who are victims of either of these situations are dramatically publicized. Shock is rapidly followed by an outpouring of sympathy, and the overwhelming desire to rescue the child is acted upon. For example:

◆ In war-torn Bosnia, a child with severe and multiple injuries is publicized in the international press; offers to help pour in from all over the world and the child goes to England where heroic measures are undertaken to save the child.

◆ 20/20 features a disabled boy who is dying, unloved and unattended, of severe malnutrition and neglect in a Romanian Camin Spital; thousands of sympathizers respond, some rushing to his side to assure him that he will at least know the touch of a loving mother's hand before he dies.

◆ Or, again in Romania, a beautiful young woman with cerebral palsy languishes in bed where she will spend the rest of her life waiting to die; when her plight is publicized, she is brought to the United States and given the opportunity to ex-

perience life with challenge rather than years of dying, denied
the pleasure of looking out of a window or hearing music on
a radio.

♦ HIV-positive children dying horrible deaths, not from AIDS,
but from starvation and neglect; when they are featured in
the publication of a large humanitarian organization, a group
of women go to their sides, and, after months of negotiation
and waiting, adopt the children and give them a chance to
have a childhood and loving home.

Although notoriety and fame are not the goal of most of these
adoptive parents, they and you are the unsung heroes in these
circumstances. Too often, you are left to your own resources
when public sentiment dies or is diverted to other disasters in
other parts of the world. Your contributions to the quality of life
of these children often go unrecognized when medical science
fails to save the children, as was the case in both the Bosnian
child and the malnourished boy from Romania. Attention is focused on meeting the scientific challenge or punishing the hei-
nous deeds of tyrants and war rather than on acknowledging
the achievements of the family and rewarding their equally heroic efforts with praise, respect, or even support for their ongoing involvement.

Quality of life is the issue in these cases—not the length of it
or the possiblity of cure. Although adoption of these children is
not for many parents, the tremendous value of enhancing the
quality of foreshortened lives or making life a joyful experience
for victims of incurable or irreversible diseases can be a rich
and fulfilling experience.

These are extreme cases brought to light by dramatic events
and mass publicity. A multitude of health problems of similar
nature have been exposed in the aftermath of these initial,
highly publicized cases in recent years. As increasing numbers
of reports have trickled out of grossly neglectful care in foreign
institutions, increasing awareness of these problems has captured the attention of both helping professionals and those interested in foreign adoption. Until that time, neither group had
much experience in dealing with children with advanced diseases or complex problems. Rickets, for example . . . :

Rickets is the well-known term for the skeletal (bone) disorder that occurs when bone is not calcified (mineralized) correctly. In the nonindustrialized world, the vast majority of rickets is caused by vitamin D deficiency. In the industrialized world, however, vitamin D deficiency rickets is a rare occurrence and most clinical practitioners have never seen a case. Other, more exotic and complex disorders of hormonal, kidney, or liver disease origin top the list of probable causes.

Some of us are old enough to remember when vitamin D supplementation became an important part of well-child care; we recall with mixed emotions the diligence of our loving parents when presented with revolting spoonfuls of cod liver oil. When their coaxing or making a game of it didn't convince us, the threat of bowed legs forever often did the trick. The advent of sugary, flavored vitamin preparations and routinely supplemented milk products changed our perception, however. Bowed legs were forgotten about and preventive care was a pleasant experience. Our family doctors enjoyed a similar euphoria.

Over time, diagnosis of rickets became a venture into exotic realms of chemicals, kidney function, hormones, and their imbalances. Once the diagnostic problem was solved, treatment was provided, aided by new technology and the wide availability of highly specialized resources. Not only did vitamin D deficiency rickets become history, most clinicians never saw advanced or complicated cases—unless or until they visited a developing country where vitamin D deficiency was endemic, or an adoptive parent brought in a child who had the condition. When that occurred, they often commented, "I've only seen this pictured in textbooks."

When children are adopted with advanced rickets, their skeletal deformities are usually far beyond the point of response to vitamin D and calcium. In addition to therapy for the child's nutritional deficiencies, the child often requires rehabilitation and long-term orthopedic care. Treatment with vitamin D and calcium prevents development of rickets rather and is only curative in earlier stages. If the bone deformities are long-standing, orthopedic problems will remain a permanent challenge.

Chronic bone and joint problems can be complications of

other problems. Parents who have adopted from large "warehouse"-type institutions often report that their most difficult encounters occurred when they were confronted with bedridden children who had severe and multiple physical deformities.

Institutionalized, multihandicapped children who are bedridden for years often develop a thinning of the bones (osteoporosis). Their bones are extremely fragile and many have sustained multiple fractures over the years. If these bones were not straightened and set when injury was fresh, as was the case in many institutionalized children, the result is grotesque deformity.

It is not unusual to see severe and advanced disorders mixed together in one child. Diagnosis of these cases is very difficult, as is treatment. The complexity of these children's medical problems would challenge the skills of the most sophisticated American medical center. Adopting parents who are visiting institutions housing older, disabled youngsters best be prepared to encounter similar situations.

Few of these severely involved children get out by way of adoption. Some are eligible for humanitarian parole, but this raises the ethical issues surrounding the return of a child to an environment that will not be prepared to meet the child's needs. (Guardianship and humanitarian parole are discussed in chapter 7.)

NEW DISEASES

Some multihandicapped children in foreign institutions have what appear to be brand-new diseases, never before described. For example, in Romania, I saw dozens of children in Camin Spitals with a complex musculoskeletal disorder resulting in:

- Genu recurvatum (back-curving of the knees).
- Fibrosis of quadriceps (hardening and scarring of anterior thigh muscles).
- Patellar dislocation and rotation (dislocation of kneecaps and rotation to back or side of leg).
- Multiple, lower-extremity joint dislocations (knees and hips, for example).

- ◆ Secondary spine problems (usually "scoliosis" or curvature of the spine).

Neither I nor any of the orthopedic surgeons I consulted have been able to give a specific name to this disease complex. Parents who are adopting or have adopted older children (above age two or three) from eastern Europe need to know that this problem occurs. I have received several reports from adoptive parents and agencies that suggest that a milder (or earlier) form of the disorder may exist.

After the initial discovery of children with all of these findings, additional children were reported with only hardening of the thigh muscles. Adoptive mothers report that "the thigh muscles feel like wires." All of these children have had histories of multiple injections (thigh muscles were common injection sites for any medication or immunizations). The relationship of multiple injections to the destruction of the muscle and the other deformities seen in advanced cases is unknown, but is highly suspicious.

Parents of children whose thigh muscles feel hardened or unusually stiff should ask their physicians to evaluate the problem. In addition, they should follow up to be sure the problem is not progressive. As the child grows in height, the hardened muscles (which have lost their elasticity) cannot stretch and keep up with the bone growth. Problems may not occur until the child is in early adolescence and experiences the adolescent growth spurt.

THINGS YOU'VE NEVER THOUGHT OF

Children in Camin Spitals often stretched my diagnostic skills to the limit. There was one medical condition I missed entirely when I first saw it. In the summer of 1990, I found a number of bedridden children with circulatory problems and discolorations of their hands and feet and sometimes their faces. Attendants reported that the condition was common and could sometimes be painful. I remained mystified about the disorder until later in the year. Winter came, and with it the relentless, pervasive cold.

When I returned to the institution, and realized how very

cold it was inside, the diagnosis hit me. Despite the fact that most of these children never went out of doors, cold injury was the only logical answer. The signs were classic findings of frostbite: circulatory problems and discoloration of hands, feet, noses, and ears.

That was an awful day. I derived no pleasure from making that diagnosis, lost a lot of my objectivity (which isn't particularly abundant), and marched into the director's office with a terrible mix of outrage and pain. It was hard enough to accept the truth that children were getting frostbitten in their beds; but it was harder still to accept the fact that there was no attempt at heating the institution one year after the revolution. When the director was approached about the problem, he called the children "the lucky ones." The unlucky ones, he added, got pneumonia, and most of them "didn't survive."

Ever since that day, which was a real low point in my first two years, it has occurred to me that some of the "lucky ones" may have gotten luckier still and have been adopted. Although none of the follow-up reports I have received reported cold injury symptoms in adoptees, the information may be helpful to adopting parents whose children have similar complaints.

WHEN PROBLEMS ARE HEAPED UPON PROBLEMS

The low standard of diagnosis in developing countries, particularly that of complex or rare conditions, adds another layer of problems onto the adoption of challenged children.

- ◆ Underlying syndromes and commonly associated disorders may have been missed even though the more obvious physical disability was well described. For example, a heart or kidney defect may be missed while the orthopedic problem is well diagnosed. Although most of the physical disabilities described earlier in this chapter occur in isolation, any one of them may be associated with symptom complexes known as congenital malformation syndromes.
- ◆ Inheritability of the problem may be overlooked or go undetected. In situations where many children are abandoned and/or access to family histories is poor, genetic disorders

are missed more often. Although the basic treatment may not vary, it is an important part of good case management to make genetic counseling part of the child's total program. He may be at increased risk of having children with similar problems.

Although less common than the sporadic (one-time-only) occurrence, disorders such as club foot, cleft palate, and congenital deafness can be genetically determined. The birth family of Vasile Michael Goldberg, for example, had a very positive history for club feet.

When either of these situations is present, consultation with a birth-defects specialist or genetic counselor is recommended.

♦ Underlying diseases, such as developmental or psychological disorders, may be masked by physical handicaps. Conditions such as mild cerebral palsy, ADHD, anxiety, or reactive behavior disorders may not express themselves until the physical problem has been partially rehabilitated and the child has gained mobility. For example, the child with unrepaired cleft palate may not reveal a serious learning problem or language deficit (beyond the mechanical problems of producing speech) until after surgical repair and functional recovery of the palate has been accomplished.

♦ Disabled children are more vulnerable to a variety of serious, "second problems" stemming from their institution placement. For example, any disabled child is likely to have been given more injections; hence he is more likely to have contracted a blood-borne communicable disease like hepatitis B. Child abuse prevention centers have documented that disabled children (in any setting) are at much higher risk for child abuse than their nondisabled counterparts. Symptoms of post-traumatic stress disorder (PTSD), phobias, and related anxiety disorders stemming from prior abuse are usually delayed reactions. When they occur in a disabled child, they may not be recognized for two reasons:

1. The child is limited in his ability to express himself.
2. All of the child's symptoms have been associated with the physical disability.

♦ Almost without exception, disabled survivors of institutions have formed a strong attachment to a peer. Some of these relationships are understandably codependent. It is not unusual, for example, to see a visually impaired child team up with a sighted child with a different sort of problem. Mentally disabled children often pair with a physically disabled child with more normal cognitive skills.

Separation from friends represents a significant loss for challenged children, both during and after adoption. The emotional reaction to this loss is variable, but usually involves some degree of depression and grief. Furthermore, deep feelings of guilt are common regarding the child-friend left behind. Unless these psychological responses are treated through psychotherapy or guidance programs, more severe and long-lasting psychopathologies can develop.

THE CHALLENGES ADOPTING FAMILIES FACE

Beside every challenged child in America stands a challenged parent (or two). Although the nature of challenge differs, they are, nonetheless, challenges. In international adoption of children with special needs, adopting parents face all the normal challenges of intercountry adoption plus another layer of challenges uniquely related to the special needs of the child after the child comes to America.

♦ Foreign adoptees may not be eligible, or may fall under quota restrictions, for rehabilitation services. Adoption agencies and adopting parents should consider eligibility factors as well as the listed "available services" when special-needs children are concerned. Services listed as "available" in a community may not be available to the foreign adoptee until he or she is a full-fledged citizen. Insurance companies, health plans, and other third-party payers may exclude children with "preexisting conditions" from coverage. When children have mental health problems requiring treatment, there may be a cap on the total reimbursement.
♦ Several adopting families have reported negative reactions, friction, and occasionally prejudice when they return to their

communities. One mother reported that her Gypsy child was discriminated against in his public school because of his darkened skin. Another reported that her friends and neighbors thought she was "hung up in some unrealistic rescue fantasy, and couldn't see reality anymore." "Maybe there was an element of that," she added. "But I was just not going to give up on my child. He needs a little more time."

Others have experienced resentment. They are continually confronted with the question that started this chapter: Why go halfway round the world, when there are so many children here who need a home and special attention?

SURPRISE PACKAGES

Challenged children, like many children with special needs, come with special gifts to offer. Sometimes these gifts take us by surprise. . . .

An adoptive mother said it best: "It's a process. For us, it has been a mix of pleasant surprises and nasty shocks. The nasty shock came when we found out about the abuse our son experienced when the orphanage attempted to toilet train him. We hadn't a clue when we visited. They told us he was one of their favorite children, and we thought he had been treated accordingly. It certainly seemed so when we were there. Fortunately for us, we have access to good therapy, and most of that problem has resolved. We're still working on it, though.

"Our 'pleasant surprise' has been the greatest help. We found out that our son is 'gifted.' He has superior intelligence and is also very talented. Parenting a gifted child has its own set of challenges. Our biggest hurdle right now is to advocate for him with the school system.

"When I talk with other parents who have adopted 'challenged' children from overseas, none of us really know why we were singled out for this experience. Challenge doesn't seem an adequate word for what we have been through. It has been a real hero's journey. Regardless of our experiences, however, we would do it all over again if we were given that choice today."

For this family, the challenge of giftedness has been a welcome one. It is, however, a real challenge for both gifted children and their families. Many gifted children need special programs at school to allow them to advance at their own pace academically and according to their abilities. Although these services may be part of the child's legal entitlements, appropriate programs can be hard to find. Many gifted children have relative degrees of social immaturity, and some may need counseling or therapy when this disparity of social and intellectual skills is pronounced. Gifted children for whom English is a second language may be delayed in achievement until their language skills improve. Any or all or the above challenges may be greater in the foreign adoptee. This is particularly true when there are psychological problems related to past neglect or abuse in institutions.

Still, the challenge of giftedness is often a rewarding one. For this small group of challenged children, most parents' experience and feelings would agree with those of the mother quoted above:

"My husband and I feel very, very blessed. And so, I believe, does our child."

REFERENCES

1. ABC, 20/20 newsmagazine, "The Shame of a Nation" (1990), "A Miracle for Michael" (1991). Janice Tomlin, producer.

2. CBS, "Where Are They Now?" (1995). Bodi and Blanki Productions, Los Angeles, CA.

3. Greti Dorr interview, "Where Are They Now?"

4. People, August 12, 1991, p. 41.

5. People, 25th Anniversary Special Issue. A Child's New Home in the Heartland. 1994.

6. Author (Bascom): This observation was made repeatedly when I was touring Romania's Camin Spitals and noticed the severe speech problems that children with repaired cleft lips had. When their palates were examined, the cleft palates were still open and there was no evidence of attempted surgical intervention. This situation is unlikely to be found in children under age six or seven years; since foreign assistance programs have been established in Romania, most cleft palates have been promptly

referred for treatment during infancy or afflicted children have been adopted.

7. *Exceptional Parent, The Magazine for Families and Professionals* (ISSN 0046-9157) is published monthly by Psy-Ed Corporation, 209 Harvard St., Ste. 303, Brookline MA 02146-5005.

7

Guardianship

Love, hope, fear, faith—these make humanity;
These are its sign and note and character.

Robert Browning, *Paracelsus*, 1835

HUMANITARIAN PAROLE

Humanitarian parole? What is it? What is it not?

Why discuss it in a book about adoption?

What is it? Humanitarian parole is the U.S. legal term for granting a "nonimmigrant visa" to a citizen of a foreign country for purposes of providing humanitarian assistance not available to the foreign citizen in his country of origin.

- Humanitarian parole is most often granted for reasons of emergent or serious health care needs.
- When humanitarian parole is granted, a U.S. citizen must be identified as the responsible "sponsor" and guarantees must be provided that the parolee will be fully provided the assistance needed. When the parolee is a minor, the sponsor, or his designee, must act as his guardian.
- Humanitarian parole is a reciprocal act of good faith on the part of the sending country and the United States. U.S. embassy personnel promise the sending country that the parolee will return to the country within the time period specified in the visa.
- Once in the United States, the humanitarian parolee is a legal alien. If the terms of parole are broken, the parolee becomes

an illegal alien and the sponsor, if housing the child, is illegally harboring an illegal alien.

What is it not?

- ◆ Humanitarian parole is not a short-cut to adoption.
- ◆ Humanitarian parole is not a back door to adoption.
- ◆ Humanitarian parole is not a temporary holding device so that a child can be brought to the country (under false pretenses), then adopted later at less expense and hassle. Nor is it a device for bringing a refugee to the country who needs political asylum.

Why include a discussion of humanitarian parole in a book about foreign adoption?

- ◆ Humanitarian parole may serve as an alternative to adoption for families who wish to provide humanitarian assistance to a desperately needy child. Most families who choose this alternative either are seeking a temporary situation or do not qualify (most often for reasons of existing family size or age restrictions) for adoption.
- ◆ Humanitarian parole may serve as a lifesaving alternative for children. who, for reasons of age or disability, are not considered adoptable. It also benefits children with parents who won't or don't wish to release them for adoption.

America is a land of almost limitless resources when compared to most developing countries. Its health care technologies are considered by many to be "the best in the world." The standard of living of the average American family far surpasses that of most other nations in the world. Known as the "sweet land of liberty," it provides unencumbered opportunity for its children to realize their potential.

Every year, hundreds of U.S. families make a family decision to share this abundance with less fortunate and needy children from abroad. Some choose to enter a "child sponsorship" program through a nonprofit, humanitarian organization. Others wish to make their sponsorship more intense and personal and bring a needy, foreign child into their home for one or two years. These are the families who act as guardians for children on humanitarian parole.

Despite its principles and its unique potential for accomplishing humanitarian goals, the humanitarian parole program is fraught with problems. It is often misused and abused, and the abuses, unfortunately, are usually related to hidden agendas of adoption. In eastern Europe, for example, there were so many instances of abuse of humanitarian parole when legislation was delaying or obstructing adoption that the entire program was imperiled.

There is no good way to police or effectively monitor an act of good faith or to bring to justice a promise broken. The fact that there was "nothing illegal about it," as was often said, did not help matters when a family failed to return a parolee and adopted the child in their home state instead.

It is true; there is nothing illegal about it. The repercussions, however, can be and usually are damaging when the program is misused or abused. In Romania, for example, when widespread misuse of the program became well known, orphanage directors and health officials were afraid to allow any other children to leave under humanitarian parole for fear of being implicated in corrupt activities.

U.S. professionals who worked for humanitarian organizations in the sending countries suddenly encountered all sorts of bureaucratic obstacles in their daily work. Children who may have been eligible for humanitarian parole were suddenly "not eligible." Some who were already in process of having their permits approved were either disapproved or put on hold indefinitely, without explanation. Several professionals and many families who were legitimately exploring the possibility of bringing a disabled child out through the program were falsely accused of having a role in the abuse of the humanitarian parole program.

In the case of problems with humanitarian parole U.S. embassy officials were not and still are not often helpful. Part of this is understandable. As the responsible agency, they bear the brunt of the criticism and negative repercussions when the system is abused. When it is abused frequently and in large numbers, then the U.S. consular corps is under tremendous pressure from the foreign government.

American and other Western medical personnel who were in

Romania working with the children in the institutions in 1990–91, recognized both the need and tremendous value of the humanitarian parole system. We saw many children leave the country (most of them to nearby European medical centers) and return rehabilitated, restored to function by surgery and sometimes completely cured. Therefore, we (Western professionals) were supportive of the program and did all we could to facilitate humanitarian parole for children we knew personally. Usually this involved signing the medical affidavit that the child required assistance or supporting the urgency of the situation.

In 1992, the entire humanitarian parole system was placed in jeopardy when abuses became frequent. This concerned those of us who were working in the medical field in Romania. If the program had closed down entirely, needy children, many of whom were ineligible for adoption, would have been denied the opportunity of treatment for their medical problems that was offered through the program. They would have to stay in Romania, where treatment for major medical problems and disabilities was not available.

Families who are interested in becoming guardians through the humanitarian parole system need to know some of the problems they may encounter when they get involved with the process. In 1993, I (Bascom) was caught up in a bad situation involving the humanitarian parole program; the problems we encountered illustrate the tainted image the program has acquired because of abuse. At that time, my husband, Jim, and I were directing our own foundation, which provided humanitarian assistance to orphanages (ROSES project) and to Romania's medical schools (MERP). We were wrongly accused of helping with false humanitarian paroles and the events were particularly painful.

In November 1993, I was in the United States for a professional meeting when I received a very disturbing phone call from my husband in Romania. Jim had just returned from the American embassy, where he was escorting a young Romanian doctor (whom we had personally sponsored), to obtain a visa for her return to the University of Alabama where she was a Ph.D. candidate in neurosciences. About the same time, he had provided a medical statement for a Romanian child to go on humanitarian parole to the United States to receive treatment for severe epilepsy.

Jim was concerned. As he prepared to leave the embassy, he was confronted and accused by the sing-song voice of the consul general, who said,

"I know what you're up to!"

After a lengthy interrogation of the young Romanian physician, it became obvious that the consul general was implying that we were involved in a conspirational "underground railroad" whose mission was to get children out of Romania by way of humanitarian parole with no intention of bringing them back regardless of consequences.

The purpose of telling this story is not for me to seize an opportunity for vindication or to prove innocence; our innocence has long since been established both officially and unofficially, and our position that parole should not be corrupted or diverted to other purposes is now well known. This story instead, is intended to serve as a warning to families who are interested in humanitarian parole. The program has a tarnished image. Humanitarian parole has so often been abused by adoptive hopefuls with hidden agendas that anyone embarking on the process may encounter suspicion. It is my personal recommendation that it is not a healthy route to adoption. There is ample, legal opportunity to pursue exceptions to policy in extraordinary situations.

The problems raised by this episode were related not so much to the embarrassment and hassle in getting the situation straightened out but to our realization that the humanitarian parole system was in jeopardy altogether. Many children who were ineligible for adoption and would benefit from the program would continue to live hopelessly in institutions where no medical services were available.

Humanitarian parole was set up for one reason: to help children who had medical or other disabilities get the help they needed by being furloughed to a foreign country and being hosted by a foreign foster family until their medical/psychological situation was stable. It was to serve no other purpose.

I have personal knowledge of two case histories in which children did come out on humanitarian parole and were adopted later. Both cases involved emergent medical situations. Although the circumstances were unusual, they illustrate the need for occasional "exception to policy" (the official title of the process that should be undertaken when the return of a child cannot be considered).

Petronella

The first situation involved a child, Petronella, who was *in the process of adoption* when adoption was halted to revise the law. Petronella, who had multiple handicaps, including limb deficiency, developmental disabilities, and emotional problems, needed help immediately. After seeing her on television, an American family responded, expressing interest in adopting this special-needs child. But they wanted to be careful and make sure the situation was right.

The year was 1991. Romanian adoptions were about to close down for the first time so laws could be written. In Petronella's case, the adopting mother, an early childhood expert, volunteered to work with the ROSES project while she waited for the adoption to be completed in Romania. This gave her an opportunity to contribute to the humanitarian effort taking place at the same time she was getting to know Petronella. When the adoption process was halted, however, it was impossible to adopt Petronella and get her to the United States, despite the fact her medical needs had become urgent.

The child was badly in need of physical therapy and orthopedic care involving surgery because of her limb deficiencies. Because Petronella had been born without hands and part of her arms, the best solution was to fit her with an artificial limb and reconstruct the partial hand she had on one side. No services of this nature were available in Romania. In addition to her physical deformities, Petronella also had educational problems and alarming new symptoms signaling that she might have mental health complications, because she developed some autistic features. She was turning three years old and would soon be moved from this institution to another and lost to the system.

After applying for parole, Petronella's future mother came to me asking for assistance. She needed a medical statement. Familiar with her case, I wrote the statement and the humanitarian parole was soon granted. The adopting family promised to return to Romania and adopt Petronella as soon as the system reopened. All parties were aware that the parents' goal was eventually to adopt Petronella and that the parole system was being used as an emergency stopgap measure to meet her urgent needs.

No one involved, however, anticipated that adoption would be closed for so very long (July 1991 to April 1992). During this time, Petronella was discovered to have a previously undiscovered medical problem, congenital dislocation of the hip, that required highly specialized services and surgical attention the family had not anticipated. In addition, she needed medical services that were not available to her as a legal alien. The family was faced with a dilemma. They couldn't return to Romania to adopt Petronella because the system was closed. Meanwhile, their new child needed to be served and the only way to do that was to adopt her. Not knowing when adoption would reopen and placing their priorities on the immediate needs of the child, the family adopted in California instead of returning to Romania where she would have been reinstitutionalized, losing not only her chances for treatment but also her home and family.

Fraga

In another case, a child named Fraga required complex neurosurgery and was sent to Ireland on humanitarian parole. It was her second trip to Ireland. Through the generosity of fund-raisers in Dublin, Fraga had been there for a consultation the year before. The Romanian staff who traveled with her was advised of the danger signals in her complex problems. After a year back in Romania, Fraga developed those danger signals. The ROSES project manager and Romanian orphanage director called Dublin immediately.

When Dublin responded, it was learned that a nurse and her family who had seen Fraga the year before had offered to adopt her. The process was delayed, however, because no Irish adoption agency had yet been approved by the RAC (Romania Adoption Committee).

Aware of the complexity and probable hazards in this situation, I asked the RAC for guidance. In a remarkable show of support, the entire RAC traveled to Iasi to confer with the staff and help solve Fraga's dilemma.

The result: The RAC voted unanimously to make an exception to policy and allow the Irish family to adopt Fraga while she was on humanitarian parole. Fraga was spared a prolonged hospitalization and an unnecessary trip back to Romania. And Fraga had a ready-made family waiting for her at the Dublin airport less than a week later.

~

In both of these situations, adoption was not an option because of barriers in the bureaucracy. The humanitarian parole system was crucial in getting both children medical help until the bureaucracy could respond. No one did anything illegal.

WHEN GUARDIANSHIP WORKS AS IT SHOULD

Although Fraga's and Petronella's cases demonstrate how children benefit from humanitarian parole, they do not represent the way the system is designed to work. There is another child who benefited from humanitarian parole, but in the true meaning of what this parole situation was set up to accomplish:

~

Petre

In 1993, a child returned to his northern village in Romania amid great celebration. After a successful eighteen months with an American family, he was able to walk home on his own. Accompanied by his American family, he had a tearful reunion with his birth parents, sisters, and brothers. They touched his clothes and face, and expressed admiration for his American haircut. The local state TV was there to record the reunion. So was the village mayor and the director of the institution that had been his home before he went to America.

On the outskirts of the village was the institution where he had spent most of his childhood. The sign in front, when translated, read "home for the deficient and unsalvageable." But Petre (not his real name) did not plan to call the institution "home" ever again. He was no longer deficient. Nor was he ever "unsalvageable."

Less than two years before, Petre had come to the attention of an American couple who had adopted three other foreign children. They had recognized his need for rehabilitative and educational services and they learned that Petre had a family that could bring him home if he received medical treatment. So they agreed to take him with them on humanitarian parole.

During his stay in the United States, Petre was part of a big "topsy-turvy" family who lived in a rural village as small as his hometown. There were two "birth children" and three other adopted children, one from his own and two others from different countries.

Petre was taken to a medical center for special treatments. He received "special education" and learned to speak English. He gained weight on a wholesome diet. Someone always came to comfort him when he had nightmares. His institution had the reputation as one of the harshest in his country of origin and the nightmares were thought to stem from conditions there. He had seen and experienced things in the institution that were difficult to talk about. Slowly, things got better and the nightmares stopped.

His American family had stayed in touch with his "waiting family" back home. They told him lots of stories about his country that he had never heard before. They even knew some songs and sang them together in his native language. He didn't feel like a stranger at all when it was time to go back home.

Humanitarian parole was the best of two worlds for Petre. He returned to his home and his family, who would never have been able to provide him with the treatment he needed if he was to walk. The intervention, through humanitarian parole, saved him from spending the rest of his life in one of the saddest and most brutal institutions in all of Romania.

WHAT IT MEANS TO BE A LEGAL ALIEN

When children come to the United States on humanitarian parole, their status is that of legal alien. Despite the good intentions of most parole programs, children on parole are particularly vulnerable. Legal or not, they are still aliens in this country.

"Petre's" story is a perfect example of how things can and should be done in the humanitarian parole system. It is, however, very idealistic. Families considering guardianship should know, however, that things do not always go so smoothly. Often, there is heartache and *always* difficult separations. Occasionally there isn't a safe environment to return to. There are difficult choices to make, involving ethical, legal, moral, and political issues:

◆ Continued treatment: The home institution may not be prepared to meet the child's ongoing needs. Often the improvements being made have not progressed as well as planned. Or programs may have lost their funding and are no longer functioning.

◆ No support resources: If children return home, instead of returning to institutions, there may be no community resources to continue treatments they need. Village schools, for example, may not have special education teachers, and hospitals may not have specialists or physical therapists.

◆ Safety and well-being: The governments of "emerging democracies" are very fragile. Many revert back to more totalitarian systems, or fall into a pattern called neocommunism. Some of the new democracies fail. Some are torn apart by civil wars.

◆ New problems have arisen that require additional services: Children on humanitarian parole may not have made as full a recovery as was anticipated. Or a second problem that still needs attention may have been discovered. They may need more time before they are strong enough to return.

Parents who are involved in guardianship programs need guidance and assistance in making the tough decisions that always come up after the child is in their home. Guardians will find the following guidance useful:

- *Always* obtain the assistance of an immigration attorney.
- Consult with a social agency and obtain guidance in developing a "permanency plan" (a plan for the child's long-term future) for the child as soon as possible after the child's arrival. "Permanency plan" is a term used for a long-range plan developed by a social service agency (usually the Department of Social Services in a state); it clearly states goals for the child's future. This is often one of two things: a child is to be successfully reunited with his/her family; or a child is to be placed in some form of out-of-family-of-origin care, such as in long-term foster care, an institution, or an adoptive home.
- Try to maintain an attitude of advocacy for the child. When decisions are tough, consider the "best interests of the child" first. When decisions cannot be made, consult a guidance counselor.

RISKS AND VULNERABILITY

Humanitarian parole/guardianship when used properly can help a disabled child from another country receive services that child would never have access to otherwise. In the best of cases, the child is then returned home to her birth family, whole and able to succeed in the foreign country.

Unfortunately, children brought into the United States through humanitarian parole can become "lost" in the American system. Without advocates, they can be subjected to exploitation or neglect or end up as illegal aliens in this country with no rights or protection. As illegal aliens they are subject to deportation.

It is up to the children's sponsors to monitor what has happened to them and make sure the child is receiving the services each individual child requires. It is up to the sponsoring individuals or agencies to report to the sending country and to responsibly pursue legal change of visa status for the child if that becomes necessary.

We will end this chapter on humanitarian parole/guardianship by telling you the tale of one child, "Nikki" (not her real name). This story illustrates what can go wrong in the humanitarian parole system when no one is looking out for the child's interests.

Nikki

Nikki came to America on humanitarian parole from an underdeveloped country. Nikki's story was featured on a major TV program. She was seven or eight years old, very pretty, and lived in a place where she was dead-ended with no medical services and no school. This obviously bright, lively young child was very appealing.

The only reason given for Nikki being in an institution was that she had congenital deformities of her hands and feet. Her hands had not completely formed and she had a club foot. Both were complex, serious orthopedic problems involving bone and tissue deformities.

Nikki had been left at the doorstep of the institution as an infant. No one knew anything about her parents. It was assumed she was abandoned because of her orthopedic problems. When her story aired on television in the United States, a volunteer coordinator for an American nonprofit with a program in Nikki's institution said, "We've just got to get that kid out. We have to get her some help."

Nikki was unadoptable because her parentage was uncertain. This volunteer was an American She called the organization and asked, "Can we sponsor this child?" The answer was, "Yes, but you have to find a guardian, a family who will provide a home and a medical facility that will promise free treatment."

The volunteer (Elizabeth) put together a film on Nikki, and it was broadcast on a local station in her midwestern hometown. The response was heartwarming. A family responded and pledged to take Nikki. Furthermore, they promised to get medical services donated from a local medical center and agreed to see that she was educated.

As part of the agreement, the family wanted permission to show some of the organization's films locally, to get additional support.

When Nikki arrived, escorted by a member of the nonprofit organization, TV cameras were there to greet her. They followed Nikki to her new suburban home, taking pictures of her first visit to a nearby park. When the film was shown, money poured into both guardian home and hospital.

No one from the nonprofit organization kept track of the money;

no one responsible for Nikki knew how much money went to either the hospital or the post office box number at the end of the news article. No one monitored the child's treatment.

Anxious for news about the child, Elizabeth finally visited the home and the hospital. While there, she discovered that the money had not been spent on Nikki's care. Furthermore, she found that Nikki's care in the home and the hospital had been far from adequate. The family responsible for Nikki had neglected her and left her for long periods of time, alone and unattended. The hospital not only diverted Nikki's funding, they never had the speciality services she required in the first place. When Elizabeth finally discovered the truth, she took the initiative and transferred Nikki's care to a responsible guardian.

─────────────── ∽ ───────────────

Nikki's story illustrates many of the inadequacies in the humanitarian parole program when it is improperly used or exploited for the personal gain of unscrupulous individuals. The first guardian was guilty of neglecting and exploiting the child. The hospital and its director were guilty of exploitation and inadequate medical treatment.

THE NEED FOR ADVOCACY AND PROTECTION

Children who are in this country on humanitarian parole are in need of advocacy. As Nikki's case illustrates, these children are at very high risk for exploitation and are unprotected if abuse or neglect occurs. They are needy and vulnerable. If they weren't they wouldn't be here.

Any family considering guardianship needs to know that there are thousands upon thousands of Nikkis living overseas in circumstances that will never foster life or development. At the same time, there are hundreds of Nikkis living in the United States, most of them in responsible environments. But some are just like Nikki. No one is watching.

The pitfalls for a child on humanitarian parole run the gamut. These are children who have no rights. They are in a foreign country with no advocates and in situations that are not monitored. The possibilities for abuse are everywhere.

It is estimated that approximately two hundred children from the former Communist country of Romania are in the United States today on humanitarian parole. Few of them are being monitored. Almost none have been returned to Romania.

The same year Nikki entered the United States, a group of youngsters was brought into the United States by a philanthropist, whose act was widely publicized by the media. After founding a nonprofit organization, the individual had mounted a campaign to "get them [the children in Romania] out of the warehouses and death traps they live in."

Donations and pledges for treatment poured in to the organization's offices, and the children were brought to the United States. Their initial dramatic rescue was televised on a major network show. Politicians, religious leaders, and members of the entertainment community got involved. What has become of these children, all of whom came into this country on medical visas (another term for humanitarian parole)? Where are they now? Some were supposed to go to families who had "plans to adopt." Although no formal action was ever taken in the country of origin, many have been reported "adopted." One guardian said there is "certainly not" any plan to return his child to his country. No single official agency has control of the record of how many children who arrive on parole ever go back.

Without visa extensions some of these children may be illegal aliens in America. Others may have been granted political asylum. And it is unknown how many are living in hospitals or institutional settings such as nursing homes and foster-care homes, without functioning guardians. No one knows how many are getting the services they really need. It is probable they are, but the problem is that no one knows.

In preparing the research and background for this chapter, the authors attempted to survey the location and future plans of guardianship for this group of children. We had the cooperation and assistance of several parents (of adopted children), responsible members of the press and media, and several concerned social agencies. The results were astonishing.

Not only were the participants unwilling to come forth with their stories, but several expressed tremendous anxiety. The research ended badly. One of the only guardians willing to talk said she received a quiet phone call "from someone at State." The word "deportation" was dropped somewhere in the conversation.

There appears to be a conspiracy of silence around the fate of these children.

A LAST WORD

We strongly support the system of humanitarian parole, when properly used, for the following reasons:

1. Children who have no other options because they are ineligible for adoption, or are extremely unlikely to be adopted, can benefit immensely from this program. For many of them, it is lifesaving.
2. Families who are unable to adopt, but have the means and motivation to parent a needy child, can experience many of the same rewards, joys, and promises of adoption through guardianship.

Recognizing the risks and problems inherent in this program, we endorse efforts toward policy changes that would (1) better protect the child while in the country as a "needy visitor" (legal alien), and (2) provide legal options for guardians who are forced to consider retention of the child in their homes for reasons that pertain to the safety and continued welfare of the child.

In all, humanitarian parole/guardianship can play a vital role in helping needy children in the world. We would hate to see the children who can benefit from this parole lose that option because some have abused the system. The example of Petre in this chapter shows how an American family and eastern European family were able to join together to provide the care and treatment so desperately needed by one child. Today he lives happily, and is healthy, in his family of origin, knowing he has another family across the ocean that also deeply cares for him.

When a child is brought to the United States and medical science has restored the child to health, the absolutely best situation is that the formerly disabled child says a loving good-bye to his "American family" and is able to return to his community and his birth family, or an adoptive family in his country of origin, where he can take his place among the productive individuals of that society.

8

Meeting the Challenges, Managing the Risks

The superior man makes the difficulty to be overcome his first interest;
Success comes only later.

Confucius: *Analects*, XII, c. 500 B.C.

What if something—*anything*—goes wrong during the foreign adoption process? Say you are pickpocketed and lose your passport soon after arriving in the foreign country where you have gone to adopt your child? What if you go to the orphanage where your child is waiting and something is wrong with him and you can't get any information? What if a foreign agency wants a document that is not included in your packet, and the court proceeding can't go forward without it? Any of these possibilities can be jolting and interrupt the joy of the moment. Any of them can place the entire procedure in jeopardy.

Most of the time, when you've done all your homework correctly, adoptions do go right. In the overwhelming majority of cases, some say as much as 95 percent of the time in regular adoptions and 88 percent of the time in adoptions of special-needs, or hard to place, children, everything goes smoothly. But statistics are only estimates, and adopting parents should be prepared for any eventuality.

WHAT CAN GO WRONG?

It goes without saying that the gravest risk in intercountry adoption is failure of the adoption. Whether during the process

246

of pursuing the paper trail, or during the time you are in the foreign country trying to fight obstacles unsuccessfully, or after months or years of trying in vain to parent a terribly wounded child, adoption failure is a painful and sad experience. Whether it occurs at home or in a foreign country, it robs families of the joy and fulfillment of bringing a child into their homes. Furthermore, it robs children of the opportunity to recapture their childhood and begin to thrive. What can go wrong?

- The adoption might not occur.
- Expectations might not be met.
- The adoption might fail after the child has been brought home.
- The adopting parent(s) might be hurt, injured, sabotaged, or victimized in the process.

If written, the individual and cumulative experience of parents who have participated in a foreign adoption during the past five years would provide adopting families a rich, and sometimes colorfully illustrated primer on intercountry adoption. In this chapter, we will explore some of the challenges and risks real adoptive parents have faced and provide guidance on how future adopting parents might best prepare themselves to manage the risks and meet the challenges. To have the joy and provide that opportunity to a child, to avoid failure and pitfalls, it is best to borrow the experience of others who have gone before you. The following stories are composites of the actual experiences of several individuals or couples. Each one depicts a scenario in which an adoption goes sour or is in jeopardy, despite the intentions of the adopting family and despite their having done all their homework correctly.

THE ADOPTION MIGHT NOT HAPPEN

You might have done everything you were supposed to do beforehand and arrived safely in a country like Romania or Bulgaria. You may have survived the bureaucracy and the waiting and the hotel room with no hot water in the bathroom for $150 dollars a day, but it was all worth it when you saw the child and knew she was the child of your heart.

You might visit her every day, take her presents, form a bond, and wait again, this time to get a court appointment, during which the child's birth parents would legally give you the right to adopt. Thinking the court date was only a formality, you might find out it wasn't when the birth mother comes, is interrogated by the judge, breaks down, and changes her mind. When your lawyer says "NO ADOPTION," your agency social worker might tell you that "it happens this way sometimes—we *warned* you," implying that you shouldn't have gotten so involved with the child until everything was certain.

Then, in the next breath, she or he suggests you start all over while you're there. If you don't, you will have to pay all over again for transportation, hotel fees, and most of the in-country expenses. While you know she is right, you can't follow through. You can barely get up out of your chair. Finally, someone might question your commitment to adopt when you say "no" because you have run out of energy, and are running out of money. You need a little time for the picture of this child of your heart to fade. You need to be with your husband, who is thousands of miles away.

～

You might have passed all the home studies, met all the qualifications, withdrawn the last penny of your savings account to go to South America and find your baby. You find one and start the legal proceedings as soon as the mother, whom you are told to meet on a street corner, says, "Yes, you can adopt my child." The birth mother even lets you take a picture of her and your soon-to-be baby. Your baby!

You might survive the wait and the traveler's diarrhea that doesn't respond to any of the medicine you brought along. You might tolerate the hotel room where you either suffocate or open the balcony doors to swarms of mosquitoes at night. You might even sail through those things and be all right, because you have the picture propped up beside your bed and it gives you strength and inspiration. You are fine until you meet another waiting mother-to-be in the hotel dining room who shows you a picture of the baby she is going to adopt. She has the same picture you have—the same baby in the arms of the same birth mother, also standing on the same street corner. Then, you might not be all right. At this point, you would, no doubt, be devastated.

But it's not over yet and you have no time to be devastated. You let your head take over your broken heart. You make inquiries at the American embassy and are told that some of these babies are "sold over and over again to parents willing to put up front money," that "it's part of the territory in this part of South America." You might want, at that point, to fly back home and start all over, but this time with an agency that will send you to *another* country where they don't sell babies on the same street corner, over and over again.

You might do just that and find a reputable agency that knows the story. They have heard it before and tell you about it. They tell you how foreign scam artists and illicit baby sellers will take front money and set up a street scene just like yours. But the birth mother may not be the birth mother because the baby, who is used as bait, over and over, may have been stolen. When you ask what happens to the babies you are told that the same babies are sold over and over again until they get too old, or too sick, or too malnourished to be "marketable." Or until they die.

Finally, you are told that the foreign government is trying to do something about the situation and you sign an application with the agency and thank them for telling you the truth. You go home to wait for at least six weeks, and while you wait you prop up a Polaroid snapshot on your bedside table and every night say a prayer for the baby who will never be your baby.

∼

You might not have gotten that far. You might have sent for an agency brochure and worn out its glossy pages of pictures until you found and fell in love with a little boy from the Philippines. You might have finished your application, paid the initial fee, completed your home study, obtained three certified copies of proof of infertility, only to get a letter in the mail that said, in essence, no adoption for you.

You didn't qualify! "WHY?" you probably shouted at the letter. Maybe a rule had changed and you were too old, according to the new policies. Or was it something about your home study? Or something in one of the personal letters of recommendation, written by someone you didn't know very well but had an impressive letterhead that the social worker told you would carry the kind of clout you needed?

Although you might wonder about all these things, you might never know why you were turned down.

∼

Maybe you were not childless or infertile at all. Maybe you sat with your family one night and watched 20/20 and said to yourself:

"I'm going there. As soon as I stop crying, I am calling ABC to ask for their information packet. I am going there, and I won't come back until I have one of those children. There may be thousands of mes, but there are hundreds of thousands of them, and they are doomed without us."

You might finish your paperwork in record time, get a loan from the bank, start a donation drive at your church, and purchase your tickets to go with a group who saw the same program and felt the same calling.

You might get to Romania and say you want to go to "one of the awful places" like you saw on 20/20, and when you finally find someone with the right connections to get you into the Camin Spital, it is a place so *awful* that it stuns your senses and makes you want to run out of the door and keep running.

But you don't. Instead, you see a bright-eyed little Gypsy boy who asks you for gum, but seems to be asking for everything in the world you have to offer. The moment is surrounded by magic and you feel the chemistry. You want to take this little boy home.

You might make final arrangements with surprising ease, and close your ears when you hear the question: "Why are you taking damaged goods when there are so many healthy babies?" You might find everyone so cooperative that you wonder about it until you go to pick him up and he's not there. "He's run away," they tell you, but their eyes shift around, and you think they are lying.

It doesn't matter, at that point, how you feel. There is nothing you can do. They say they will call you if the child is found. But you don't count on it. After all, he is a Gypsy.

They do not call. No one answers the phone at the number you were told to call. When they do answer, the line is disconnected as soon as you begin to speak. You know you have to give up, but you don't want to and cannot. Some internal force has taken over and is driving you. You have less than two weeks left in the country to answer your calling.

With one week left, you go to the orphanage where you had heard the comment about "damaged goods and lots of healthy babies," but you don't see the babies, and instead you are taken to a room full of toddlers who are doomed to the awful place you've just come from unless they are adopted.

Twenty toddlers sit in their beds, silently rocking, in a tiny, darkened room. One of them stops her rocking to look at you. Her eyes follow every step you take. When you look at her, you see an unusually beautiful child, a curly-haired girl with eyes that take up half of her face. You connect. Cautiously, because you were burned before and you are trying very hard not to hope too much, you examine the medical record with the Romanian doctor, who says "she is dystrophic" (or failure to thrive) but is otherwise "normal." Then she adds, "But who knows? She has just arrived here from the dystrophic unit and no one knows her case."

You go ahead with her adoption, and, in less than a week, she is with you alone in a hotel room. She throws the food in your face when you attempt to feed her. She screams. She won't stop screaming and you can't stop her. She is inconsolable.

She doesn't stop screaming on the airplane either. And you sit beside her searching your mind for answers and only find questions. And you say to yourself what you know is true: "My life will never be the same."

EXPECTATIONS MIGHT NOT BE MET

You might get off that plane and take your screaming child home, and expect that she will stop when she has a chance to adjust. Your hopes might rise a little when she gets better and starts eating. But the mood lift doesn't last because she still has spells and goes completely out of control. You take her to the doctor then. And you learn that she may be seriously disturbed and so developmentally delayed that she may never recover and may be permanently damaged or retarded. You're told to take her home and love her. You wonder if you can.

You knew something was wrong, but you didn't expect your adopted child's situation to be so severe.

Once you start to accept the diagnostic possibilities, you expect that there are community-based services for your child, but the ones she really needs are the very ones that she is not eligible for unless you pay for them yourself. Why? Because your insurance company has a cap on allowable reimbursement for anything labeled "mental health." But you don't even have a label yet because it seems that every expert you talk to says something different, or are they all saying the same thing, but using different terms, and they seem to be speaking different languages.

You might get a referral to a big medical center in California where there is an in-patient unit for diagnosis and initiation of therapy and two psychologists who have special knowledge and experience with children from the same foreign country you went to. When the referral is accepted, you might expect they have some realistic payment plan for people like you, who are still paying for your adoption, but they don't, so you take a deep breath and ask "how much?" and they say "$67,000." **$67,000!**

You are somewhat relieved because at last you know what your child needs, but how will you pay this price? You know insurance will pay only $6,000 of that because of its cap. You decide not to take that route yet, but instead take your adopted child to the public school system, where by law she should get the kind of services and attention she needs. They drag their feet and don't provide the services until you call the California psychologist and get a strong letter in reply that forces the school to provide them.

What went wrong? Or, more accurately, what didn't?

 ◆ You did not expect the child to have such a serious problem, because she didn't look much different from the others in her group at the orphanage and the doctor there told you she was just small, but otherwise normal. She did have serious problems and she wasn't normal.

- ◆ You expected her to improve over time and with loving attention, but she didn't. Instead, she got worse.
- ◆ You expected that even in the face of serious complex problems, professional specialists would agree regarding her diagnosis and therapy. But they didn't.
- ◆ You expected your health insurance plan to pay for most of the care your child needed. They didn't. They would pay for less than 10 percent of it.
- ◆ You expected your school system to provide the services your child was qualified for under the law. It didn't.

You might have been one of the twenty families who were in the military services and adopted children whose screening tests for hepatitis B were positive, but you had been told "no problem" by the foreign doctor because the child had never had any illness that suggested active liver disease. You believed her. After all, she was a pediatrician working in the orphanage.

But when you saw the pediatric gastroenterology specialist at a big research hospital, your child was put in the hospital for liver tests and a biopsy, and you sat with your husband, and heard the words "Your child has active liver disease and it is progressive." Next, you heard that the only treatment was "still in the experimental stages." Experiment? You wonder about that word and can't get it out of your mind.

The rest of your story might go like this:

"The studies are very promising," the doctor continues, "and although the drug trial being used is very expensive, your child will probably qualify for inclusion in the national study under way."

Before you enroll in the national study, you ask what would happen without the "drug trials" and are told, "According to what we know now about this disease and its natural history, unless its progress is arrested medically, your child will be a candidate for liver transplant by the time he is thirty years old."

Meaning what? Meaning that unless a "medical cure" is discovered in the interim, your child will die of liver failure before he reaches full manhood. The only thing that will save him when his liver fails is organ transplant, and that has its own set of problems.

You had expected the parasites, anemia, and even the vitamin deficiency, but had not expected a progressive, life-threatening medical disorder. When that disorder was a communicable disease stemming from an infection, you had not expected it to be incurable. You had not expected a disease that, even when progress was slowed or "in remission" or "arrested," could still be communicated to others around him.

~

Or, you might have been the family who completed an adoption of a little boy in Romania, and everything was progressing perfectly until you learned during a medical exam (that was supposed to be a formality) that your new child had tuberculosis and couldn't immigrate to the United States, whether he was adopted or not. "It doesn't matter," the consular staff person at the U.S. embassy said to you in a matter-of-fact tone of voice, "that he is your child now. What matters is that he will not be admitted to the United States with active tuberculosis."

You might learn, for the very first time, that it is a rigidly enforced policy of the CDC (Centers for Disease Control in Atlanta, Georgia) not to permit your child to immigrate until he was cured, or the disease was *fully arrested* and you could prove it.

You learn that the treatment process, if all goes well (and it doesn't always), will take a minimum of one year, and probably more than that.

"Furthermore," the staff person continues in a not-so-matter-of-fact voice, "this doesn't change his adoption status. He is your son now, and your responsibility. You must ascertain that he receives the treatment he needs."

But this is not easy. It is not easy because you must convince a foreign government, one that is very short of medical re-

sources, to provide precious treatment and long-term hospitalization for your child. At the same time, there are many like
him with the same problem, who need the same treatment and
who have not been adopted by foreigners. The government officials may feel those children should be given priority over
your child, because they are not going to emigrate as soon as
the huge investment of time and energy is productive and the
disease is arrested.

It is not easy, but you do it anyway.

You leave your little boy behind in a hospital where there are
not any ancillary services like education or social work, but you
leave him there because they are willing to take him IF you
are willing to send/donate the pharmaceuticals and medical
supplies that are not available in the country. For at least one
year.

It is not easy, but you do it.

It gets harder. It is harder when you hear that the expensive
medicine you are mailing to him is being pilfered off somewhere and sold on the black market and never gets to your
child. It is hard to find someone who is going into the country
to hand-carry the medicine and hand-deliver it to your child,
who is lying there not getting any better and is so far behind
on his treatment schedule that another year's delay is predicted.

Hearing nothing but bad news, you might respond to advice,
accept what seems inevitable, and fully prepare yourself to give
this child up, then start all over with another adoption. You
might be in the midst of this process and consider it the hardest
thing you have ever done in your life, and suddenly another
family comes forward and offers to adopt the child.

You might seize the opportunity to make a private arrange-
ment with this other family, who are willing to assume all the
risks and responsibility. You agree to allow them to adopt your
child if they find a way to help him enough to get him to this
country.

You might go through this, but think you are in a recurring
nightmare when you hear that as soon as he was brought to the
United States by the new family, he was taken to a doctor who
put him in the hospital for tests and discovered that their little
boy—your little boy, once—never had tuberculosis at all. He
had been misdiagnosed in the first place.

～

The nightmare finally ended for this boy and for both of his families. Today he is thriving, healthy, and normal. He is doing well in school and is described as a "very happy child." Both families are pleased, especially the first American family who did so much and went through so many heartaches to save a little boy. The two families stay in touch with each other.

The nightmare could start all over, however, for another foreign child who has been diagnosed with tuberculosis and cannot immigrate to the United States. The nightmare could recur, and is likely to, because tuberculosis is a major health problem in many developing countries where there are adoptable children.

We cannot prevent the nightmare of tuberculosis in children and the effect it has on their lives when they have no possibilities unless they find homes and can immigrate to a country that has health care resources. We can, however, reduce the number of nightmares.

How? By telling this child's story and letting it serve as an example for other courageous families to follow. In telling the story, many of the events that went wrong with this child's adoption and immigration can be prevented next time around.

Nothing went wrong with this adoption. It proceeded almost perfectly. What went wrong was immigration. Immigration to the United States is restricted for certain communicable diseases, and tuberculosis is one of them.

～

The above two stories are about communicable disease and how many things can go wrong when American families adopt children who suffer from them. There are many others. Even though the diseases are different, the major points are the same.

♦ Immigration to the United States is restricted for several communicable diseases. Tuberculosis is one of them; HIV is another. To confirm the diagnosis of tuberculosis, good X-ray and laboratory services are required.

♦ Because the incidence of TB is very high in many developing countries, many children are immunized with a vaccine (usually called BCG). Effective vaccination will often cause the TB skin test (TINE test or PPD) to be positive.

♦ Because the diagnosis can be very confusing in children, it is advisable for adopting parents to attempt to get a second opinion before giving up on an adoption. Often, but not always, the U.S. embassy has a health officer or a list of licensed physicians. Even if in-country consultation is obtained, however, it is advisable to communicate with your personal physician or pediatrician at home and ask for advice. It is surprising the amount of consultation that can take place with modern communications and express mail.

♦ Tuberculosis is a treatable disease, and most children who have it can be cured with appropriate therapy. Because of the characteristics of the TB germ, treatment is prolonged, as was the case with this boy. Some families may desire to make arrangements for treatment of the child in the foreign country rather than give the child up. Usually, this is prolonged and can be expensive. But it can be lifesaving.

A child might be spared misdiagnosis and unnecessary treatment if proper medical attention is obtained early. Parents and children might be spared the agony of separation. A child may be cured or saved—one who really has tuberculosis.

HOW TO MAKE YOUR ADOPTION A SUCCESS

You might have been one of the parents who came forward, even went public, with a story in order to spare those who come after you. But you're not. "There, but for the grace of God go I," you think. Then you might wonder "What can I do to avoid this?" How can I make my adoption a success?

While there are no guarantees with adoption, there are certain steps you can take to help ensure yours will proceed smoothly. That is what the rest of this chapter is all about. We can only make suggestions, based on our personal experiences, which have been, in turn, highlighted and influenced by the personal experiences of others. Before we continue, we would like you to have our personal version of your rights. Read them. Then read them again. Keep them in mind as you read the rest of this chapter.

We believe it is okay to:

◆ Want a child desperately.
◆ Feel more desperate as your age increases and your nest stays empty.
◆ Want to "replace" a loss.
◆ Want to rescue or "save" a child.
◆ Be mushy, sensitive, have empathy, and respond instinctively to the *pull, calling,* or *chemistry* of the situation.
◆ Seek guidance and need advice.
◆ Fail to rescue and let go.

Once you have given yourself permission to have these feelings and motivations, you will be able to bring them to a level of awareness, called consciousness, instead of keeping them buried. If they stay buried, they tend to pop out like little demons and will do so at inopportune moments. When that happens, they, not the cooler head that is needed, take control of the situation.

Many adopting parents feel embarrassed about these very normal, human motives and the feelings attached to them. They find them difficult to discuss. There is an underlying fear that if these motivations are expressed, the would-be parents will be perceived as people who are unrealistic or who have their head in the clouds and will lose it in a tense situation, like adoption. Underlying that fear is the dread that someone will misinterpret, pass judgment, and send a name to the bottom of a list.

When anyone fears or dreads negative repercussions, particularly when those repercussions may negatively affect one of the most important things they have done in their lives, like adopting a child, they stop talking about them. To keep them from popping out unexpectedly in conversations, they are often suppressed, hidden away in the subconscious. Communication stops, both internally and with others. This is exactly the opposite of what should be happening in the inner process of adopting a child.

THE FIRST STEP IN THE INNER ADOPTION PROCESS

The most important communication that takes place during the long and complex process of adopting a child is communication with yourself. Some of your feelings and motives may be buried or under the surface. If so, it is important to fish them out—for your own sake, not someone else's.

Before you consider all the what-to-dos of the adoption process itself, take a little time to put words to your own feelings and motives. Assess your own needs and try to describe how the adoption will answer those needs. Remember your rights while you do this. This is an essential part of taking good care of yourself and building the self-confidence you will need when you go through the process.

In his workbook on writing screenplays,[1] author/screenwriter Syd Field writes a chapter on character definition. Characters in a screenplay, like people in real life, are defined by their actions, by how they do what they do, and how they say things rather than what they say. Before writing the play or anything else, Field advises the would-be script writer to define the dramatic need of the main characters. Defined as "what your character wants to get, gain or achieve," dramatic need provides the energy that fuels all of their action. Without it, the character has no definition and action cannot take place. Without action, there is no play. (Or no one would produce it.) It doesn't happen.

Think of yourself as the main character in a play you are writing. The plot of the play is the story of your adoption. The ending is your dream of how it will be to hold that child in your arms. Define yourself in terms of your dramatic need. What is it? Do you need to love, to nurture, to procreate, to fill an emptiness, to be needed, to save someone? Identify and define your needs. *Your needs*, not your spouse's or the social worker's or the child's.

Do you have a need for a child of your own? Do you have a need to give, to rescue a child who may be doomed by circumstances? Are both factors present? Have you lost a child in the past, or had miscarriages? Do you have a need to replace that child, to fill up the emptiness that has created? Is your only living child suffering some serious illness or a handicapping condition?

Once you have answered these questions in words, you will have identified your needs. Now it is time to define those needs, to give each one three dimensions. You may find it helpful to write down what comes to mind when you elaborate. Write it in your personal journal or diary or open a new file on your computer. No one else needs to ever see it. Write as much as you can about your needs and motivation in this adoption script you are writing. Write down the ending. Your dream.

Most professionals who have written about the psychological process of adoption write about the dream child or fantasy child that most adoptive parents have. The fantasy child is always there. Sometimes the child has a name, a face, a certain personality. Other times, the fantasy child is featureless, but has a certain aura. Although it may be important for you not to let this fantasy child be too specific, too much of a prescribed expectation (a setup for disappointment), it is important for you to know what your fantasy is. It won't go away. It is best for you to know it. Write a description of your fantasy child. If you are married, ask your spouse to do the same. Record it so that you cannot change it.

When you have completed this personal assessment, when you have spelled your needs out, when you know how your dream ends, you will find it much easier to cope with the normal stresses of adoption. Once you have written your thoughts, you will find it much easier to communicate with others about the adoption. It is even easier to fill out forms or be specific about your "preferences" (sex, age, etc.), if and when you are asked.

But, most importantly, you will have started a valuable process. You will have a power you did not have before. You will be better prepared to cope with the stress and anxiety because of an increased self-awareness. Consciousness is a powerful tool. Your reactions in a tense or stressful situation will be under control.

MANAGING RISKS

By now, you have learned a lot. You know the basic process of foreign adoption. You are aware of many of the special needs that abandoned children will bring with them. You are in touch with your own feelings and understand your motivation. After you have made the decision to embark on an intercountry adoption, you borrowed the experience of other parents by talking to them or reading their stories. You know the risks. It is time to put yourself in the picture. How will you manage those risks so that they are minimized or avoided entirely in your adoption?

Because the road ahead of you looks very long right now, and because it has many unmarked branches, you probably need some kind of map. A travel guide might be helpful, and a compass.

The following basic primer of risk management for intercountry adoption is merely a guide. Because a systematic approach is needed, we have divided it into three stages representing the time segments of the adoption process: preadoptive, intraadoptive, and postadoptive. All three must be planned ahead. Most of these plans can be accomplished only within the window of opportunity provided you early in the process.

PHASE ONE: THE PREADOPTIVE PERIOD

The preadoptive phase is that period of time you spend in your home country getting prepared to adopt. Being well prepared involves many things: assembling documents, developing a plan and a fallback plan, obtaining professional guidance, continuing the inner adoption process and taking good care of yourself in the process.

Be Prepared, Be Prepared, Be Prepared. If there is ever a time in your life to be a little compulsive, this is it. Make lists. Check them, not twice or thrice, but daily. Make a PERT chart or action plan—whatever you want to call it—and assign a due date to each task or action. Establish deadlines and try to stick to them.

Assemble Forms and Information Packets. Focus on requirements and eligibility criteria. There are four major sources of this information:

1. U.S. Department of Immigration and Naturalization Services (INS).

2. U.S. Department of State.
3. Adoption agencies
4. Parent organizations and periodicals written for adoptive parents.

INS provides packets of information that contain all U.S. government requirements for immigration, visa clearance, and any restrictions to immigration of children adopted in foreign countries. The State Department provides information on the specific requirements of the "sending government," including the most recent legislation pertinent to intercountry adoption. The State Department also provides current advisories to any U.S. citizen who is planning to travel to a foreign country.

You can obtain these packets by telephone request. INS is listed under the Department of Justice in the federal government section in the yellow pages of your local telephone directory. Or you can call INS in Washington, DC, and make the same request. Be prepared to wait for a telephone line; be prepared to never hear a real voice; be prepared to play telephone roulette and respond to a mind-boggling menu of questions. Be prepared to state the specific country or geographic region in which you are interested.

When you receive the packet, do everything on the list, even if someone tells you that it isn't necessary for adoption. Many of the regulations have nothing to do with adoption per se, but are requirements for immigration.

Complete, Sign, and Date All Forms. Some government agencies still discard any incomplete forms. Others require you to fill documents out in black ink or number 2 pencils. Follow any and all directions explicitly. Don't expect anyone to return a form to you for completion. Make copies of everything you fill out and file them. When photographs are required, always get extra copies. If the original requires notarization, have all copies notarized.

Be prepared to feel some invasion of your privacy. You will be mug-shot, fingerprinted, and checked for any police records. You may be required to provide confidential medical records, such as affidavits of infertility.

There are lots of war stories about adopting parents who had to delay their adoptions because of a missing piece of paper. One adopting family discovered, on the day before departure, that their fingerprint files were missing. Several have arrived in foreign countries and discovered an expired home study. (Most home studies are good for only one year.) Incomplete paperwork always threatens to delay adoption.

Be Prepared Financially. Adoption is big business, and foreign adoption is very big business. As obnoxious as the thought might be that children are viewed as commodities, accept it. It is reality. Be prepared for a $20,000 minimum cost (an average total that includes both out-of-pocket expenses and agency fees, compiled from six adoption agencies working in Romania in 1993[2]). Be prepared financially to spend longer than you planned in hotels in the country of your destination, and be prepared to spend almost twice what you anticipate during the intraadoptive period. You may not have to. But be prepared.

Anticipate. Expect the unexpected, out-of-pocket expenses for your child in the postadoptive period. If your child needs special services or certain kinds of specialty care, he may not be eligible for those services until he is a U.S. citizen—and that may not occur until months after the adoption is finalized. Even if the child qualifies or meets eligibility criteria, some of the specialty care required (or desired) for the child may not be covered by insurance or other third-party payers.

Know your health care coverage policies inside out. Mental health care is the most common problem. There is a cap on allowable reimbursements for most mental health care. In medical care, some insurance companies will not cover conditions that are categorized as "preexisting." Find out all you can about your insurer's policy on mental health care. The more you know at this stage, the less likely you are to have an unpleasant shock later on. You may never have to utilize mental health coverage but it can't hurt to know the details.

Research Adoption Agencies. Obtain information from several adoption agencies, even if you have selected one or even if you are planning a private adoption. Their brochures and pamphlets are filled with valuable information that is not available elsewhere. If you plan to select an agency (and it is always recommended that you do), compare notes, prices, and requirements. They vary.

The agency you select is the first important choice you will make in a long process of decision making. Consider your choices carefully. Do their fees meet your budget? Do you meet their basic eligibility requirements? Does their mission statement mesh with your own philosophy?

Some agencies are religious organizations. It may be important to you to be sure that your spiritual values and beliefs are compatible. You may be asked to sign a statement of faith and intent regarding the child you plan to adopt.

If possible, talk to a family who has been through an adoption with the agency you favor before signing up. Be prepared to pay part of your fee up front, when you apply, and the balance as you go along. Remember this: Fees are not refundable. There is no such thing as a money-back-guarantee-if-you-are-not-satisfied or a refund if things go wrong.

Discuss and Sketch Out a Fallback Plan. Chances are, you won't need it. But if things go wrong mid-process, you will be glad you have it. If, for example, you get caught in an unannounced adoption shutdown in the country you plan to go to, or if that occurs just after you arrive, a fallback or alternative plan may enable you to complete your adoption elsewhere. Most international adoption agencies serve several countries in the region.

Get Professional Guidance. Anticipatory guidance is counseling or professional guidance that you receive to prepare you for a future event. It is worth its weight in gold. Adoption agencies provide some limited guidance, but they focus on the *process of adoption* rather than health concerns and psychosocial issues. They are experts at making arrangements and serving as an interface between the governmental, legal, and procedural facets of adoption.

Many adoption agency social workers are not "clinical" caseworkers. If you are assigned a caseworker, find out what kind of social worker he or she is. (Don't be embarrassed to ask.) If you have psychosocial issues you wish to discuss—at any phase of foreign adoption—ask for a referral or seek out a guidance counselor. This may be one of the most valuable ways for you to avoid serious problems during and after adoption.

Anticipatory guidance may identify areas that need more attention or counseling in order to prevent serious problems. Marriage counseling is the most frequent area of need. In general, couples who adopt are more likely to have disrupted marriages than couples who do not adopt their children. Managing stress is a major factor in risk management. The stress of long, complex infertility workups is often underestimated. Applying to an agency and going through all the red tape adds another layer of stress to those already encountered. A third layer is added if and when the adopted child has serious health, mental health, or developmental problems.

Change, whether adverse or positive, is always stressful. Adoption of a child represents major change in any family. Even the smoothest adoption, therefore, is stressful. Although stress, in and of itself, is not a problem (or a pathological process or a disease), it has a way of seeking out the weak points in relationships. Old marital issues often resurface with a vengeance when a child is being added to the family. When the child is coming from a foreign environment, and particularly when the child has been wounded by that environment, the normal stress factors multiply exponentially. "It's like walking through a psychiatric minefield," one adopting parent said.

Professional guidance before and during stressful events should be viewed as both preventative and interventive. Prevention allows you to identify risks and plan how to deal with them. Intervention is called for if the anticipatory guidance reveals serious underlying issues that may jeopardize either the successful completion of adoption, the marriage, or the successful parenting of the child.

Be aware of the "actuarial tables": Statistically, your marriage is in more jeopardy than the adoption if things go wrong. What are the two most common marital risk factors?

1. The marriage is jeopardized when one parent, most often the

mother, is forced to choose between the child and the spouse. In the majority of such instances, the mother chooses the child.

2. The marriage is jeopardized when fundamental differences exist regarding childrearing practices and philosophies. Conflicts arise that are not resolvable. Disagreements about childrearing quickly snowball into major conflicts when children have problems. The bigger the problem, the bigger the snowball.

Even in ideal marriages, parents are not always in agreement regarding childrearing philosophies. The preadoptive phase is the ideal time to discuss these issues. If there are significant points that do not seem to be resolved by frank discussion, a session or two with a professional guidance counselor may prove invaluable.

Anticipatory Guidance on Health Matters. In all foreign adoptions, a visit to the family physician, nurse clinician, or pediatrician is an important and often overlooked event. This appointment should be scheduled during the preadoptive phase. It is your "prenatal" visit.

Make a list of questions and take the list with you. Parents-to-be often report that they "forgot to ask the most important question." Don't be afraid to know more than the doctor about the part of the world you are going to, or the special needs inherent in all foreign adoptions. The physician is a resource, not always an expert. For example, all physicians have access to current CDC (Centers for Disease Control, Atlanta, Georgia) advisories and regulations.

Many communicable diseases (tuberculosis and AIDS, for example) and some other health conditions carry restrictions or quotas that restrict or prohibit immigration. A known diagnosis of mental retardation, for example, places a child under a quota restriction and requires a different kind of visa for immigration. CDC is the regulatory agency, and your physician is a good source of "anticipatory guidance" on how those regulations may affect your adoption.

Remember: These communicable disease issues may have no

effect on adoption. They do, however, affect your child's immigration. You do not want to leave your newly adopted child in a foreign country because of an immigration restriction that you did not know about.

Finally, be certain to discuss finances with your primary health care provider. Review your health insurance policy and pay special attention to:

1. Any restrictions for coverage if there are preexisting conditions.
2. The extent and limitations of coverage for mental health conditions.

Do this regardless of the age of the child you are adopting. Babies less than six months of age can develop significant mental health problems later as a result of early trauma or disturbed relationships with a caregiver in an orphanage.

Ask the doctor what kind of information or records he or she may want and be prepared to locate them on your own. Neither agencies nor adoption councils require all of the records your physician may want or need to care for your child optimally.

Birth records are the most commonly omitted documents. When a medical record is being set up, the birth record is the first piece of paper in any standard file. When any growth, developmental, or health problem arises, information contained in birth records is not only the starting point, it is often the most important. If you possibly can, get birth records.

Plan to get hospital records if your child has any history of hospital care. You may not know this until you arrive in the foreign country. Be aware that smaller hospitals are called "clinics" in many foreign countries. If so, get in-patient records from the clinic. Be aware that when children are institutionalized, hospital records are often kept separately. They are usually not included at all in the orphanage files. Take note:

♦ Birth records and hospital records are not routinely included in most foreign adoption dossiers.
♦ These records are likely to contain vital information regarding your child's health.
♦ These records are rarely destroyed in the "sending county" (except in circumstances of war or natural disaster).

♦ Most likely, you will have to request—or even track down—these records on your own.

Remember the one-page sample "medical summary" from chapter 4? If not, reread it now. It is a perfect example of an incomplete record. It is a perfect example of what you *do not want* to show up with as your only medical summary.

Write It Down. If you have not already done so, develop the habit of documenting systematically. You do not need an elaborate scheme. Develop your own. There are a surprising number of how-to books available on the subject of journal keeping. We offer the following model:

Divide your journal into three sections: a log/appointment calendar, a to-do list, and a narrative journal. If you use a computer, the journal portion can be cut-and-pasted to a separate and protected file. Cut/copy and paste is also useful for the log/appointment and to-do sections. Unfinished to-dos can be rolled over to the following day. Put done to-dos in **bold**. They leap off the page and give you a boost each morning.

By the end of your preadoptive phase, you will have generated a surprising amount of systematically organized information. This includes addresses, telephone numbers, lists, notes, anecdotes, information and personal resources, appointments, and reminders. You will also be into the habit of telling your story—as it happens.

Taking Care of Yourself. All of the things you have done so far are part of taking care of yourself. You are preventing inconvenience or (sometimes) agony, when you wade through paperwork systematically. You are making things easier for yourself when you make a careful choice of agencies, because a compatible agency is your best friend if things begin to go wrong. You are giving yourself a sense of security about parenting when you talk to the doctor, make plans to get the records, and arrange the insurance so that the problems will be covered.

You are learning a lot about yourself when you keep that journal. You will be able to apply that knowledge with competence when things get tense or stressful. Your mushiness won't get in the way. When stress occurs, your head will rule your heart because you understand that heart and can control it. You will be able to think on your feet, and your heart (we promise) will continue to beat.

You are taking care of yourself when you seek out guidance or see a counselor. There are two situations that cry for this:

- One, if you identify a serious difference of opinion when you review things with your spouse and can't seem to talk it out. Guidance is called for then, or marital counseling.
- The second issue is less common, but calls for guidance. When you thought about your dream child and your relationship to him or her, no doubt you reflected on your relationship with your own parents and/or had some flashbacks about when you were a child. If, in the course of these recollections, you recalled anything painful about your relationship (with your parents), patterns of parenting you do not want to recycle in your own parenting, or particularly if there was abuse or rejection, then get some guidance at once.

You are taking care of yourself because you are healing old wounds that have never before had an opportunity to heal. Adoption has provided that opportunity. You have put those issues in cold storage and put off dragging them out because they were not relevant to your life before adoption. Don't be afraid to drag them out. Professional guidance will work with you to see that your adoption goals are realized. If you were wounded as a child, it might interest you to know that wounded healers are the best healers. But before you are empowered to use your special gifts of intuition, sensitivity, and strong, fighting spirit, you need to be in touch with your feelings. As Clarissa Pinkola Estés said in her audiotape "Warming the Stone Child,"[3] "if you can't feel, you can't heal."

You are not only taking care of yourself, but you are taking care of the child you plan to adopt. You are preventing the recycling pattern that often occurs when significant stress arises.

Prepare Yourself for the Trip. Take care of yourself in tangible ways as well as psychological ones. Leave some room in your suitcase for personal items, like your cosmetics, or a soft pillow to sleep on, a book to read, or your favorite brand of coffee. Take something out of your bags if you have to. You are not being self-indulgent. You are taking care of yourself. Remind yourself that you are doing this so that you can be a more secure base for your child.

Don't forget your own health care. It's surprising how many adopting parents do. In addition to the baby formula and Tylenol and liquid vitamins and antibiotics you are taking for your child *just in case,* pack up a health maintenance kit for yourself. Take along over-the-counter medicines like Imodium for diarrhea, decongestants, and analgesics even if you never have colds or traveler's diarrhea or headaches. You don't want the first time you are afflicted to be in a foreign country that might have a limited supply of pharmaceuticals.

Be sure to take more than you need of any prescription medications. If you are an average adopter, you will be in your child's native country longer than you planned. If you wear glasses, take a copy of your prescription along, or a spare pair of glasses, if you have one. If you wear contacts, take plenty of solution.

Be certain to take an emergency ID bracelet or dog tag if you have a severe allergy or a medical condition that requires special attention. Wear it at all times, even when you are "dressed up." Don't rely on your passport or the card in your wallet. They can be stolen. An unconscious accident victim is a common target for street predators. In any country.

Start well ahead of time on your shots and immunizations. Review the ones you need for the specific country you are entering and the ones every foreign traveler needs "just in case." Be aware that some immunizations, like hepatitis B, require a series of shots, spaced apart, at monthly intervals. If you slip up on the time schedule, ask your doctor if you can take a syringe and a vial of vaccine along.

Be informed about hepatitis. Hepatitis is a big killer. There are several hepatitis viruses at large out here, and by the time this book is in print, there may well be more. Although they all cause liver disease, they behave differently, like people in the same family. In infants and young children, the medical jargon for the way different strains of virus are transmitted from one person to another differs.

Hepatitis A, for example is transmitted through the gastrointestinal tract and is caught by contact with contaminated material coming from the intestinal tract of someone ill or coming down with the virus. Hepatitis A is most contagious during its incubation period—*before there are any signs of specific illness.* Poor hand washing in institutions is commonly the way the staff or visiting adults become infected. Children, being children, spread the disease easily from one to another— particularly in the crowded conditions usually found in institutional settings. Children, however, may never show the yellow jaundice that differentiates the disease from other systemic illnesses. In institutions, hepatitis A spreads like wildfire.

Hepatitis A does not yet have a vaccine, per se. However, the disease can be prevented by a single injection, albeit a large one, of gamma globulin. Remember: The so-called half-life for the period of effective immunity is limited for any gamma globulin shot. After ninety days, there is no longer reliable protection unless you get another shot. Gamma globulin, however, is widely available in many countries. If you anticipate having to get a GG injection somewhere overseas, it is best to bring along your own disposable syringes.

Hepatitis B is blood borne, like HIV (AIDS virus). It is most commonly transmitted by contaminated needles. The screening test for hepatitis B done in many foreign countries only indicates that the child has been exposed. It does not tell whether or not the child has, or has ever had, active liver disease. There is immunization for hepatitis B.

As hepatitis viruses multiply and march through the alphabet, the information about them is outdated as soon as it is in print. The best way to keep yourself and your family protected is to take advantage of educational activities. Go to lectures for parents on the subject. Ask your primary health care physician for copies of information bulletins and alerts. Ask for the current recommendations of the CDC (Centers for Disease Control) or from the American Academy of Pediatrics "Red Book," which is updated and published annually.

CDC information bulletins, published periodically, will also provide current updates on visa and immigration limitations and quotas for all communicable diseases that fall under restrictions. Keep current.

If you are taking any controlled-substance drugs, like sedatives, tranquilizers, or major painkillers, be sure to carry a doctor's letter that lists them by the same name that is on the bottle and states clearly that they are medically necessary and are for your personal use only. Be prepared to show this letter at customs when you arrive. Do not bury it in a suitcase. Put it in your carry-on luggage or in your purse. Remember: Customs officials are always on the lookout for drug traffickers. Anyone carrying "suspicious material" without a doctor's note attached may be subjected to body searches, interrogation, or even detainment.

PHASE TWO: THE INTRAADOPTIVE PERIOD

The intraadoptive phase is that period of time you will spend in the foreign country. Three things will be happening during this time: you will be finalizing the selection of the child you want to adopt; you will be finalizing the foreign adoption and U.S. immigration procedures; and you will be initiating the process of transition of your chosen child into your family.

One adoptive parent described the intraadoptive period as "herky-jerky." Things are either moving at a crash-course pace with several things happening at once or everything seems to bog down and screech to a crawl. The latter, the bog-down period, is most difficult to tolerate.

During the intraadoptive period, the most valuable assets a parent can have are a high level of consciousness, strong intuition, and good observational skills. The latter are particularly important when you visit the orphanage where your child is waiting.

Be Aware, Be Attentive, Beware. A heightened state of awareness and strong intuition are the best friends one can have on foreign soil. Maintaining attention may be difficult and requires some discipline at first. The combination of jet lag and the tension of an adoption-about-to-happen is very distracting.

Instinct and intuition are powerful tools. Adopting families should trust them. They can save you from dangerous situations or circumstances that may jeopardize your adoption.

A mother who was adopting a child told us the following story:

> "I don't know what made me walk away from that street mob," the adopting mother commented. "They erupted right after I turned the corner. I was standing there in the midst of them, and they looked pretty innocent. One of them even helped me locate myself and pointed out things on my map.
>
> "I just got this creepy feeling on the back of my neck. Then I heard this voice inside my head saying *attention!*—just like my driver says when he takes me across the street. The next thing I knew, I had folded my map and was walking real fast in the opposite direction. I was out of there."

Trust Your Instincts: Act on Them Both Emotionally and Objectively. The signals you get internally are rarely wrong, and even if you've had a false alarm, no harm is done. The rules apply to offices and orphanages as well as city streets. It helps to be one of those people who notices everything. Little details can be big tips that something is wrong.

> "Although everything seemed to be going smoothly during my final conference, I couldn't shake the feeling that something was wrong. We were going through that coffee ritual they do every morning. The director was droning on and on, reviewing all the stuff we had been through before. *Why are we sitting here like this?* I asked myself. *We've been through this before. Yesterday, in fact.* Then I noticed something and I knew. I looked at his hands and saw them shaking. His hands never shook before.
>
> "I had my child out of there in less than an hour. When we got to court, a clerk kept asking if I was from Italy. *Italy?* I wondered about that. Later, when the court procedure was over, I asked about it, discreetly—I wasn't out of the country yet. I was told that the orphanage director had some kind of deal going with the Italians. That explained why the director was pretty nervous when I showed up early and why he was

even more nervous when an Italian family showed up moments after I had left. It was never made clear what kind of "deal" it was, but it was inferred that it wasn't altogether legal.

"I was pretty lucky."

Yes, she was. But more than luck was involved.

Preparation, intuition, and good observational skills are your best weapons against things going wrong. Preparation will have familiarized you with the procedures and processes that are standard or usual. Armed with that knowledge, you are better able to recognize anything that is out of line, not quite right, or dishonest. You are protected from charlatans, opportunists, and corrupt baby dealers. When something is wrong in this regard, it is unusual for anyone to tell you. Some of the most valuable clues are:

◆ A sudden departure from expected routine (*you are taken to a street corner to meet the mother instead of some official office*).

◆ Behavior change in someone you are dealing with (*his hands are shaking, or his eyes shift around*).

◆ A person you have not met before shows up on your doorstep or in your hotel lobby and offers "assistance" or facilitation. Or someone you know in another capacity, like your driver, suddenly changes hats and wants to work as a facilitator.

◆ Almost anything involving an unanticipated request for money or material gifts.

Be Careful: Check It Out with Your Agency. This is a very difficult and sensitive topic. In some foreign countries, the money under the table, *bakshish,* or *dash,* is an expected part of any transaction. In others, it is not only unethical but illegal and punishable by the law if it constitutes bribery.

In the latter case, the attempt to make any kind of payment like this results in a tragic lose-lose-lose event: *The individual accepting the "bribe"* is fined, often jailed, and may be subjected to harsh punishment. *The bribing party* is also subject to fines and, although rarely detained, is usually asked to leave the country. *The child is not adopted and is, although I have never been clear exactly why, very unlikely ever to be adopted.*

Many adopting families are deeply moved by the circumstances in poor, underdeveloped countries, and are determined to make some contribution or donation. Their motives are humanitarian rather than bribery. When these humanitarian instincts are undeniable, it is usually advisable to act on them only after the adoption has been completed and you are out of the country. If that is your choice, be certain to make no promises, sign no papers, and tell no one of your intent when you are in-country. When you are back home, you can plan your donation with a much cooler head. And you can remain anonymous, if you wish.

You should also be aware that donations are always needed by the nonprofit organizations that are operating programs in developing countries. Some of these organizations allow the donor to specifically earmark donations. Others do not. In large humanitarian organizations that do allow this type of specified donation, for example, you may select one of a number of ongoing projects for your contribution. Some of the larger organizations have thousands of projects. If a food program for hungry refugee children is more to your liking than a water well development project, you can specify your wishes at the time you make your donation.

Many adoption agencies have a nonprofit wing if their adoption activity is not classified as nonprofit. One of the adoption agencies in Romania, for example, conducted a training program for social workers. Another had an orphanage-based program that facilitated the return of young children to their birth families. You may want to inquire about your agency's nonprofit activities and ask them what you can do to help support them.

Guidance During the Intraadoptive Period. *You're largely on your own. Read, review your material and ally with others like you.*

Your most powerful allies are other parents-to-be who are waiting for completion of adoptions. Among them, there may be some who are going through the process for the second or third time. They are not only a good source of practical advice, they are often a source of inside knowledge.

By the same token, beware of gossip and rumors that may be

circulating. They run rampant through the community of foreign adopters. Use good judgment in these situations. But don't let them scare you off. Chances are, the networking you do with other adopting families will continue into the postadoptive period. It is likely that you will make some close friends through your shared experiences.

Many needy foreign countries have international programs that employ professionals. These professionals may be available to you for consultation or guidance when you have questions, particularly those of an emergent medical nature.

Be careful. Inquire about any professional's background and credentials. Foreign environments are notorious hiding places for con men, charlatans, and impostors. Remember this when and if any person offers professional assistance. If someone introduces himself as "Doctor," ask him what kind of doctor he is. Ask to see a card or license. Don't ever be embarrassed to ask. No legitimate professional will be affronted or object to this type of question.

Write Everything Down and Review It Periodically. *Continue your journal.* It is easier to do if you have brought along a laptop computer—preferably one that runs on dual voltage or has easily rechargeable batteries. *A warning tip:* The current converters that are included in travelers' kits are not appropriate for computers. Most are manufactured with hair dryers in mind. Because computers run on very low voltage, the 1,500 watt current required for appliances like hair dryers will burn out most computers. Check with your manufacturer for appropriate converters. And remember: Adapter plugs *do not convert* current. Ever!

Document All Meetings with Officials. Take notes. Or take your laptop with a fresh supply of batteries. *Always* date your notes.

"I started having trouble with the social assistant assigned to our case," said one adopting mother. "She would say one thing one day and another the next.

"One day I got fed up. I had kept everything on my laptop, and I just called her over and showed it to her. 'See,' I said, pointing out my notes of January 4th, 'this is what we discussed and this is what you said then. I am sure you just forgot.'

"Of course, she remembered when I showed her the computer, even though she didn't read English well. There was no trouble after that. The girl was probably more inept than devious."

Document Your Observations When Visiting Your Waiting Child at the Orphanage. While you are going through transition/waiting periods and observing your child, one of the most valuable bits of documentation is an "average day description." Take one full day, get the needed permission, and simply follow your child through an average day. Keep a log. Write down everything he does and when he does it. Take pictures or videos if you are permitted—and if you are convinced that personnel will act "natural" when a camera lens is present. Add your "average day description" to your journal. When you are home, use the material you have gathered together to begin his or her baby book.

If your child has a developmental problem and you seek assistance at a child development clinic during the postadoptive period, you may encounter a request for your "average day description." In addition to providing a new one that describes an average day in your home, by all means add the original you did in the orphanage. The child development team you are seeing will welcome this material and find it very helpful in evaluating your child's problems.

Because transition periods are so important, we have devoted the next chapter in its entirety to this topic.

Take Care of Yourself. When you do, it is like putting on your own oxygen mask before you put on your child's when an airplane is in trouble. If you are whole and healthy, you are much better able to care for a child and meet the challenges of parenthood.

When you enter adoption with open eyes, know yourself and your dreams and motivations, and when you take care of yourself, having learned from another's experience, you have managed the risks involved in foreign adoption. Not all the risks can be eliminated. But all of them can be managed.

If risks are managed well, lives and the quality of lives are no longer in such terrible jeopardy. Dreams have not been destroyed. You, as an adopting parent, are less likely to suffer the kind of wounds that carry scars for a lifetime. Your family, although stressed and challenged, is unlikely to be demolished. For a waiting child in need of a family, your family is most likely to succeed in becoming his "forever family."

REFERENCES

1. Syd Field, *The Screen Writer's Workbook* (New York: Dell, 1984), pp. 53–61.

2. B. B. Bascom, *International Adoption,* Instructional Session presented at the Annual Meeting of the American Academy of Pediatrics. Washington, DC, November 1993.

3. Clarissa Pinkola Estés, *Warming the Stone Child: Myths and Stories About Abandonment and the Unmothered Child* (Boulder, CO: Sounds True Recordings, 1990). Write to 735 Walnut Street, Boulder, Colorado 80302.

9

Transition

Out of the dusk a shadow, then a spark;
Out of the cloud a silence, then a lark;
Out of the heart a rapture, then a pain;
Out of the dead, cold ashes,
Life again.

John B. Tabb: *"Evolution,"* 1884

Making the adoption process work for you and doing it right is the goal of every adoptive parent. In this chapter, the reader will find specific information on the intraadoptive and immediate postadoptive periods. Taken together, this time span marks the end of most of the red-tape process of adoption and initiates the inner process of establishing a permanent parent-child relationship. While parents are completing the legal processes of adoption, immigration, and naturalization, the child is undergoing the psychological process of transition from orphanage to the new home and parent. For foreign children coming out of institutions, many for the first time in their lives, this time of transition is often a critical period.

Adoptive parents need to be aware of the impact of the huge life-change their child is experiencing at this juncture. Very little is written about transition and its effect on adoption outcomes. Very few, if any, agencies include a planned or supervised transition program in their adoption package. In terms of adjustment, however, transition is an important first step in ensuring the emotional security of the child. With the proper approach at this phase, stressful and/or traumatic events that may permanently affect the child's adjustment to adoption can be minimized or avoided.

By now, the reader has a good idea of the social and physical world of children in institutions of eastern Europe and elsewhere. For the children incarcerated in the orphanages worldwide, that social and physical world is often the only one they have ever known. Until . . .

One day there is a commotion in the institution and strange people come into the room. They pick up a child and look the child over. They count fingers and toes. Maybe they smile, tickle, or even feed the child. They don't speak the child's language, they smell different and are dressed strangely. After a little while they leave.

Later, they return, these strangers with the strange smell and the strange looks. Then they do something really terrifying to the child. They take the child away from the only world he has ever known. They take the child away from the familiar smells and sights and away from the other children.

Imagine the anxiety a child removed from the only environment she has ever known experiences. Children are easily overwhelmed by new sights and activities, such as a ride in a car or on an airplane, a meal in a restaurant, staying in a hotel, or a walk along a noisy, congested street. For many institutionalized children, the trip home may be the first trip ever outside the confines of the orphanage. For some, it may be the first venture out of a building, or a room, or a crib.

Before bringing your child home, you will want to know as much as possible about your new family member.

- ◆ Before leaving your home, learn as much as possible about the developmental stage of the child by reading, observing other children in the family or neighborhood, volunteering at nursery schools, or attending adoptive family meetings and activities. For example, if you have never had a child, how are you to know what the normal activities of a, say, two- to three-year-old are?
- ◆ Prior to the adoption, send or take pictures of your entire family (including pets) to the orphanage of the child. Some-

times a tape of you speaking is helpful to leave with the child, especially if there is a delay in the adoption process (and assuming that a tape player is available). Have someone explain to the child any procedural delays during the adoption process, so he/she doesn't feel abandoned again.

◆ After adoption, but before leaving the foreign country, learn as much as possible about the child whom you have made part of your family, including specific details of the child's background. You may have to do some detective work.

BECOMING A NEW PARENT

Parents who are adopting children from foreign institutions begin the process of becoming a parent while the child is still in the institution. The process begins during a time of upheaval and change for both parent and child. The successful use of this transition time is the first challenge of adoptive parenthood. To avoid some of its pitfalls and take advantage of the opportunities it offers, adopting parents may wish to borrow another experience. A California couple has a story to tell that illustrates how much difference a good transition plan can make.

Catarina

Catarina's story starts in a remote village in the heart of Transylvania. As an infant, Catarina was abandoned to an orphanage. Her birth mother was a single parent, a vagrant Gypsy woman, impoverished and uncertain of the child's paternity.

I (Bascom) didn't know anything about her parentage or family situation when I first became aware of Catarina. She was one of a large group of dystrophic toddlers we decided to include in our ROSES project. The dystrophic children were always the most severely affected by the deprivation in orphanages. Catarina was no exception.

Slim and somber eyed, she wore the close-cropped haircut that most children had in orphanages. She was quiet and withdrawn and didn't interact with adults in her environment. But she did have a playmate and was much more animated when they were in the crib together.

A few months before opening our project site in this particular orphanage, I had gone to a Los Angeles church, La Canada Presbyterian, to make a presentation to a group that was interested in Romania. They were very moved by what they heard that morning; soon after, the church made Catarina's orphanage one of their missions for the following year. In 1991, a La Canada team of professionals and volunteers came to Romania to help the children in the dystrophic unit.

By the time the group arrived, we had (with her little friend's help) coaxed Catarina from her crib, and although her response was very slow, she was beginning to make progress in a preschool program run by the ROSES psychologist, Jeff. Something very special began to happen with Catarina, however, when the La Canada volunteer team arrived. Two of the volunteers—a childless, married couple—took a special interest in her and she began to respond. The two lost their hearts to Catarina.

Later, when the couple called from California, I was not surprised to hear that they had decided to try to adopt Catarina. Because adoption was closed at the time, they asked for my advice. I referred them to an agency that would handle their case as soon as Romanian adoption was reopened. In 1992, when adoption reopened, another obstacle presented itself: The new law didn't permit a family to choose their child. Exceptions were often made, however, when the family had selected the child before the process was put on hold or if the child had special needs.

The director of Catarina's orphanage was a shy and strict woman who refused to say the word "adoption" aloud. Aware of her sensitivity to the topic—she lived in fear of being accused of cooperation "under the table" and of being fined or punished—I had avoided the subject in my discussions with her. Still, her orphanage was so full of obviously abandoned babies and toddlers, I did not understand why she wasn't referring more for adoption. When I asked about the abandoned children in her orphanage, knowing that we had never seen a parent visit the dystrophic unit, the director's only reply was, "There is not one single abandoned child in this entire orphanage. All of them have parents and the parents come at least every six months."

Well. We had never seen a parent, not in more than a year. Not at night, when we made spot checks, or on weekends, when we came in. Not ever. Furthermore, we had documentation to confirm our suspicion of Catarina's abandonment. All visits were recorded in the file, and Catarina's files showed that there had been no parental visits since the day she was born.

Although those of us who worked for humanitarian organizations were strictly forbidden to work directly in adoptions (for many understandable reasons), we could give assistance when requested by agencies or adopting parents. Despite the promise I had made to never say the "A" word in the orphanage director's presence, I had to break the promise when the agency social worker called and asked if I would just inquire (or find out somehow) if Catarina was abandoned. The director, the agency worker told me, had refused to cooperate with them. When I met with the director and expressed an interest in Catarina's case (which was true) and told her honestly that someone had developed an interest in adopting Catarina, she made no reply, but was attentive.

I will never know what happened, but, over time, all of the pieces came together somehow. Soon after our conference, Catarina's orphanage director sent a letter of notification of Catarina's abandonment, and the local authorities began to search for the mother. At first, she didn't respond. We assumed that she, like many Gypsies, was wary of authorities and might not respond to a visit from the local police, which was the way parents were notified that an abandonment petition had been filed. Then one day, the birth-mother just appeared. The faith and persistence of the couple from California paid off. Two years and lots of hard work by an excellent case worker from the adoption agency later, the adoption went through.

The next time I saw the orphanage director, her attitude had softened. She opened her desk drawer and showed me a small stack of letters and photos that adoptive parents had sent her from all over the world. They had adopted their children before the law, she assured me, as she passed them to me for a look. Although she expressed some confusion about why the adoptive parents were so excited about the beautiful children in the photos, I think she knew in her heart what adoption had done for those children. Besides, she had kept those letters like treasures in her drawer, accessible for her quiet moments in that huge orphanage with all its nonabandoned children.

Although the director was committed to Catarina's adoption, there was a lot of tension for everyone while we waited through a series of monthlong periods. During this time, Catarina was beginning to slow down in her progress. She looked despondent much of the time. Her friend was still her only companion. She, like many other toddlers in programs, was outgrowing the resources available to her and really, really needed to go home. We could scarcely get her out of her room and couldn't imagine what she might do when her new parents came to pick her up.

With this thought in mind, we designed a transition program for Catarina. A team came together and began to function—case worker, adoptive parents, and psychologist. I stayed on the sidelines as consultant. We called it Catarina's Customized Exit Plan. (*Exit* is the word used in Romania for discharge.) Together, we prearranged psychological follow-up that would begin as soon as she arrived in California. Jeff worked with the adoptive parents and carefully planned a gradual, step-by-step program of transition. He estimated that the plan would take about one month, and Romanian friends of the adoptive parents opened their home to the family so they could avoid the expense of hotels. When the adoptive parents arrived to finalize Catarina's adoption, the transition plan was already in place.

The first challenge was getting Catarina to begin a separation process. Despite its inadequacies, she felt very secure in the rooms and halls of her section of the orphanage. Most of her outside time had been spent on a large balcony because her unit was on an upper floor and outside play areas were not accessible. At first we took her on walks with her new parents, then arranged overnight stays, then weekends away from the orphanage with them. Jeff supervised all orphanage visits and held frequent conferences with the new parents. One month turned into two, and the family wasn't home for Christmas as they had hoped. But the child was setting the pace and we were only setting the stage. Finally, the day arrived that all agreed would be Catarina's last one in the orphanage.

Catarina balked on the final day. She, like so many wounded children, had that wonderful intuition. Somehow, she knew this was no weekend visit. She knew her departure was going to be final. And she knew the changes that had recently come into her life were permanent. And she wasn't so sure she could deal with it. So she attached herself to her playmate and refused to let go. Then Jeff agreed to a plan to enlist the help of Catarina's best friend. She was finally convinced to leave by her friend, who walked out with her.

Today, Catarina attends school (her new mother says she's very smart) and is learning at a normal pace. Her attachment to her family is growing stronger every day. She sees a psychologist regularly to work out her residual problems. Her appearance is changed; her face has filled out and there is a happy glow in her eyes. Her orphanage haircut is gone. She is very lovely and has long dark curls.

Things weren't always easy for this child and her new parents. Catarina had her bad days in the first few months after adoption. The first night she was home she banged her head so violently that she drove a hole through the drywall of her new bedroom. But now, two years postadoption, she looks and acts like a normal child. This adoption story, no doubt, will continue its happy ending.

Several months after her adoption, I received a picture from Catarina's adoptive parents. Catarina is being held up in the air by her mother. Their faces are only inches apart and are full of joy and the wonder of discovery. The bond between them is almost visible.

Catarina's success story has not come easily. A lot of people have worked very hard: Her new parents persevered when everyone else was pessimistic. A skilled caseworker worked diligently with all the local authorities. Jeff never gave up on her at the orphanage, worked with her every day, then nurtured the family through transition. A gifted LA psychologist has provided treatment for Catarina and guidance for the family (but stays realistic and is always willing to work some more). A new mother and father have known the joy and fulfillment of parenting and healing a wounded child.

What made the difference? Why doesn't Catarina have a more severe attachment disorder? Why is this little girl growing and thriving developmentally? A lot of things made the difference. But one of the determining factors of importance—perhaps the most important one—was Catarina's Customized Exit Plan.

TRANSITION PLANNING

Children who have been in orphanages, or some other form of institutional environment, have a more critical need for transition than children who have been in homes.

1. Generally speaking, larger institutions are more neglectful of children's needs because of lower staff child ratios.
2. Qualitatively, the relationship between primary caregiver and child is usually much less nurturing in orphanages.
3. Abuse is more common in institutions. Child care practices that we would consider abusive, such as harsh punishment during toilet training, may be routine.

The institutional environment provides a very constricted, limited experience for children, even if there is no abuse or gross neglect. When a child leaves this life of dull monotony abruptly, that child is catapulted into a world of strangeness and sensory overload for which they are unprepared, both physiologically and emotionally.

Adopting parents are often unprepared to cope with the adopted child's behavioral response to leaving his orphanage environment. It helps to understand and be consciously aware of the challenges a child faces when he begins the transition and leaves his former home.

UNDERSTANDING A CHILD'S SEPARATION AND LOSS

It is difficult to think of adoption as a time of loss for children who are gaining an adoptive family. Children, however, will always react in some way to separation from and loss of the only home they have ever known. Often, children experience grief and sadness when they make these separations, particularly when friends and playmates are involved. Children, even abandoned and unattached children, do experience grief when they suffer a loss. In children, the grieving process probably lasts much longer than we think. When children come from an environment like Catarina's, the grief is often more pronounced because they harbor guilty feelings of having abandoned, deserted, or betrayed a friend.

Many adoptive parents will encounter this situation in the orphanages, particularly when they adopt a child more than two years of age. They often will find the child has a friend who is not a birth sibling, but with whom she is as closely attached as other children become to their true brothers and sisters. An important part of transition planning is to recognize the feelings the adopted child has when he or she must separate from that friend. Some adoptive parents have enabled their child to keep in touch with the friends they leave behind through correspondence or even telephone calls. Other parents have tried adopting both children. This is a complex issue for which we've seen mixed results, no matter how it's been handled. Adoptive parents can only observe their child's situation and make the decision they feel most comfortable with. It's a decision that's best made with the help of professional guidance.

Older children who have grown up in institutions have often had multiple placements, diminishing their opportunity for strong attachments and adding repeated separation and loss to their psychological histories. But, as I've said, toddlers and youths in institutions have often become strongly attached to a peer. Separation from and the loss of that friend will be emotionally traumatic and needs to be handled very sensitively.

UNDERSTANDING ATTACHMENT IN INSTITUTIONS

Children of institutions are often more attached to their physical environments than to any individual in that environment. It may take weeks, for example, before such a child is comfortable leaving her crib, his room, or the building.

The behavior of a child who is attached to a crib or room is very difficult for most adopting families to understand. They will probably focus on the fact that the object the child is attached to is scarred, old, dirty, or ugly. It is difficult to understand, for example, why a toddler will cling tenaciously to the rusting bars of crib with a sagging mattress that smells bad.

That the physical facility is in deplorable condition does not matter to the child, however, because it is the only environment that child has ever known and it often represents his only security. Remember that the crib is his fortress, and he guards it very well.

UNDERSTANDING THE CHILD'S BEHAVIOR

Throughout the period of transition your child will tell the story of his own experience through behavioral reactions. This is because institutionalized children rarely have verbal skills at a level that enables them to communicate effectively. It is important that adopting parents understand that many of the behaviors their child exhibits at this time are related to stress and are not necessarily reflective of the child's basic personality.

When you go to the orphanage to observe or interact with your child, you should watch for any signal of stress and anxiety: for example, increased rocking, withdrawal or retreat (the latter most often seen in young children), hiding under a crib, and/or retreating to a corner of a crib. Occasionally, the cues are not visible. An increase in heart rate may be the only sign that a child is experiencing stress from being removed from her familiar environment. While this is not a physical problem and does not represent any health threat, it is a sign of anxiety. You should recognize it as such; it may be your only clue that your child is stressed.

Self-injurious behaviors are a common sign of more severe distress or deeper psychological disturbance, such as picking at skin, slapping of face or head, or biting, most commonly the back of the hand.

PLANNING TRANSITION

A transition plan is a do-it-yourself project for most adopting parents. Transition programs are rarely, if ever, part of foreign adoption agency programs. Nor are they part of orphanage discharge, often called exiting, routines.

When you visit an orphanage, you are often entering a world as strange to you as the outside world is to the child you are adopting. In addition to adapting to the orphanage environment, you are initiating the bonding process with your child.

To be prepared for this dual task, you need some basic guidelines and goals. Although we recognize that the process is complex and deserves a manual of its own, we offer the following tips to make the transition more smooth and productive.

Your goals during this period should be to:

◆ Reduce your child's stress and anxiety by providing security.
◆ Establish trust with your child by providing consistency and structure that will carry over after adoption.
◆ Acquire knowledge by learning as much as possible about your child.
◆ Build a foundation for a strong parent-child relationship by providing a secure base and making the getting-to-know-you experience a constructive, pleasant one.

There are two basic considerations you should focus on in transition: pacing and staging. You, as the parent, set the stage, while your child sets the pace. Allow the child to set the pace and rely on her cues to decide when she is ready for the next step. Be flexible, but remain encouraging and keep the child moving in the right direction.

To set the stage, establish routines for your time with the child. Be consistent; show up at the same time each day if you can. Repeat routines such as taking a walk, looking at pictures, and so on. *Routines are structure and structure is security to any child in transition.*

You can accomplish these goals in a number of ways. To build trust, confidence, and security set a regular schedule of visits with your child. During these visits, establish a routine of activities—playing, changing, washing, holding—which will give your child a sense of structure and help you get to know each other. You should be a beacon of strength and steadiness in your child's world, so step in and take control of things when you visit. You should relay a strong feeling of security that your new child will be able to connect with and trust during this time of transition.

When your child gets upset, hold him and offer empathetic consolation. If your comfort is shunned, don't leave. You should not expect your child to accept consolation right away. Give him time to accept you. Establish and stick to the daily routine you have started by always being there when he expects you to be. This sets the foundation of trust.

Let the child cue you when he is ready for more or when you are moving too fast. For example, if you find the child is comfortable with just walking along with you inside the orphanage, but he becomes upset when you first try to take him outside, then postpone the outside trip for some time and continue inside visits.

Enter and become a part of your child's institutional environment before expecting him to enter yours. Find out as much about that environment as you are allowed. At first you will just inspect the plumbing and the physical environment, noting any specifics such as how the child is bathed or fed. When you've absorbed that, then you can focus on your child's behavior and concentrate more fully on his interaction with peers and caregivers.

Make some judgment about your child's ability to relate. During early visits, ask to observe the child with his primary caregiver. Not the director or the doctor, but the nurse or attendant who usually takes care of him. Watch your child during caregiving routines, such as dressing, bathing, feeding, play, and so on. Learn about the food he eats, his likes and dislikes, and how he responds to dressing and bathing. Take notes, so that later you can duplicate the experiences and help your child feel more comfortable with you in his new home. Familiarity is calming and makes the child feel more secure.

Learn *the child's* routines, even if you plan to discard them at a future date. (You may not want, for example, to get up every morning at 5:30 A.M. for his bath!) Join in and work with the caregiver the first few times you are involved with routines.

Take extensive notes on the interactions that take place. Observe both quantity and quality of interaction between the caregiver and your prospective child. How much time does she spend with the child? How much talking is going on? Any singing? Is there any sign of affection? Does the child smile? Laugh?

Learn how to do things the way they are done in the orphanage. Ask the caregiver to teach you the songs they sang in the institution, if there were any, and any games or play routines she does with the child. Spend some time in the kitchen and learn how your child's food is prepared. Familiarize yourself with any other programs that are taking place in the orphanage. Document and write down what you see.

Some orphanages have educational programs. Others have so-called infant stimulation or early intervention programs. These programs may be run by foreigners or may be indigenous. It doesn't matter. Observe, document, and find out as much as you can about whatever programs are in place.

Ask for copies of any individualized records on your child that the program may be keeping. Don't worry about translating at this point. It is more important for you to watch your child's interaction and responses than to be distracted by trying to locate a translation service.

Some adopters who have had long waiting periods have joined the program staffs of orphanages as volunteers. The value of this experience for the adopting parent is often positive. If nothing else, it gives a parent an inside view of the facility where their adopted child has been raised, which provides valuable information that isn't available any other way. The value of his new parents joining in his environment varies for the child. Some children are delighted. If the child seems to react negatively to your participation, drop out. Or volunteer for another project activity that does not have your child as a participant.

One of the most common problems occurs in the child who is quick to begin to attach to the adopting parent. These children may experience fear or jealousy when their new parent begins to interact with other children. They may not be ready to share. They may be afraid the new parent will "choose" someone else.

A note of caution: If you observe severe problems, like abuse, harsh punishment, or emotionally damaging caregiving, accelerate your transition. Sacrifice your transition plan if you must, and get your child into a safe, secure environment. When in doubt, always decide in favor of the child's safety.

One of the highest risk times for abuse to erupt in an orphanage is after the child is "spoken for" for an adoption. Be aware. Be suspicious of any signs of physical injury, regardless of the explanation. *The most common phony explanation* for bruises and so forth is that the child was fighting another child for a toy.

Should an event that you think points to abuse occur, be very careful about reporting it. Do not question or reprimand the staff. A previously sympathetic director can become defensive and sometimes hostile under such circumstances. An adoption can suddenly go wrong or a child can be seriously injured.

If you do report the incident, report it to your agency. In addition, if you know and trust any Western personnel in the orphanage program, report it to them in the strictest confidence. They will know what to do and how to do it.

IN RETROSPECT

When it comes time to leave the orphanage with your child, you may feel that you have not yet accomplished enough. It is important to remember that, at this point, transition has only begun and that orphanage time was an opportunity to build a foundation, not begin intervention or change behaviors. If not aware of these pitfalls, adoptive parents may find themselves wondering why the child cannot accept and respond to them. If you expect your new child to respond immediately to your love, or even feel grateful, you may be disappointed.

One of the surprising things about orphanages is how little is done to set limits or establish boundaries with children. Children who are no longer crib-bound are often treated very permissively. If you suddenly set too many rules and try to enforce them too quickly, your newly adopted child could rebel.

SOME TIPS ON HOW TO SMOOTH TRANSITION

Many children, particularly younger ones, will sail through transition in a matter of days. For others, it may take weeks. Sometimes children do not adjust quickly to new parents or any new environment. When everything in their lives has changed, children often react with anger, confusion, fear, and frustration. Remember the food and water taste different, and even the smells are different. To you, it may seem as though everything has improved for the child you are adopting.

When a small child is dealing with change, he or she will

often reference the past as a model. Any positive reminder of his past will help him adapt to an entirely different life and make him feel more secure. For example, he may have come to know and trust someone else, like an orphanage worker, and although that person is now gone, the memory of her may be important in helping the child transfer affection to a new parent. Remember Hayley Rose Lansing (from the introduction) and how the orphanage caregiver sprayed perfume on Suzanne before they parted?

THE TRANSITION CONTINUES
ON THE HOME FRONT

When adopted children arrive in their new homes, parents often find they have brought along some baggage. Adoption expert Joan Warden calls it "reality baggage."[1]

Reality baggage, Joan explains, means many things. It means the child's likes and dislikes and mannerisms, or it can mean fearful memories that cause distress or signal early symptoms of post-traumatic stress disorder. The "baggage" can be psychological: sadness, despair, anxiety, fear, anger, or even rage. Or it can be physical: milk allergies, ear infections, parasites, malnutrition, or even chronic illness. Parents who adopt a child need to know how to deal with this baggage. As Worden puts it:

> Somewhere between success and failure, liking and disliking, acceptance and rejection, your child lives. He lives independently of you and yet is completely dependent on you. He is his "own person" and yet he is, needs to be, and wants to be a part of you and your family. He is the child that will grow up to be the one that challenged you the most and yet gave you the greatest sense of pride and success in yourself and in him.[2]

Children develop behaviors or habits in orphanages that are adaptive in an institution and may be maladaptive in a family home. Just to survive, a toddler in an institution may have become manipulative, learned how to lie, or learned to be a bully to meet basic physical needs. Children in institutions may have been rewarded or gained approval for behaviors that are unacceptable in a family. So when the child from an institution comes into your home, there will be a period of adjustment that you and he will go through as you work to first understand and then modify or change these behaviors.

There are some behavior issues that may take a little longer to resolve after arrival home. Adoptive parents may have concerns about their child's sleeping, toileting, emotions, or food habits, or about clinging behaviors, jealousy and sibling rivalry, passivity, and poor self-esteem.

FIRST, TAKE CARE OF YOURSELF

It is common for adoptive parents to become frustrated and exhausted quickly. After arriving home from the adoption trip with the new child, your entire household will probably be in flux and can be upset for months on end. It is disappointing and faith shattering to bring a new child into your home who is upset, who will not eat, who cries or shrieks, and who won't be comforted.

When things go wrong, the first reaction of adoptive parents is often to begin questioning their parenting skills. They may also question the wisdom of adoption. On particularly bad days, they may even question their love for the child. Those who feel they "got the wrong child" can feel cheated. In this situation sometimes the child is blamed instead of the "baggage" the child brought to the home. Along with the frustration can come anger at the adoption agency, at the system, at the child, and at themselves.

Adopting parents who are experiencing these feelings need to reach out to others who understand what they are going through. Otherwise, you are at risk for becoming isolated and feeling that you are the only ones in the country who are experiencing the problems you are. This is especially true if you don't have a support system upon which you can rely. If you find yourself in this situation, it's time to join a support group of other adoptive parents.

When parents read stories or see media coverage about other adoptive families who have no problems and live happily ever after, which, by the way, is usually not the full and true picture, their feelings of isolation and low self-esteem increase. A support group of other adoptive parents will help to establish the proper perspective.

Most of these issues aren't issues at all but simply a normal part of childrearing. Checking with other parents who have adopted from your child's country can give you a wealth of information. In the meantime, we offer the following strategies to help during the first few months after bringing your new child home.

SLEEPING ISSUES

Sleeping habits generally will change as a child adjusts to a family. For example, the child may have nightmares, be unable to sleep alone, have sleep irregularities, be resistant to sleeping in the bed the parents have provided, or cry or fight on being awakened. These are normal behaviors to be expected and are caused by the child's fright and insecurity.

Although no adoptive parent can or even would want to replicate the circumstances from which the child came, sometimes it is helpful to adjust your habits a bit during the first few months. A child from Korea, for example, will come to the home accustomed to sleeping on a mattress on the floor. Parents can let the child sleep on the floor for a while, perhaps on a futon, and then slowly introduce the child to the normal bed.

Richard Darby in *International Adoption, Inc.*, discusses how one family dealt with this issue:

> On the first night, all the family members slept on the living room floor with the new child. Each night one member would leave the living room to sleep in a bed. When all the family had left the living room floor, the new child readily accepted a bed.[3]

As with all issues involving fear, new parents must reassure the child.

TOILET TRAINING

This is an area in which many families run into problems.

Some children who were reported to be toilet trained will regress after coming to the new environment. Fear and anxiety can lead to bed-wetting. The child may use toileting to express anger and frustration. If there are problems, the parents can begin regular toilet training all over again, making sure the child goes to the bathroom after eating and before bed; use protective plastic sheeting, or traning pants or diapers at night. Don't use shame or punishment after an incident. The act may be unconscious.

If a child is having problems toileting, by all means make sure there is no medical problem on the child's part for the difficulties. Many children from foreign countries have parasites that can cause digestive problems and result in diarrhea or a similar lack of control. Consult with your pediatrician. Have a stool sample tested for parasites as soon as possible after arrival. Some children experience problems with the food and water; either can also cause changes in patterns of elimination, discomfort and/or diarrhea.

WITHDRAWN BEHAVIORS

Many children react to severe change by withdrawing from their environment. They can even display severe grief symptoms. Fear of the unknown can paralyze them and institutionalization can also cause children to become passive. Children who have grown up in orphanages many times do not know how to respond on a normal emotional level. Often children from an institutional environment have learned not to get close to anyone, to rely only on themselves and to trust no one. It will take time, patience, and sometimes a skilled professional to help a child to bond with you, their new family.[4]

Let the child gradually acclimate to her new home. Introduce as few new people as possible to the new child, until she has sufficiently bonded with you as a family. When the child is comfortable that you are her forever family and has begun to attach to you, she can then use you as a secure base from which to explore the world. Don't plan a family reunion or get-together to introduce the new child to the extended family right away. Don't take the child into new circumstances until she is comfortable and happy in your home. Don't plan a family cele-bration visit to a place such as Disneyland until she has become accustomed to life in your environment. Just keep daily life in your home as calm and insulated as possible until the new child adjusts and then gradually introduce her to friends and family and new environments.

Many adoption agencies require new parents who both work to have a plan that will allow them to spend undivided time with the child upon returning home. One or the other parent should try to take a leave of absence so he or she can be with the child. The best possible scenario is to have one parent, often the mother, become a stay-at-home parent during this time of transition. Any new child will react better if she has one-on-one time to be nurtured during this period.

HOARDING

Some children who were deprived in the institution will hoard and gorge on food. This does not always indicate hunger or malnutrition, but more often indicates a history of psychologi-cal neglect. Other children will hoard belongings. Remember, however, they have come from an environment where they have not only missed the necessities but have never had private own-ership of anything. The very concept of possession is meaning-less to most children from institutions. When their language skills develop, for example, there is usually a lack of any pos-sessive words, such as *my* and *mine*, or *your* and *yours*.

Older children may steal and hide items they needed or wanted to keep. Now they are in a place with many wonderful things. They may feel these items are there for the taking and they must grab them before someone else does. Still other chil-dren will share excessively; they have come from a place where there was no "ownership." The parent can try to help a child who does this to establish boundaries and to understand what is theirs and what belongs to someone else.

CLINGING

At first, the child may feel secure only with the one person he connects with; usually that is the person who physically brought him home from his original country. Although this person is still a stranger to him, and a strong attachment has not formed, this person represents the only tie to the past the child has. The child will cling to this person.

JEALOUSY AND SIBLING RIVALRY

Jealousy and sibling rivalry can arise between the adopted child and siblings who were in the family before the child's arrival. The special attention given most foreign adoptees often worsens the situation. It is advisable to follow traditional guidelines for preparation of children in the family, both before and after adoption. Be aware that jealousy and rivalry may be delayed reactions.

NO REACTION

Adoptive parents sometimes say their new child went through no adjustment period, that the expected "honeymoon period" didn't occur at all. If the child is pleasant, smiling, and obedient, this may or may not be a good sign. All human beings respond to new situations in some way. Having no reaction to the adoption isn't typical. However, parents who see no adjustment problems may just have gotten lucky and gotten a child who is very resilient and has adjusted well and quickly.

However, this "no reaction" scenario might mean the child is not attaching to you as he should. It can mean the child is holding back unpleasant reactions to you and your home. Very young children are good at hiding anxiety by being passive. Sometimes this reaction looks like that of a child who is nice and quiet. Even if the child is quiet, the adoptive parents must make sure the child is interacting with the rest of the family and learning about how to act in the new home. Passivity may mean the child is having difficulty forming relationships. If this is the case, either you as the parent or a professional must help the child learn how to develop the capacity to feel and attach. Excessive passivity can also mean the parent should explore if something is emotionally or physically wrong with the child. If so, the parent should explore these alternatives through appropriate professional channels, such as consulting a developmental pediatrician, child psychologist, or a therapist who specializes in attachment work.

POOR SELF-ESTEEM

Many older adopted children arrive at their new home feeling inadequate. This is a condition that can persist for years after being adopted. The children may feel bad because others, such as their birth parents, have rejected them. Often these are children who have had several moves and placements before being adopted. Or, they may feel inadequate because they had to wait until they were older before they found adoptive parents. The postinstitutionalized child may also feel guilty and "bad" because he abandoned his friend or friends in the institution.

Some children become almost compulsive about compensating for a sense of badness they have about themselves. They can self-abuse, correct themselves, or call themselves bad names as a result. Often a child who exhibits this kind of behavior needs professional help.

But, if these symptoms have just appeared or your child does not exhibit them with great frequency you can offer some help. There are techniques you can try to help boost your child's self-esteem in these situations. They are called claiming techniques and they help the adopted child understand the process through which you were able to bring the child home. For example:

- ◆ Explain to the child that you understand her life has been disrupted at a time when security was very critical.
- ◆ Recount how long and hard a task it was for you to find the child or what an adventure it was. Tell the child that you feel that even though the child was born in a different place, the child was born for you. Explain the time it takes to go through an agency and the long adoption process. This may help the child understand that being adopted at an older age isn't the result of his own shortcoming. You can keep a detailed file

of correspondence, newspaper clippings, and documents to show your child how much work it was to be able to adopt him or her.

♦ Explain that through circumstances beyond his control, such as poverty, illness, state pressures, his birth parents simply were unable to care for him. Discuss the issue that the birth parents felt the child would get better care and find better parents to take care of him if they gave the child up.

♦ Prepare a *life book* with your child that explains the events and pictures about her life and the birth parents. Parents can include in the life book their struggles to find the child and joy in welcoming the child into their family.

♦ Sometimes it helps a child to adjust and identify with his new family by giving the child a middle name of family significance. If you are an Anglo family and adopt a boy with the first name of Wong, for example, you may wish to name your son after the husband by calling him Wong Samuel Smith. Later the child can pick the name he wishes to use officially and in public.

♦ Help your child realize that everyone has experienced losses and disruptions from familiar things and places. This might help your child deal with the feelings he or she is having. Try to teach your child that new loves can be as good as old ones.

PROFESSIONAL HELP

If your adopted child does not begin to respond after being in your home usually about three months and continues with the behaviors listed above, it is time to let the family physician know. The doctor may refer or consult with a child development clinic or professional therapist. In doing so, parents are seeking guidance in understanding and dealing with the following:

♦ Tantrums.
♦ Disobedience.
♦ Complete disregard for the possessions of others.
♦ Refusal to fit in or enjoy life.
♦ Gluttony and hoarding.

Getting Help. Sometimes these symptoms point to a more severe problem than poor adjustment to the new situation. Parents should always seek professional help and guidance if they suspect this is the case. Adoptive parents can always use the additional support of a professional guidance counselor.

Understanding Your Own Reactions. If and when problems and difficult behaviors surface in a child, it is easy to develop bitterness about the country of origin, and/or assign blame to the institutional staff. While this may be a natural response, it really does not remedy the situation at all. Adoptive parents should always remember that often foreign adoption workers, orphanage staff, and foreign professionals do not have the time or the training to detect existing emotional or physical problems. Sometimes the child is too young, or too unknown for problems to become obvious. It is a lot to expect of orphanage caregivers, whose task is continuous schedules of feeding and changing in overcrowded facilities, to notice that one child doesn't turn his head as she approaches.

It is during this adjustment period that parents most often begin to revise their expectations about the child they have adopted. A big part of that adjustment is the gradual letting go of the ideal, or fantasy child you might have held in your heart and transferring affection to the real child in front of you. Accepting your child as she actually is will be one of the most important things you can do for her.

Remember, with an adoptive child, the arrival at home is just the beginning of the journey.

FOSTERING BONDING AND ATTACHMENT

One of the first major steps of becoming a new parent is to foster a bond with your newly adopted child. This task is easier if a child or baby has had other attachments in the past. Once a child has been able to trust and attach to *someone*, it is much easier to repeat the process and transfer the bond to the new parent. The institutionally adopted child is often one who has not had the opportunity to complete the necessary *Bonding/Attachment Cycle* he needs to. Before he is able to develop trust, he needs a positive attachment. The accompanying diagram illustrates this cycle.

BONDING / ATTACHMENT CYCLE

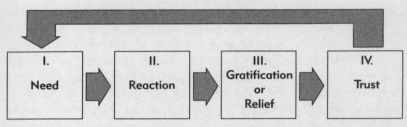

Adopted children who require professional help are often those who never trusted anyone to take care of them. They missed the gratification of the cycle described in the diagram. We offer several tips that have been proven to help the child with the attachment process in this situation:

- ◆ At first make sure your child is exposed to only a few people, like those in your immediate family. This will allow for a quiet, comfortable "honeymoon" period.
- ◆ To increase confidence in your abilities as new parents, you can read about child-rearing theories. Many good books are available. (See the reading lists in the Appendix.) Talk to other adoptive families and read publications put out for the adoption community.[5] One idea is to baby-sit for other adoptive parents of children the same age as your child. Talk to your adoption agency about how to accomplish this.
- ◆ Do whatever you can to help your new child feel at home, especially in her new room. You may wish to provide the same type of bed she had while she was in her country of origin. Were the lights on in the room where the child slept? If so, you may want to keep your child's light on at night. Here, the notes you took in the orphanage will become invaluable. Limit the space a child can explore at first. This will allow the child to slowly get used to her new environment. Start by giving your child only one or two toys and gradually introduce more as the child seems able to handle them. Chil-

dren from institutions can become overwhelmed when presented with too many choices at first. Slowly introduce family pets; many institutionalized children have never seen a cat, a dog, or a fish. Teach the child how to take care of the pets and be responsible. As with any child, you must teach yours to be gentle.

♦ Remember, establishing an attachment with your child is a long-term, dynamic process. Refer to the bonding chart on the previous page and be creative about replicating it with your newly adopted child. If your efforts do not seem to be working, seek professional help. Feel free to ask the adoption social worker and parent support group for advice. Read books and, by all means, be prepared to seek a therapeutic situation for yourself and the child if your child's behavior problems persist or she does not respond to the things you are doing at home.

It is very important not to jump too quickly to a "diagnosis" of a serious behavior or adjustment problem. Adjustment periods are normal, and any adopted child will react in some way to a new environment. Not every difficult behavior is a disorder. Most of them are not. Promotion of healthy attachment is a major issue in adoption, but children will form those attachments at different paces and often take giant steps forward, then retreat a bit to regroup. This is not regression. Nor is it reactive attachment disorder. Tantrums and/or nightmares probably occur in most children during periods of adjustment. Your first concern should not be that your child has post-traumatic stress disorder!

All difficult-to-manage behavior doesn't require psychotherapy; most of it does not. Parenting classes in which common child-rearing issues are discussed can be of tremendous value to any new parent and are highly recommended for adoptive parents, even when there are other children in the family and you are experienced parents. Most communities offer a variety of resources for parents that may be of help in learning to manage common behavior problems.

♦ Learn as much as possible about the specific details of the child's background (culture, history, if they were in foster homes or orphanage, etc.). For example, in some cultures children do not talk at the table; adults always touch children when speaking to them; Asian boys are superior to girls; kissing may not be common; in some countries pets do not live indoors; babies are not given solid foods until after one year old; and so on. Be aware of these differences and the fact they might add to the issues you must help your child work through during the transition period. Sometimes your child just needs to become accustomed to the way your family does things and you can teach this as you go along.

◆ Evaluate the mental and physical health information about the child and consult with your family's physician or pediatrician. A visit to the family pediatrician should be one of the first steps taken soon after the child's arrival.

It is not unusual for a child adopted from abroad to arrive with such things as ear infections, upper respiratory infections, skin conditions such as scabies, infected sores (impetigo), and/or head lice. Some of these conditions are communicable and medication is often required; attend to them immediately but also be aware that most of these conditions pose no long-term health problems.

Remember that family physicians and pediatricians are as interested and committed to your child's wellness as they are to treating acute diseases. Most primary care physicians will recommend and want to see your child for his first "well-child visit" as soon as possible after arrival.

◆ By all means, learn some crucial words in the child's native tongue: I love you, sweet or pretty boy/girl, toilet, water, what do you want?, come here, stop, go, stay, mother, father, sister, brother, etc.

Throughout transition, it is important for you to pay close attention to cues presented by the adopted child. Let your child take the lead and help her *ease* into your family and environment. With time and effort, parents and child can make transition a holistic, health-promoting experience for the entire family.

REFERENCES

1. Joan Worden, *Report on Intercountry Adoption* (Boulder, CO: International Concerns Committee for Children, 1995), p. 21.

2. Ibid.

3. Richard Darby, *The Report on Foreign Adoption, 1986,* edited from 1977 *International Adoption, Inc.,* International Concerns Committee for Children.

4. For more information on helping an adopted child bond with a family it may be helpful to refer to books such as Dr. Martha Welch's *Holding Time* (New York: Simon & Schuster, 1988).

5. An excellent resource is the "Adoption Book Catalog" published by Tapestry Books and Patricia Irwin Johnston, M.S., P.O. Box 359, Ringoes, NJ 08551-0359.

Home

Do not try to jump over your own shadow.

Gypsy proverb

In the life of every adopted child, there comes a time when he feels and expresses a strong need to know more about his birth parents, his country of origin, his cultural ties and roots. This phenomenon is more than curiosity. It represents a need that is, most probably, fundamental to all human beings. Adoption only makes the need more acute.

Although spoken questions may arise as late as adolescence, this need to know is always subconsciously present in the mind of an adopted child. Adoptive parents often want to know more about how and when to answer these questions, how to make the answers both less painful and more constructive. Also, they are often confronted with decisions about when and why it may be important to return with their adopted child to the youngster's homeland and arrange a reunion with birth families.

Reunion and rediscovery of roots can be critically important in the emotional development of the uprooted, transplanted child, however well the transplant has taken. For some adopted children, healthy attachment to adoptive families is not possible until the child has a clear sense of who he is, where he came from, and why he was "given up for adoption." Maintaining a sense of belonging to a culture and family can be vital in the long process of healing and becoming whole again.

While every adoption has distinctly individual characteristics and variations, the recent experience of parents who have adopted internationally gives credence to the value of keeping an adoptive child's cultural heritage alive in his mind. Not only does successful transition go smoother and faster, but also the capacity of the adopted child to form strong, long-lasting attachments is enhanced.

American mother Lynn Lansford describes vividly the exact moment she encountered and began to understand the importance of her adopted child's heritage. Like many other adoptive families in the early 1990s, Lansford had adopted a special-needs infant of Gypsy descent from an Eastern European orphanage—in her case, Romania. This meant, however, that little Juliana's roots went deeper than the Romanian culture. Juliana was Gypsy, and although Gypsies have no homeland, they have a strong cultural heritage.

Gypsies, or the Rom, are descendants of ancient travelers who came to Europe after being forced from their ancestral lands in India. They are talented and colorful people. Musicians, animal trainers, and skilled craftspeople, they often work from roving caravans or settlements. But despite their very real talents and the romantic depiction most of us associate with Gypsy life, the Rom have lived for centuries as victims of discrimination, rejection, persecution, oppression, and poverty. As a result, many of their children have been placed in orphanages. This is particularly true in eastern Europe. When a return to their original homes is impossible, Rom children are truly lost youngsters. Not only have they lost home and family; they have lost all connection with their heritage.

For Lynn Lansford's adopted daughter, reconnection with her Gypsy heritage began soon after her adoption. One day, on a family outing, Lynn found herself with her baby on her back in a carrier at the annual Renaissance Festival in her community. Suddenly, a thunderstorm broke out, with rain and lightning overhead. Seeking refuge, she ducked into a canvas shelter with the baby.

Lynn had stepped back in time.

There before her was a "Gypsy" couple whom she assumed were actors for the festival. They were selling handmade wares and were dressed in medieval garb. Before she knew it, the man had pulled out a violin. He turned to her, admiring little Juliana on her back. Lynn's daughter Juliana is typical of other Gypsy children, being very beautiful with dark, sparkling eyes and dancing black curls.

"Is she Gypsy?" he asked.

Taken aback, Lynn replied, "Why, yes, she's from Romania."

With a twinkle in his eye, he said, "I know how to tell if she's true Gypsy, you just watch."

Puzzled, Lynn began to realize this couple were no impostors, but the real thing. The Gypsy man began playing an ancient Gypsy song. It was a famous Rom lullaby.

Juliana, who had not been paying much attention, sat quietly in her little backpack. As the song was played, she was immediately attentive. Her little eyes glowed. Then, she began to weep softly, with tears running down her little dark face.

"She is true Gypsy!" the man cried out. "Gypsy children are born with this song in their hearts and always cry when they hear it! Bless you both!"

Lynn says she learned volumes that day about her little girl and vowed to make sure she knew her wonderful heritage.

Today, Juliana is a happy, well-adjusted lively child who has settled nicely into her new American family. Her mother has taken her back to her native land to meet with her Gypsy birth parents and their relatives. Juliana understands the meaning of being a true Gypsy and feels very special about herself because of the reunion trip.

~

A Personal Story of Love
By Lynn Lansford

When we decided to adopt in Romania in 1990, we deliberately went into it not only in full force, but with full intentions of adopting a child with special needs. We expected developmental delays and nutritional neglect, possible irreparable physical damage (such as rickets) and emotional problems. I had posed as many questions as I could think of to developmental specialists, pediatricians, and psychologists. The advice was all over the map, but the single piece of advice that floated through them all was to choose a happy child over an angry one, because it shows how capable that child will be in adjusting to its environment. It sounded logical.

Because we didn't go through an agency, and represented ourselves instead of hiring an attorney, we jumped through every hoop alone. We wanted it this way. I wanted to be in complete control from choosing the child to meeting the birth parents, hopefully knowing as much as I could about its prenatal care, birth history, siblings, grandparents, mental illness (or lack of), cancers—everything. I wanted the freedom to inspect, dissect, and possibly form long-lasting family ties which were protected from danger by oceans, visas, and economic problems. In other words, I was terrified of adopting a child sight unseen with little or no knowledge of its past, one that I might have to fear a birth parent appearing again to reclaim my adopted child. A parent-initiated foreign adoption was definitely our answer.

After arriving in Romania, I realized that every Romanian child who was institutionalized was in one way or another a special-needs child. My choice would have to be more specific; I wanted a child whom no one else would probably choose.

When I went to the cradle in Hunedoara and told the director that I wanted a child no one else would want, she said she had several children who at age three would be sent to institutions for the handicapped, and she would show me those.

The first little face I saw peeking around the door was a tiny stubble brown-haired child with big dark brown eyes and a smile that melted my heart. He appeared to be a year or so, maybe eighteen months, although his hands were frail and thin. He walked like he had been walking only weeks, and his body proportions seemed odd, but he had a light that brightened the room. The other child they brought for me to see was slightly bigger, blue eyed, with light brown hair. He cowered in the corner and glared at me. I immediately went back to the advice I was given, and decided to focus on the happy child.

He was charming, sweet, and knew right away how to hook the people around him. I was definitely hooked. I asked to see his medical records and didn't get the helpful response I wanted. They didn't have them, they said.

"What made this child destined for a handicapped institution?"

I asked. The only response was that he was globally retarded, but with fresh food, he would maybe recover. I asked for his birth certificate, but they said they had lost it, saying they thought he was about eighteen months old. I did get his birth parent's name and address, which I felt was a partial success.

They brought me more children, but the happy little boy had won my heart.

So did a seven-month-old baby they said was brain damaged at birth. They hadn't had her long, only a few weeks, but she never cried or laughed. She only opened and shut her eyes, and her legs didn't work. When they handed her to me, she was wrapped in blankets from the tip of her head to her toes. All I could see were these huge brown eyes and wide little nose. I took my finger and tried to get her to follow its movement from side to side, but nothing. I stroked her cheek to see if she would turn toward the touch, but again just a blank stare. As I tried to unwrap her to look at her legs, she immediately was taken from me with the words, "You don't want her. She is a Gypsy."

I knew of the prejudice against the Gypsies, but I also knew that this baby was a child that would languish and die. I saw a sparkle in her eye, even though I wasn't sure anyone was home inside her little brain. I decided I wanted her also.

Fortunately, locating the birth families wasn't difficult. My son's parents were in a coal-mining town called Petrosani (Pet-ro-shawn) in Transylvania. His father was a coal miner and his mother had had several illnesses that left her at home. Alex, the name we chose for our son-to-be, was the sixth child in the family, yet only three children lived in the home.

The minute I met his birth parents, Dorel and Iona, I liked them immensely. They were simple people, kind, honest, and very worn down by poverty and Communism. I could tell they wanted the best for their son.

In one of our several visits, I found out that Alex wasn't eighteen months old. He was almost three. He was born prematurely at twenty-eight weeks and weighed seven hundred grams (one pound nine ounces). Iona had endured a dry uterus for over a week before getting to the hospital for a cesarean, which left her with an infection. Instead of a stillborn birth, Alex was alive but termed "nonviable"—a birth certificate wasn't even to be issued.

She was told to go home, they would make the arrangements. Alex continued to live in an isolette equipped with a forty-watt Communist light bulb. Iona returned to the hospital with several illnesses ranging from "nervous disorder" to "operation illness"— probably a staph infection. She was treated with morphine.

When Alex was three months old, his birth parents went to pick him up at the hospital. They kept him at home for less than three weeks and returned him with pneumonia and dehydration. He was only three pounds ten ounces, and they never went back for him again.

After talking with them, I realized they honestly believed that he was a healthy, normal three-year-old surviving well in an orphanage that was providing him with everything they couldn't. Clothes, toys, medicine, food, and fresh air. When I tried to tell them that Alex was barely the size of a one-year-old with absolutely no speech or communication skills, they looked at me like I was from another planet.

They felt they had done the best for him by giving him to the state. I left it at that.

I also realized that Alex's problems were more complex than I thought, but I was determined to adopt and give this child every chance in the world to heal.

Juliana's birth family was another matter. When we went to the mayor's office to pick up the social study on her family, the mayor had refused to do it all, saying he was afraid of her father—a Rombaro or *bulibasha*—a clan leader. I was fascinated by the Rom (Gypsy) culture, and was openly excited that her roots were so colorful. When we visited her birth family, we found them living in a large house surrounded by a fenced-in yard full of horses, wagons, and chickens. She was the youngest of eight children, all of whom still were in the house. I was impressed by the father. He was always well dressed in coat and tie or sweater with a hat. He had a wonderful smile, and treated us with friendliness and respect.

Her mother was a hard-looking, crude woman who seemed untrusting and angry. She rarely spoke, yet I felt she was the last word in the house. I felt very uneasy around her and kept my distance, yet remained friendly. Juliana's brothers and sisters were beautiful, yet all were dirty and ragamuffin in appearance. All six children shared two beds, which were all in the same room as the parents' bed, and it was filthy.

During our negotiations and plans for the adoptions, I took special care to soak in everything and everyone, yet I wasn't able to get as much information about them as I had hoped. I did discover that the father believed that Juliana was conceived while he was in jail; therefore, he wouldn't allow her to be brought home after birth. That explained a lot.

I became more fascinated by the Rom sixth sense I'd heard about, which dealt with their ability to foresee the future or to read minds, and it seemed her mother was capable of it. The town of Deva is rather large, and Juliana's mother was everywhere we were, watching us. We would be at the courthouse and she would be on the corner waiting for us. We'd get in the car, drive two or three miles to the hotel, and she'd be waiting near the front door. I never understood how she did it, yet we never lost her.

I was always disappointed that my relationship with Juliana's birth parents was never going to be as open and friendly as my relationship with Alex's birth family, but that's how it had to be.

In our thinking about adoption, we always felt that we wanted our children always to know the truth, always feel we loved them not only for who they are but for what they were born from and what they could be. The birth parents were included in the package.

Once on U.S. soil, our work really began. Juliana had lost the ability to use her leg muscles because of being bound so tightly. She also had begun to give up, realizing that crying was of no use, since no one would respond to her. We did a lot of physical therapy to build muscle tone and held her constantly. Within one year, she was back on track and developing normally. She wears glasses today because of strabismus (crossed eyes), which was probably caused by never having things to look at except her nose. We think she's beautiful in her red specs.

Alex had multiple problems as most of the "older" Romanian children had, but we managed to live through it and help him through it, including not being able to eat solid foods, hyperactivity, poor muscle control, constant diarrhea, compulsive behaviors, and self-abuse. Throughout it all, he remained happy, charming, controlling, manipulative, obsessive, and totally ripped our family apart with the symptoms of attachment disorder.

He was a class-act con man from the start—stealing, lying, urinating in his room, down the heat vents, and on his toys. He destroyed his room from top to bottom in a matter of days, leaving us with no place safe for him to sleep but in our shower, where we could be sure he couldn't hurt himself or us. It took us two years to get him to eat meat, and he still has some trouble swallowing.

I began doing Dr. Martha Welch's holding therapy on Alex when I couldn't reach him in any other way, and noticed an improvement almost immediately, especially when I did holding with control discipline, which is where the parent takes total control of the child's life and tiny minute-by-minute gives it back as he earns it through trust. An example is coloring. I would allow him "the privilege" to color, but at first I would choose the book, the picture, and two colors. If he could be trusted to color nicely, not eating the crayons or tearing the book, I added another crayon, or a different page. Now, he chooses not only the book, but all his crayons. If he reverts to destructive behaviors, he loses the privilege to color completely—then we begin again.

I was finally feeling an attachment after having Alex for four years, but something was still missing. Yes, I was his mother, but he didn't depend on me. In some ways, I could have been an aunt or a neighbor; the motherness hadn't clicked for him. I knew the healthy bond wasn't there.

Because Alex never bonded with one specific person in the first eighteen months of his life, he didn't realize that need for me to be his security blanket, his trusted person, the mother who loves him no matter what. That could be fulfilled by anyone and it was, but I knew for him to be a healthy child capable of complete trust with himself and with other people, he had to become attached to me. I felt to achieve that, I had to go back to the first three years of his life.

As part of my openness about my children's adoptions, we have always talked about the circumstances of their birth families as if it was a natural occurrence. They have always known about the abandonment, the orphanage, their birth siblings, and for Juliana, the Rom roots. In fact, many dinner conversations centered around the birth families and answering questions, so when I suggested that we return to Romania to visit the orphanage and birth families, it was met with great excitement by both children.

I had always anticipated taking Alex and Juliana back to Romania when they were a lot older, but that time had come now. I didn't want to wait until the turmoil of adolescence or the search for identity as an adult. I felt to really reach Alex and for Juliana to fully understand her story, I had to make them live it while it was still fresh and with their open, understanding little souls. I also knew that as the only mother they have ever known, they would have to trust me completely.

I wrote to Alex's birth family six months before we were to go to Romania and asked them if they would like to meet him.

I received a positive answer just weeks before we were to leave, and didn't have time to tell them when to expect us. Unable to contact them by phone, we took our chances and pulled into the block of apartments in Petrosani late one afternoon. Our friend and translator went to the door to ask if they would still like to see Alex, and tears immediately came to their eyes. Alex was sitting quietly in the car, fully aware and anxiously awaiting the meeting. Before we could get out of the car, his birth father was racing toward us. "Alex, there is your birth father!" I said, pointing to an older, gentle-looking man dressed in the clothes I had sent them at Christmas. Alex reached up and hugged his birth father, who kissed him gently, then hugged me. As we all walked to the block of apartments, I held one of Alex's hands, while his birth father held the other. We were all quiet. Inside the tiny, hot apartment, Alex hugged his birth mother and birth sister, Dori, then wanted to see their house.

It was how I remembererd it, only covered with four years of pictures of Alex that I had sent them. They hugged him, held him, and asked him lots of questions. He told them he loved Chuck E Cheese and Discovery Zone, which was hard to explain to people who barely have running water. We laughed and we cried, and I saw Alex very slowly attach to me.

He would sit with his birth mother, and then, for the first time, walk over to me and nestle into my body, then go to his birth father, then return to me.

I finally said to Alex that this was the time to ask them questions. What did he want to know? Was he unsure about anything? He got very quiet and said, "I want you to tell them something. Tell my birth mother 'thank you' for giving me to my mom." It was then that I fell in love with my son, and he finally had a mother he genuinely loved. I knew I had done the right thing.

I hadn't planned on taking Juliana to see her birth family. I planned to take her to the hospital and the orphanage, which I did, but after seeing what happened to all of us during Alex's birth family reunion, I knew I couldn't leave Romania without giving that experience to Juliana. Honestly, I was afraid of her birth family, and wasn't sure how we could do it safely.

We agreed to find her birth family and arranged to meet them in a public park next to the apartment where we were staying. Yet when we finally located the house in the late afternoon, Chilly, our friend and translator, made other plans. He saw what it meant to Alex to be inside of his birth parents' house—to feel the poverty, the pain, and the love. He also knew that if we met in a public park, Juliana would be just meeting strangers without a connection, a piece of the puzzle that she couldn't complete. He was right. Within one hour after locating the house, the family, and preparing Juliana, we were in front of the house and in front of the entire Rom clan, including her birth mother, birth father, four sisters, three brothers, and an aunt, uncle, and cousin. They grabbed her, held her, played with her hair, talked to her, kissed her, and everyone sobbed. When her birth mother took off Juliana's glasses, the resemblance to her birth father was undeniable. Juliana was his child, and they all knew it. Juliana touched her mother's scarf, touched her tears, and as her birth mother hugged her, Juliana looked at me and smiled, then said, "Thanks, Mom."

Since we've returned, Alex has a special peace within him he has never had before, and the bizarre behavior is gone. Juliana feels a specialness about herself, and about being a Rom, that only the experience of being loved by them could give her.

They both start kindergarten this fall, and for the first time since the adoption, we are complete.

Today, in mid-1996, Lynn and Jim's incredible journey continues. Lynn travels to Romania and its institutions at least twice a year. Her mission is not to bring home more children to her own home but to open doors for the children still there. Her purpose is to get them out of the persecution and oppression that is their fate in their country. To date she has privately "facilitated" (without any monetary gain to herself) more than a hundred private adoptions in the formerly Communist country. Most of the children have been of Gypsy descent. Lynn expects and hopes to do more in the future through her organization, Romanian Ties.

Through her work with Romanian Ties, Lynn regularly returns to Romania to help disadvantaged children, particularly street children. As a contribution, she and her children (seven in all) make handmade Gypsy dolls (out of dark-haired Barbies!) and sell them to raise money.[1]

My (McKelvey) personal interest in adopted children, especially those from eastern Europe, comes out of family experiences with adoption and the friends and colleagues I have found through writing several books on high-risk children and adoption. It is through my writing that I found my friend Lynn Lansford and so many others, including the coauthor of this book, Barbara Bascom.

As a writer and editor, I've always focused on the needs of families and children and I was the Lifestyles editor at the (Denver) *Rocky Mountain News* for years pursuing this interest. After writing *High Risk: Children Without a Conscience* and *Adoption Crisis: The Truth Behind Adoption and Foster Care*, I received virtually hundreds of letters and phone calls about adoptive children. Through my writings and speaking contacts I discovered the rich world of international adoption and the families who plunge in, taking the risk to help the children and add to their families. One of these families was that of Jim and Lynn Lansford, who have since become very close to me.

There is another reason I am personally so involved in adoption issues. I have an adopted stepdaughter. As with most families today, the circumstances are rather convoluted, but through my personal, family experience I have benefited by knowing and loving a daughter who is not biologically related to me. Through my stepchildren I have been privileged to know and love three stepgrandchildren who are half Native American and one great-grandchild.

On my shelf today, as I write this, sit three beautiful Gypsy dolls with long, flowing multicolored voile skirts—all made by the Lansford family. Each doll came with a certificate of authenticity and a story about their Gypsy heritage. Each has a name.

The stories they arrived with tell about traditional Gypsy life in Romania. "Bianca," with long braids and a fur vest and hat, comes from a small farming village called Sintu Han where she lives with her father, mother, and two brothers; they farm the land and harvest potatoes and turnips each fall. "Gianina," with her warm babushka and sweater, lives in the Transylvanian village of Hateg in a wagon with her father, mother, and four sisters; her father is a blacksmith who roams the countryside finding work. Her mother sells trinkets she finds and trades for in the local markets.

Since it is almost Christmas as I write this, my friend Lynn made the dolls especially for me. I intend to give Bianca (the bell maker) and "Gianina" (the painter) to my two granddaughters. My granddaughters are both Native American and they love collecting ethnic dolls, especially those with long, flowing, black hair like theirs. One of these girls, Calico Rose, is the daughter of my own adopted stepdaughter. She and Autumn Rose are just as beautiful as the dolls I will give them. (The third doll? Well, Bianca is mine to keep.)

It is from my three grandchildren, all half Native American heritage (with the last name of McKelvey!), that I have personally learned how important it can be for a family to grow and love alongside children of a different ethnic culture. It has not always been easy, but never dull. Parenting a child of another heritage can be a challenging, rewarding joy. Adoption gives us this marvelous option.

> *Who can tell what a baby thinks?*
> *Who can follow the gossamer links*
> *By which the mannikin feels his way*
> *Out from the shore of the great unknown,*
> *Blind and wailing, and alone,*
>   *Into the light of day?*

J. G. Holland, *Bitter Sweet*

REFERENCES

1. Romanian Ties, a not-for-profit organization; all proceeds benefit Romanian street children and Gypsy children living in Romanian orphanages. For more information on Romanian Ties, you may write Lynn Lansford at 5565 Broadmoor Bluffs, Colorado Springs, CO 80906.

APPENDIX I

Reading List

BOOKS

Arms, S. *Adoption: A Handful of Hope.* Berkeley, CA: Celestial Arts, 1990.

Bowlby, J. *The Making and Breaking of Affectional Bonds.* London: Tavistock Publications, 1984.

Brodzinsky, A. *The Mulberry Bird: Story of an Adoption.* Indianapolis: Perspectives Press, 1986.

Cline, F., M.D., *Hope for High Risk and Rage Filled Children,* Evergreen, CO: EC Publications, 1992.

Cline, F., M.D., and Fay, J. *Parenting with Love and Logic—Teaching Children Responsibility.* Golden, CO.: 2207 Jackson St., 80401. Love and Logic Press, 1991.

Committee for Single Adoptive Parents, *Handbook,* new edition, $15, P.O. Box 15084, Chevy Chase, MD 20925.

Delaney, R., and Kunstal, F. R. *Troubled Transplants.* Portland, ME: University of Southern Maine, 1993.

Dorris, M. *The Broken Cord.* New York: Harper & Row, 1989.

Dunn, L., ed. *Adopting Children with Special Needs: A Sequel,* Washington, DC: North American Council on Adoptable Children, 1993.

Fahlberg, V., M.D. *Attachment and Separation,* 1979, Spaulding for Children, P.O. Box 337, Chelsea, MI 48118.

Gabel, S. *Filling in the Blanks: A Guided Look at Growing Up Adopted,* Indianapolis: Perspectives Press, 1988.

Jewett, C. *Helping Children Cope with Separation and Loss.* Harvard Common Press, 1982.

Johnston, P. *An Adopter's Advocate.* Wayne, IN: Perspectives Press, 1984.

———. *Perspectives on a Grafted Tree.* Wayne, IN: Perspectives Press, 1983.

Keck, G., and Kupecky, R. M. *Adopting the Hurt Child: Hope for Families with Special-Needs Kids.* Colorado Springs, CO: Pinon Press, 1994.

Krementz, J. *How It Feels to Be Adopted.* New York: Alfred Knopf, 1982.

Mansfield, L. G., and Waldmann, C. H., *Don't Touch My Heart,* Colorado Springs: Pinon Press, 1994.

Melina, L. *Making Sense of Adoption: A Parent's Guide,* New York: Harper & Row, 1989.

McKelvey, C. A., ed. *Give Them Roots, Then Let Them Fly: Understanding Attachment Therapy.* The Attachment Center at Evergreen, CO, 1995.

McKelvey, C. A., and Stevens, J. E. *Adoption Crisis: The Truth Behind Adoption and Foster Care.* Golden, CO: Fulcrum Publishers, 1994.

McKelvey, C. A., and Magid, K. *High Risk: Children Without a Conscience.* New York: Bantam Books, 1989.

National Committee for Adoption, *Adoption Factbook.* Washington, DC, 1989.

Randolph, Elizabeth. *Children Who Shock and Surprise: A Guide to Attachment Disorders,* 1994. RFR Publications, 8655 Water Rd., Catati, CA 94931.

Verny, Thomas, M.D. *The Secret Life of the Unborn Child.* Toronto: Doubleday, 1981.

Welch, Martha, M.D. *Holding Time.* New York: Simon & Schuster, 1988.

DEVELOPMENTAL MEDICINE READINGS

Anderson, W., et al. *Negotiating the Special Education Maze: A Guide for Parents and Teachers,* 2nd ed. Woodbine House Publ., 1990.

Batshaw, M. *Your Child Has a Disability: A Complete Source Book of Daily Medical Care.* New York: Little Brown, 1991.

Finston, P. *Parenting Plus: Raising Children with Special Health Needs.* New York: Penguin Books.

Miezio, P. *Parenting Children with Disabilities.* Marcel Dekker Publ., 1983.

Minshew, D. H. *The Adoptive Family as a Healing Resource for the Sexually Abused Child: A Training Manual.* Washington, DC: Child Welfare League of America, 1990.

Pueschel, S. ed. *The Special Child: A Source Book for Parents of Children with Developmental Disabilities,* 2nd ed. P.H. Books Publ., 1995.

Sobol, T. *We Don't Look Like Our Mom and Dad.* Coward-McCann Publ., 1977.

Stein, S. *About Handicaps,* 2nd ed. Walker & Co., 1984.

PERIODICALS AND NEWSLETTERS

Adopted Child, P.O. Box 9362, Moscow, ID 83843

The Adoption Advocate, 401 E. Front St., Port Angeles, WA 98362

Adoption Advocates Press, 1921 Ohio NE, #5, Palm Bay, FL 32907

Adoption Today magazine, P.O. Box 88948, Seattle, WA 98138

Adoptive Families magazine (formerly OURS), 3333 Highway 100, N., Minneapolis, MN 55422

Adoptalk, North American Council for Adoptable Children (NACAC), 1821 University Ave., Suite N-498, St. Paul, MN 55104

The African Connection, Americans for African Adoptions, Inc., 8910 Timberwood Dr., Indianapolis, IN 46234

Growing in Friendship Together (GIFT), (Romanian adopted children) 138 Cardinal Circle, Quitman, TX 75783

Our Romanian Children, P.O. Box 8318, Argonne, IL 60439-8313

Children in Common (Eastern European Children), P.O. Box 21016, Cantonsville, MD 21228

Our Chosen Children (Eastern European), P.O. Box 401, Barre, VT 05641-0401

National Directory/Registry (Adoptive Families of Romanian Children), 5924 Wildwood Ave., Sarasota, FL 34231

Romanian Orphans Support Group, P.O. Box 3392, Langley, BC, Canada V3A 4R7

Romani Information Packet, International Romani Union, Manchaca, TX 78652-0822

Chain of Life, P.O. Box 8081, Berkeley, CA 94707

The Children's Voice, 22705 Koths, Taylor, MI 48180

Connections, (Children from India), 1417 E. Miner, Arlington Heights, IL 60004

Romanian Ties, Lynn Lansford, 5565 Broadmoor Bluffs, Colorado Springs, CO 80209

The Communique (Interracial families), P.O. Box 16248, Houston, TX 77222

F.A.C.E. Facts, P.O. Box 28058, Northwood Station, Baltimore, MD 21239

FAIR Newsletter, P.O. Box 51436, Palo Alto, CA 94303

ICCC Newsletter, 911 Cypress Dr., Boulder, CO 80303-2821

Los Ninos News, 1600 Lake Front Cir., #130, The Woodlands, TX 77380-3600

News Digest, National Information Center for Children & Youth with Disabilities, P.O. Box 1492, Washington, DC 20013

Parents of Peruvian Adoptees, RD 4, Box 4303, Glen Rock, PA 17327

Parents Network for the Post-Institutionalized Child, 217 N. Wade Ave., Washington, PA 15301 (Thais Tepper)

Roots and Wings, 30 Endicott Dr., Great Meadows, NJ 07838

Single Mothers by Choice, P.O. Box 1642, Gracie Square Sta., New York, NY 10028

Stars of David (Jewish), 9 Hampton St., Cranford, NJ 07016.

APPENDIX II

Resources for Support and Assistance

There are numerous support groups and organizations and much information available on international adoption. Inclusion on this list does not reflect our recommendation and a lack of inclusion only reflects our lack of awareness and is not an intent to exclude. This information is offered to the reader for further exploration. Where phone numbers are omitted, please consult information.

ADOPTION INFORMATION AND HELP

AASK (Adopt a Special Kid)
2201 Broadway, Suite 702, Oakland, CA 94612
510-451-1748

Access to Respite Care and Help National Resource Center
800-473-1727 (information and referral)

Action for Child Protection
4724 Park Road, Suite C, Charlotte, NC 28209
704-529-1080

Adopted Child, monthly newsletter covering a variety of topics
P.O. Box 9362, Moscow, ID 83843
208-882-1794

Adoptee Liberty Movement
P.O. Box 717, Radio City Station, New York, NY 10101-0727
212-581-1568

Adoption Assistance Hotline (resource through NACAC)
800-470-6665

Adoptive Family, bimonthly magazine published by Adoptive Families
of America
3333 Highway 100N
Minneapolis, MN 55422
800-372-3300

Adoption Service Information Agency (ASIA), 7720 Alaska Ave., NW,
   Washington, DC 20012
202-726-7193

ADPN (Attachment Disorder Parents Network), Gail Trenberth,
   P.O. Box 18475, Boulder, CO 80308
303-443-1446

American Academy of Adoption Attorneys
Box 33053, Washington, DC 20033

American Adoption Congress
1000 Connecticut Ave., NW, Suite 9, Washington, DC 20036

American Psychiatric Association
1400 K Street, NW, Washington, DC 20005
202-682-6133

American Academy for Cerebral Palsy and Developmental Medicine,
American Academy of Pediatrics, local state chapters (consult the
   telephone book)

ATTACh, 2775 Villa Creek, Suite 240, Dallas, TX 75234
214-247-2329

Attachment Center at Evergreen, Inc.
P.O. Box 2764, Evergreen, CO 80439
303-674-1910

Centers for Disease Control (CDC), Atlanta, GA

C. Henry Kempe National Center for the Prevention and Treatment of
   Child Abuse and Neglect
University of Colorado Health Sciences Center
420 E. 9th Ave., Denver, CO 80262

Child Help USA National Child Abuse Line
800-422-4453

Child Welfare League of America, 67 Irving Place, New York, NY 10003
212-254-7410

Committee for Single Adoptive Parents, P.O. Box 15084, Chevy Chase, MD
   20815

Connell Watkins & Associates, 28753 Meadow Dr., Evergreen, CO 80439
Provides pre- and post-adoption counseling, as well as intensive
   attachment therapy. Coauthor McKelvey can be contacted at this
   location.
303-674-6860

Federation for Families for Children's Mental Health
Attn: Barbara Huff, 1021 Prince St., Alexandria, VA 22314
703-684-7710

Friends of Man
800-337-4377

Health Resource Center
1 Dupont Circle, Washington, DC 20036
202-939-9320

How to Adopt in Romania, Lynn Lansford, Romanian Ties, 5565 Broadmoor
Bluffs, Colorado Springs, CO 80209. Not an adoption agency, but a
resource regarding Romanian orphans and Romanian street children,
particularly of Rom heritage.

Human Passages Institute, 777 S. Wadsworth Blvd., Lakewood, CO 80226.
303-914-9725. Therapeutic interventions, consultations, therapy with
special needs children, adoptees and families.

INS (Immigration and Naturalization Service) Look in the telephone book
for the listing in your location. Or contact the U.S. Department of State,
202-647-3444. The INS puts out the helpful booklet *The Immigration of
Adopted and Prospective Adoptive Children.* Write to 425 I St., Washington,
DC 20536.

Mercy Ministries: The Mothering Center
Attn: Karleen Dewey
1543 Marion Street
Denver, CO 80204

Mothering Center
Martha Welch, M.D.
952 5th Ave., New York, NY 10021
212-861-6816

National Adoption Information Clearinghouse, 11426 Rockville Pike, Suite
410, Rockville, MD 20852 (The Clearinghouse publishes the booklet
National Adoption Directory with a listing of adoption agencies by state,
parent support groups, adoption exchanges, and legal resources.)
202-842-1919

National Adoption Center, 1218 Chestnut St., Philadelphia, PA 19107
800-862-3678

National Alliance for Mentally Ill Children and Adolescents Network
2101 Wilson Blvd., Suite 302, Alexandria, VA 22201
703-524-7600

National Center for Clinical Infant Programs
733-15th St., NW, Suite 912, Washington, DC 20005
202-347-0308

National Child Welfare Leadership Center
P.O. Box 3100
Chapel Hill, NC 27515
919-966-2646

National Clearinghouse on Family Support
Childrens Mental Health
Attn: Connie Wagner
Portland State University, P.O. Box 751, Portland, OR 97207

National Clearinghouse for Professionals in Special Education
1800 Diagonal Rd., Suite 320, Alexandria, VA 22314
703-519-3800

National Council for Adoption (NCFA)
1930 Seventeenth St., NW, Washington, DC 20009
202-328-1200

National Information Center for Children & Youth with Disabilities
   (NICHCY)
P.O. Box 1492, Washington, DC 20013
800-695-0285

National Information Systems for Health Related Services
800-922-9234

National Legal Resources Center for Child Advocacy Protection
1800 M. St., NW, Washington, DC 20036
202-331-2200

National Mental Health Association
1021 Prince St., Alexandria, VA 22314
703-684-7722

National Resource Center on Special Needs Adoption
16250 Northland Dr., #120, Southfield, MI 48075
313-443-0300

National Special Needs Center
800-233-1222

North American Council on Adoptable Children (NACAC)
970 Raymond Ave., #106, St. Paul, MN 55114-1149
612-644-3036

Parent Network for Post-Institutionalized Child
P.O. Box 613, Meadowlands, PA 15347
412-222-1766

Report on International Adoption, 1995, International Concerns Committee
   for Children, AnnaMarie Merrill, 911 Cypress Drive, Boulder, CO
   80303-2821
303-494-8333

Resources for Adoptive Parents (RAP)
Attn: Peggy Meyer
4049 Brookside Ave. South, Minneapolis, MN 55426
612-926-6959

SEARCH Institute
700 South Third St., Suite 210, Minneapolis, MN 55415

SNAP (Special Needs Adoptive Parents)
Linda Kuelen or Peggy Hannon
9800 Academy Hills, NE, Albuquerque, NM 87111
505-822-0921

SNAP (Special Needs Adoptive Parents)
Brad Watson, RSW, executive director
Granville St., Suite 1150-409, Vancouver, BC, V6C 1T2 Canada
604-687-3114

Specialized Training of Military Parents of Adopted Children
12208 Pacific Highway SW, Tacoma, WA 98499
206-565-2266

Technical Assistance for Parent Programs
Federation for Children with Special Needs
95 Berkeley, Suite 104, Boston, MA 02116
617-482-2915

The Brooke Foundation (ROSES)
1070 Race St., Unit C, Denver, CO 80206
Consultant work, emphasis on special needs adoption and transition
    planning (Dr. Barbara Bascom)
303-333-5886

Three Rivers Adoption Council
307 Fourth Ave., Suite 710, Pittsburgh, PA 15222
412-471-8722

U.S. Department of Health and Human Services (HHS)
Children's Bureau, 200 Independence Ave., SW, Washington, DC 20201
202-619-0257

UAPs (University Affiliated Programs) in Child Development; affiliated
    with medical universities, at least two in every U.S. state. Check the
    phone directory under Universities.

Youth Law Center
Attn: Alice Bussiere
114 Samford St., Suite 900, San Francisco, CA 94104
415-543-3379

INFORMATIVE WORKSHOPS

To further inform, the authors cofacilitate a series of workshops/lectures:

- ◆ International Adoption: What to, How to and Why
- ◆ Children of Institutions: Truth or Consequences

- ◆ Adoption Crisis: The Truth Behind Adoption/Foster Care in America
- ◆ Transition: The Critical Missing Link
- ◆ Attachment in Adoption
- ◆ High Risk Children: Statistics and Solutions
- ◆ High Risk Children Without a Conscience
- ◆ International Adoption: Lessons Learned in Eastern Europe
- ◆ So You'd Like to Develop a Program in Foreign Orphanages? Let's Talk
- ◆ The Adopted Child: Nurturing the Family Tree
- ◆ How to Succeed with the Adopted Child: A Basic Primer
- ◆ Special Needs Adoption and the Drug-Exposed Child
- ◆ Developmental Issues and the Adopted Child
- ◆ Developmental Attachment Disorder: Uncovering the Mystery
- ◆ Disenfranchised Children: Attachment Issues (Children of war, the streets, the institutions)
- ◆ Temperament, Resiliency, and Survival in the Adopted Child
- ◆ Also offered are consultation, evaluation, therapy teams and support groups

For additional information please write to:

Howard Pelham, agent
2290 Suite-C East Fremont Road
Littleton, CO 80121

APPENDIX III

Resource List

International adoption agencies are in the business of specializing in arranging and coordinating international adoptions. The best agencies will be familiar with the adoption process in each of the countries in which they have programs, as well as U.S. rules and regulations. A "direct, full-service" agency means all phases of the adoption (homestudy, referrals, placement, and postplacement counseling) can be covered by the placing agency.

Upon accepting your application, an agency is able to assist you in collecting all the necessary documentation and submitting the adopter's package to adoption authorities in the foreign countries. Usually, they will introduce the adopter to one or more children available for adoption and help in that decision.

Once a child is selected, they will coordinate the adoption process, assist with travel arrangements, and ensure all necessary documents and hurdles have been finished and overcome. Should a problem occur in the document-preparing process or in the foreign country, the wise agency will be there for the adoptive parent and provide the resources needed.

As professionals the authors will not and cannot recommend specific adoption agencies. For the sake of resources, however, we print here a listing of international adoption agencies listed by state; we are grateful to the International Concerns Committee for Children for allowing us to reprint this list.

For current addresses and phone numbers consult the appropriate telephone book; the authors submit this list as being accurate in 1995 and cannot be held responsible for any changes, errors or omissions. The reader is advised that the status of foreign adoption agencies changes regularly, as do the circumstances of the countries served. For additional resources see Appendix I.

ALABAMA
  Villa Hope
  P.O. Box 131267, Birmingham, AL 35213
  205-870-7359

ALASKA

Adoption Advocates International (WA), Port Angeles, WA
136 Old Black Diamond Road, Port Angeles, WA 98362
206-452-4777

Fairbanks Adoption and Counseling, Fairbanks
P.O. Box 71544, Fairbanks, AK 99707
907-456-4729

Adoption Services of WACAP, Seattle, WA
P.O. Box 88948, Seattle, WA 98138
206-575-4550

ARIZONA

Dillon Southwest, Scottsdale
3014 N. Hayden Rd., Suite 101
Scottsdale, AZ 85251
602-945-2221

Hand-in-Hand, Tucson
3102 N. Country Club, Tucson, AZ 85716
602-327-5550

ARKANSAS

Families Are Special, N. Little Rock
Box 5789, 2200 Main, N. Little Rock, AR 72119
501-758-9184

Small Miracles International, Inc., Midwest City, OK
7430 SE 15th, #204, Midwest City, OK 73110
405-732-7295

CALIFORNIA

ACCEPT—An Adoption & Counseling Center, Los Altos
339 S. San Antonio Rd., #1A, Los Altos, CA 94022
415-917-8090

Adopt International
121 Springdale Way, Redwood City, CA 94062
415-369-7300

Adoption Horizons, Eureka
630 J St., Eureka, CA 95501
707-444-9909

Adoption Services International, Ventura
2021 Sperry Ave., Ventura, CA 93003
805-644-3067

Adoptions Unlimited, Chino
P.O. Box 462, Chino, CA 91710
909-902-1412

Bal Jagat, Chatsworth
9311 Farralone Ave., Chatsworth, CA 91311
818-709-4737

Bay Area Adoption Services, Mountain View
465 Fairchild Dr., #215, Mountain View, CA 94043
415-964-3800 (9:00–2:00 weekdays)

Children's Home Society of California
2444 Moorpark Ave., #312, San Jose, CA 95128-2625

Chrysalis House, Fresno
2134 W. Alluvial, Fresno, CA 93711
209-432-7170

Family Connections, Modesto, Sacramento, Fresno
Main Office
P.O. Box 576035, Modesto, CA 95357-6035
209-524-2139

Family Network, Inc., Monterey
Main Office
284 Foam, #103, Monterey, CA 93940
800-888-0242

Help the Children, Inc., Stockton
41 W. Yokuts Ave., #107, Stockton, CA 95207
209-478-5585

Heritage Adoption Services (CA), Sacramento
P.O. Box 188408, Sacramento, CA 95818-0408
916-442-5477 (10:00–5:00 weekdays)

Holt International Children's Services
3807 Pasadena Ave., # 170, Sacramento, CA 95821
916-487-4658

Life Adoption Services, Tustin
440 W. Main St., Tustin, CA 92680
714-838-LIFE (5433)

North Bay Adoptions, Windsor
9068 Brooks Rd. S., Windsor, CA 95492
707-837-0280

Partners for Adoption, Santa Rosa
P.O. Box 2791, Santa Rosa, CA 95405-0791
707-578-0212

Sierra Adoption Services, Nevada City
P.O. Box 361, Nevada City, CA 95959
916-265-6959

Universal Family Services (Liaison), Mill Valley
P.O. Box 2505, Mill Valley, CA 94942
415-388-3561

Vista Del Mar, Los Angeles
3200 Motor Ave., Los Angeles, CA 90034
310-836-1223

COLORADO

AAC Adoption & Family Network, Inc., Berthoud
307 Welch Ave., P.O. Box W, Berthoud, CO 80513
303-532-3576

Adoption Alliance (CO), Aurora
3090 S. Jamaica Ct., #106, Aurora, CO 80014
303-337-1731

Chinese Children Adoption International, Littleton
1100 W. Littleton Blvd., #435, Littleton, CO 80120
303-347-2224

Colorado Adoption Center, Fort Collins, Wheat Ridge
1136 E. Stuart, #2040, Fort Collins, CO 80525
303-493-8816

Connell Watkins & Associates, (adoption consultants) Evergreen
28753 Meadow Dr., Evergreen, CO 80439
303-674-6860

Covenant International, Inc., Colorado Springs
2055 Anglo Dr., #104, Colorado Springs, CO 80918
719-531-5100

Friends of Children of Various Nations (FCVN), Denver
1756 High St., Denver, CO 80218
303-321-8251

Hand-in-Hand, Colorado Springs
1617 W. Colorado Ave., Colorado Spring, CO 80904
719-473-8844

Hope's Promise, Castle Rock
309 Jerry St., #202, Castle Rock, CO 80104
303-660-0277

Human Passages Institute, (Consultants, therapy) Lakewood
777 S. Wadsworth, Bldg. #1, Suite 105, Lakewood, CO 80226
303-914-9729

CONNECTICUT

Adoption Resource Center at Brightside, W. Springfield, MA
2112 Riverdale, W. Springfield, MA 01089-1099
413-788-7366

International Alliance for Children, New Milford
23 S. Main St., New Milford, CT 06776
203-354-3417

Jewish Family Service (CT), Winfred
740 N. Main St., Winfred, CT 06117
203-236-1927

New Beginnings Family & Children's Services, Inc., Mineola, NY
141 Willis Ave., Mineola, NY 11501
516-747-2204

Spence-Chapin Services, New York, NY
6 E. 94th, New York, NY 10128
212-369-0300

Thursday's Child, Inc., Bloomfield
227 Tunxis Ave., Bloomfield, CT 06002
203-242-5941

Welcome House Social Services of Pearl S. Buck Foundation, Perkasie, PA
P.O. Box 181, Green Hills Farm, Perkasie, PA 18944-0181
215-249-1516

Wide Horizons/Wide Horizons for Children, Inc., New Britain
Main Office
282 Moody St., Waltham, MA 02154
215-249-1516

DELAWARE
Child and Home-Study Associates, Wilmington
1029 N. Providence Rd., Media, PA 19063
610-565-1544

Welcome House Social Services of Pearl S. Buck Foundation, Perkasie, PA
P.O. Box 181, Green Hills Farm, Perkasie, PA 18944-0181
215-249-1516

DISTRICT OF COLUMBIA
Adoption Center of Washington
1990 M. St., NW, #380, Washington, DC 20036
202-452-8278 or 800-452-3878

Adoption Service Information Agency (ASIA), Washington
7720 Alaska Ave., NW, Washington, DC 20012
202-726-7193

American Adoption Agency, Washington
1228 M. St., NW, 2nd Flr., Washington, DC 20005
202-638-1543

Barker Foundation, Washington
1200 - 18th St., NW, #312, Washington, DC 20036
202-363-7751

Children's Adoption Support Service, Inc., Washington
3824 Legation NW, Washington, DC 20015-2702
202-362-3264

Cradle of Hope Adoption Center, Inc., Washington
1815 H. St., NW, #1050, Washington, DC 20006
202-296-4700

Datz Foundation, Washington
4545 - 42nd St., NW, #307, Washington, DC 20016
202-686-3400

International Families, Inc., Washington
5 Thomas Circle, NW, Washington, DC 20005
202-667-5779

World Child, Washington
4300 - 16th St., NW, Washington, DC 20011
202-829-5244

FLORIDA
The Adoption Centre, Maitland
341 Maitland Ave., #260, Maitland, FL 32751
(Look in the phone book.)

Jewish Family and Community Services
3601 Cardinal Point Dr., Jacksonville, FL 32257
904-448-1933

Suncoast International Adoptions, Inc., Largo
14277 Walsingham Rd., Largo, FL 34644
813-596-3135

Universal Aid for Children, Inc.
1600 S. Federal Hwy, 2nd Flr., First Union Bank Bldg., Hollywood, FL
   33020
305-925-7550

GEORGIA
Family Partners Worldwide, Atlanta
1776 Peachtree St., NW, #210, Atlanta, GA 30309
404-872-6787

Heart to Heart Adoption Services (a program of Lutheran Ministries
   of GA)
756 W. Peachtree St., NW, Atlanta, GA 30308
404-607-7126

The Open Door Adoption Agency, Inc., Thomasville
P.O. Box 4, Thomasville, GA 31792
912-228-6339

Partners in Adoption, Alpharetta
1050 Little River Lane, Alpharetta, GA 30201
404-740-1371

HAWAII
Hawaii International Child Placement & Family Services, Inc., Hawaii
P.O. Box 240486, Honolulu, HI 96824-0468
808-377-5095

IDAHO
Idaho Youth Ranch Adoption Services, Boise
7025 Emerald, Box 8538, Boise, ID 83707
208-377-2613

New Hope Child & Family Agency, Seattle, WA
2611 NE 125th, #146, Seattle WA 98125
206-363-1800

World Association for Children & Parents/WACAP, Seattle, WA
P.O. Box 88948, Seattle, WA 98138
206-575-4550

ILLINOIS
Bensenville Home Society, Bensenville
331 S. York Rd., Bensenville, IL 60106
708-766-5800

Bethany Christian Services, Evergreen Park
9730 S. Western, Suite 203, Evergreen Park, IL 60642-1814
708-422-9626

Catholic Social Service (IL), Bloomington
603 N. Center, Bloomington, IL 61701
309-829-6307

Children's Home and Aid Society of Illinois, Rockford
910 - 2nd Ave., Rockford, IL 61104
815-962-1043

Family Network, Inc.,
9378 Olive St. Rd., Rm 320, St. Louis, MO 63132
314-567-0707

Love Basket, Hillsboro, MO
4472 Goldman Rd., Hillsboro, MO 63050
314-789-4100

Lutheran Child & Family Services, River Forest, Addison
P.O. Box 5086, River Forest, IL 60305
708-771-7180

Lutheran Social Services of Illinois
6525 North Ave., #212, Oak Park, IL 60302
708-445-8352

INDIANA

Americans for African Adoptions, Inc., Indianapolis (central IN only)
8910 Timberwood Dr., Indianapolis, IN 46234
317-271-4567

Bethany Christian Services, Indianapolis
6144 Hillside Ave., #10, Indianapolis, IN 46220-2474
317-254-8479

Coleman Adoption Services, Inc., Indianapolis
615 N. Alabama, #419, Indianapolis, IN 46204
317-638-0965

Sunny Ridge Family Center, Highland
9105A Indianapolis Blvd., Highland, IN 46322
219-838-6611

IOWA

Heart International Adoption Services, Johnston
5335 Meek Hay Rd., Johnston, IA 50131
515-278-4053

Hillcrest Family Services, Cedar Rapids
205 - 12th St., SE, Cedar Rapids, IA 52403
319-362-3149

Holt International Children's Services, Carter Lake
Midwest Office (serving IA, NE, SD)
2200 Abbott Dr., #203, Carter Lake, IA 51510
712-347-5911

KANSAS

Adoption by Gentle Shepherd, Overland Park
6310 Lamar Ave., #140, Overland Park, KS 66202
913-432-1353

Children's Foundation—Adoption and Counseling, Inc., Louisburg
930 Carondelet Dr., #300, Kansas City, MO 64114
602 W. Amity, Box 1133, Louisburg, KS 66053
913-837-4303

Small Miracles International, Inc., Wichita
550 S. Oliver, Wichita, KS 67218
316-686-7295

KENTUCKY

Children's Home of Northern Kentucky, Covington
Devou Park, 200 Home Rd., Covington, KY 41011
606-261-8768

Methodist Home of KY/Mary Kendall Campus, Owensboro
193 Phillips Ct., Owensboro, KY 42303
502-683-3723

LOUISIANA
Holy Cross Child Placement Agency, Inc.
929 Olive St., Shreveport, LA 71104
318-222-7892

MAINE
International Adoption Services Centre, Alna
P.O. Box 55, Alna, ME 04578
207-586-5058

Maine Adoption Placement Services, Houlton, Portland, Bangor
18 Market Square, P.O. Box 772, Houlton, ME 04730
207-532-9358
P.O. Box 2249, 6 State St., Bangor ME 04401-2249
207-941-9500
565 Congress, #206, Portland, ME 04101
207-775-4101

Sharing in Adoption, Gorham
2 Springbrook Land, Gorham, ME 04038
207-839-2934

MARYLAND
American Adoption Agency, Baltimore
1228 M St., NW, 2nd Flr., Washington, DC 20005
202-638-1543

Creative Adoptions, Inc., Columbia
10750 Hickory Ridge Rd., #109, Columbia, MD 10044
301-596-1521

Datz Foundation, Gaithersburg
16220 Frederick Rd., #404, Gaithersburg, MD 20877
301-258-0629

World Child, Silver Spring
1400 Spring St., #410, Silver Spring, MD 10910
301-589-3271

MASSACHUSETTS
Adoption Resource Center at Brightside, W. Springfield
1221 Riverdale, W. Springfield, MA 01089-1099
413-788-7366

Alliance for Children, Wellesley
40 William St., #G80, Wellesley, MA 02181
617-431-7148

Beacon Adoption Center, Great Barrington
66 Lake Buell Rd., Great Barrington, MA 01230
413-528-2749

Cambridge Adoption and Counseling Association, Inc., Cambridge, Watertown
P.O. Box 190, Cambridge, MA 02142
617-923-0370

Florence Crittenton League, Lowell
119 Hall St., Lowell, MA 01854
508-452-9671

Love the Children, Duxbury
2 Perry Dr., Duxbury, MA 02332
617-934-0063

Lutheran Child and Family Services of Massachusetts, Worcester
416 Belmont St., Worcester, MA 01604
508-791-4488

New England Home, Boston
161 S. Huntington Ave., Boston, MA 02130
617-232-8610

Protestant Social Service Bureau, Inc., Quincy
776 Hancock St., Quincy, MA 02170
617-773-6203

Southeastern Adoption Services (SEAS), Marion
P.O. Box 356, Marion, MA 02738
508-996-6683

Wide Horizons for Children, Inc., Waltham
282 Moody St., Waltham, MA 02154
617-894-5330

MICHIGAN
Americans for International Aid and Adoption, Birmingham
877 S. Adams Rd., Birmingham, MI 48009-7026
810-645-2211

Bethany Christian Services, Grand Rapids, Madison Heights
901 Eastern NE, Grand Rapids, MI 49503-1295
616-459-6273

Children's Hope, Shepherd
7823 S. Whiteville Rd., Shepherd, MI 48883
517-828-5842

Evergreen Children's Services, Oak Park
21590 Greenfield, #204, Oak Park, MI 48237
810-968-1416

Family Adoption Consultants, Kalamazoo, Rochester
P.O. Box 489, Kalamazoo, MI 49005
616-343-3316

Golden Cradle International, Ypsilanti
1660 Cliffs Landing, #3, Ypsilanti, MI 48103
800-566-5368

International Adoption Consultants, Wyandotte
4064-7th St., Wyandotte, MI 48192
313-281-4488

MINNESOTA
Children's Home Society of Minnesota, St. Paul
2230 Como Ave., St. Paul, MN 55108
612-646-6393

Crossroads Adoption Services, Minneapolis
4620 W. 77th St., Suite 105, Minneapolis, MN 55435
612-831-5707

Forever Families International Adoption Agency, Eveleth
2004 Highway 37, Eveleth, MN 55734
218-744-4734

HOPE Adoption & Family Services Intl, Inc., Stillwater
421 S. Main, Stillwater, MN 55082
612-439-2446

MISSISSIPPI
Heart to Heart Adoption Services, Jackson
P.O. Box 12246, Jackson, MS 39211
601-977-9948

MISSOURI
Adoption Associates, St. Louis
100 N. Euclid, #206, St. Louis, MO 63108
314-367-1557

Children's Foundation—Adoption and Counseling, Inc., Kansas City
930 Carondelet Dr., #300. Kansas City, MO 64114
913-837-4303

China's Children, St. Louis
10245 Chaucer Ave., St. Louis, MO 63114-2330
314-890-0086

Family Network, Inc., St. Louis
9378 Olive St. Rd., Rm. 320, St. Louis, MO 63132
314-567-0707

Love Basket, Hillsboro
4472 Goldman Rd., Hillsboro, MO 63050
314-789-4100

Lutheran Family Children's Services of Missouri, St. Louis
4625 Lindell Blvd., Suite 501, St. Louis, MO 63108
314-361-2121

Universal Adoption Services, Jefferson City
124 E. High St., Jefferson City, MO 65101
314-634-3733

MONTANA
Montana Intercountry Adoption, Bozeman
109 S. 8th Ave., Bozeman, MT 59715
406-587-5101

NEBRASKA
Adoption Links Worldwide, Omaha
4911 Pinkney, Omaha, NB 68131
402-342-1234

Holt International Children's Services, Carter Lake, IA
2200 Abbott Dr., #203, Carter Lake, IA 51510
712-347-5911

NEVADA
Nevada State Welfare: check county name in phone book

NEW HAMPSHIRE
Vermont Children's Aid Society, Winooski & Woodstock, VT
P.O. Box 27, Winooski, VT 05404-0127
802-655-0006
32 Pleasant St., Woodstock, VT 05091
802-457-3084

Wide Horizons/Wide Horizons for Children, Inc., Concord
5 S. State St., Concord, NH 03301
603-224-5174

NEW JERSEY
Adoption and Infertility Services
P.O. Box 447, Lincroft, NJ 07738
980-946-0880

Adoptions International, Inc., Philadelphia, PA
219 Montrose, Philadelphia, PA 19147
215-334-3801

A.M.O.R., Matawan
12 Grenoble Ct., Matawan, NJ 07747
800-596-2273

Casa del Mundo, Inc., Flemington
P.O. Box 2142, Flemington, NJ 08822
908-782-3367

Child and Home-Study Association, Media, PA
1029 N. Providence Rd., Media, PA 19063
610-565-1544

Children of the World, Verona
635 Bloomfield Ave., #201, Verona, NJ 07044
201-239-0100

Children's Aid and Adoption, Marshtown, Orange, Morristown
575 Main St., Hackensack, NJ 07601
201-487-2022

Family Focus Adoption Services, Little Neck, NY
54-40 Little Neck Parkway, Suite 3, Little Neck, NY 11262
718-224-1919

Holt International Children's Services, Trenton
340 Scotch Rd., Trenton, NJ 08628
609-882-4972

Homestudies, Inc., Teaneck
1182 Teaneck Rd., Suite 101, Teaneck, NJ 07666
908-946-1014

Jewish Child Care Association, New York, NY
575 Lexington Ave., New York, NY 10022
212-303-4722

Love the Children, Quakertown, PA
221 W. Broad St., Quakertown, PA 18951
215-536-4180

New Beginnings Family & Children Services, Inc., Mineola, NY
141 Willis Ave., Mineola, NY 11501
516-747-2204

Option of Adoption, Philadelphia, PA
504 E. Haines, Philadelphia, PA 19111
215-843-4343

Small World Ministries, Hermitage, TN
401 Bonnaspring Dr., Hermitage, TN 37076
615-883-4372

Spence-Chapin Services, New York, NY
6 E. 94th, New York, NY 10128
212-369-0300

Today's Adoption Agency, Hawley, PA
P.O. Box G, Hawley, PA 18428
717-226-0808

Welcome House Social Services of Pearl S. Buck Foundation, Perkasie, PA
P.O. Box 181, Green Hills Farm, Perkasie, PA 18944-0181
215-249-1516

Wide Horizons for Children, Inc.
282 Moody St., Waltham, MA 02154
617-894-5330

NEW MEXICO
Rainbow House International, Belen
19676 Highway 85, Belen, NM 87002
505-865-5550

NEW YORK
International Adoption Home Study Agency, Brooklyn
41 Schermerhorn St., #144, Brooklyn, NY 11201
718-390-7274

Jewish Child Care Association, New York, NY
575 Lexington Ave., New York, NY 10022
212-303-4722

New Beginnings Family & Children Services, Inc., Mineola, NY
141 Willis Ave., Mineola, NY 11501
516-747-2204

Wide Horizons for Children, Inc.
282 Moody St., Waltham, MA 02154
617-894-5330

Spence-Chapin Services, New York, NY
6 E. 94th, New York, NY 10128
212-369-0300

NORTH CAROLINA
Carolina Adoption Services, Greensboro
106 E. Northwood St., Greensboro, NC 27401
910-275-9660

Christian Adoption Services, Matthews
624 Matthews-Mint Hill Rd., #134, Matthews, NC 28105
Matthews, NC 28105
704-847-0038

Datz Foundation, Cary
875 Walnut St., #275-23, Cary, NC 27511
919-319-6635

Lutheran Family Services in the Carolinas, Raleigh
P.O. Box 12287, Raleigh, NC 27605
919-832-1620

NORTH DAKOTA
New Horizons, Bismark
2823 Woodland Dr., Bismark, ND 58504
701-258-8650

OHIO
Crittenton Family Services, Columbus
1229 Sunbury Rd., Columbus, OH 43219
614-252-5229

European Adoption Consultants, N. Royalton
9800 Boxton Rd., N. Royalton, OH 44133
216-237-3554

Family Adoption Consultants Macedonia
8536 Crow Dr., #218, Macedonia, OH 44056
216-468-0673

Jewish Family Service (OH), Sylvania
6525 Sylvania, Sylvania, OH 43560
419-885-2561

Lutheran Social Services of Central Ohio, Columbus
57 E. Main St., Columbus, OH 43215
614-228-5209

OKLAHOMA
Dillon International, Inc., Tulsa
7615 E. 63rd Pl, S., Tulsa, OK 74133
918-250-1561

Project Adopt
3000 United Founders Blvd., #141, Oklahoma City, OK 73112
405-848-0592

Small Miracles International Inc., Midwest City
2550 S. Oliver, Wichita, KS 67218
316-686-7295

OREGON
All God's Children, Portland
4114 NE Fremont, Portland, OR 97212
503-282-7652

China Adoption Services, Portland
P.O. Box 19764, Portland, OR 97280
503-245-0976

Dove Adoptions International, Inc., Portland
3735 SE Martins, Portland, OR 97202
503-774-7210

Heritage Adoption Services (OR), Portland
516 SE Morrison, #714, Portland, OR 97214
503-233-1099

Holt International Children's Services, Eugene
P.O. Box 2880, Eugene, OR 97402-9970
503-687-2202

New Hope Child & Family Agency, Seattle, WA
2611 NE 125th, #146, Seattle, WA 98125
206-363-1800

Plan International Adoption Services, McMinnville
P.O. Box 667, McMinnville, OR 97128
503-472-8452

PENNSYLVANIA
Adoption Unlimited, Inc., Lancaster
2270 Weston Rd., Lancaster, PA 17603
717-872-1340

Adoption Worldwide, Inc., Jenkintown
Benjamin Fox Pavilion, #419, Jenkintown, PA 19046
215-885-5670

Adoptions International, Inc., Philadelphia
219 Montrose, Philadelphia, PA 19147
717-399-7766

Child and Home-Study Association, Media
1029 N. Providence Rd., Media, PA 19063
610-565-1544

Children's Adoption Network, Langhorne
245 Bradley Ct., Holland, PA 18966
215-860-3353

International Assistance Group, Pittsburgh
21 Brilliant Ave., Pittsburg, PA 15215
412-781-6470

Love the Children, Quakertown
21 W. Broad St., Quakertown, PA 18951
215-536-4180

Lutheran Children and Family Services, Philadelphia
101 E. Olney Ave., Box C-12, Philadelphia, PA 19120
215-276-7800

Lutheran Service Society of Western Pennsylvania, Greensburg
1011 Old Salem Rd., #107, Greensburg, PA 15601
412-837-9385

New Beginnings Family & Childrens's Services, Inc., Matamoras
8 Pennsylvania Ave., Matamoras, PA 18336
717-491-2366

Option of Adoption, Philadelphia
504 E. Haines, Philadelphia, PA 19111
215-843-4343

Today's Adoption Agency, Hawley
P.O. Box G, Hawley, PA 18428
717-226-0808

Welcome House Social Services of Pearl S. Buck Foundation, Perkasie
P.O. Box 181, Green Hills Farm, Perkasie, PA 18944-0181
215-249-9657

RHODE ISLAND
Alliance for Children, Pawtucket
500 Prospect St., Pawtucket, RI 02860
401-727-9555

Wide Horizons for Children, Inc., Waltham, MA
282 Moody St., Waltham, MA 02154
617-894-5330

SOUTH CAROLINA
Christian World Adoption, Inc., Charleston
270 W. Coleman Blvd., Mt. Pleasant, SC 29464
803-856-0305

Lutheran Family Services in the Carolinas, Columbia
P.O. Box 21728, Columbia, SC 29210
803-750-0034

SOUTH DAKOTA
Holt International Children's Services, Carter Lake
Midwest Office (serving IA, NE, SD)
2200 Abbott Dr., #203, Carter Lake, IA 51510
712-347-5911

TENNESSEE
Christian Counseling Services (TN)
P.O. Box 60383, Nashville, TN 37206
615-254-8341

Holston United Methodist Homes for Children, Greeneville
P.O. Box 188, Greeneville, TN 37744
615-638-4171

Small World Ministries, Hermitage
401 Bonnaspring Dr., Hermitage, TN 37076
615-883-4372

Williams-Illien Adoptions Inc., Memphis
3439 Venson Dr., Memphis, TN 38135
901-373-6003

TEXAS

Adoption Resource Consultants, Richardson
P.O. Box 1224, Richardson, TX 75083
214-517-4119

Adoption Services, Inc. (TX), Ft. Worth
3500 Overton Park W., Ft. Worth, TX 76109
817-921-0718

Bright Futures, Killeen
2212 Sunny Lane, Killeen, TX 76541
817-690-5959

Dillon International, Inc., Tulsa, OK
7615 E. 63rd Pl, S., Tulsa, OK

The Gladney Center, Ft. Worth
2300 Hemphill St., Fort Worth, TX 76110
817-922-6000

Heart International Adoption Services, Seabrook
2951 Marina Bay Dr., #130, League City, TX 77573
713-326-3063

Los Ninos International Adoption Center, Dallas, Austin,
The Woodlands
1600 Lake Front Cir., #130, The Woodlands, TX 77380-3600
713-363-2892

UTAH

World Association for Children & Parents/WACAP, Seattle, WA
P.O. Box 88948, Seattle, WA 98138
206-575-4550

VERMONT

The Adoption Centre, Burlington
278 Pearl St., Burlington, VT 05401
802-862-5855

Lund Family Center, Burlington
P.O. Box 4009, Burlington, VT 05406-4009
215-536-4180

Vermont Children's Aid Society, Winooski and Woodstock
P.O. Box 27, Winooski, VT 05404-0127
802-655-0006

VIRGINIA

American Adoption Agency, Richmond
1228 M St., NW, 2nd Flr., Washington, DC 20005
202-638-1543

Barker Foundation, Washington, DC
7945 MacArthur Blvd., Cabin John, MD 20818
301-229-8300

Catholic Charities of Richmond (VA), Richmond
1512 Willow Lawn Dr., P.O. Box 6565, Richmond, VA 23230-0565
804-285-5900

Datz Foundation, Vienna
404 Pine St., #202, Vienna, VA 22180
703-242-8800

WASHINGTON
Adoption Advocates International (WA), Port Angeles
401 E. Front St., Port Angeles, WA 98362
206-452-4777

Leap of Faith, Kent
22601 SE 322nd St., Kent, WA 98042
206-886-2103

New Hope Child & Family Agency, Seattle
2611 NE 125th, #146, Seattle, WA 98125
206-363-1800

World Association for Children & Parents/WACAP, Seattle
P.O. Box 88948, Seattle, WA 98138
206-575-4550

WEST VIRGINIA
Burlington United Methodist Family Services, Inc., Scott Depot
P.O. Box 370, Scott Depot, WV 25560
304-757-9127

Catholic Charities of Southwestern Virginia, Roanoke
820 Campbell Ave., Roanoke, VA 24016
703-342-8627

WISCONSIN
Adoption Advocates, Inc., (WI), Madison
2601 Crossroads Dr., Madison, WI 53701
608-246-2844

Adoption Services of Green Bay & Fox Valley, Inc., Green Bay
529 S. Jefferson, #105, Green Bay, WI 54301
414-432-2030

Bethany Christian Services, Waukesha
W255 N477 Grandview Blvd., #207, Waukesha, WI 53188-1606
414-547-6557

Community Adoption Center, Janesville, Madison, Manitowoc
3701 Kadow, Manitowoc, WI 54220
414-682-9211

Division of Community Services, Madison, WI
See local phone book for listing in your community

HOPE Adoption & Family Services Inter., Inc., Stillwater, MN
421 S. Main, Stillwater, MN 55082
612-439-2446

Lutheran Social Services of Wisconsin and Upper Michigan, Madison,
  Milwaukee
1101 W. Clairemont Ave., #2H, Eau Clair, WI 54701
715-833-0992

New Horizons, Bismarck, ND
2823 Woodland Dr., Bismarck, ND 58504
701-258-8650

Pauquette Children's Services, Portage
P.O. Box 162, 315 W. Conant, Portage, WI 53901-0162
608-742-8004

Special Children, Inc., Elm Grove
321 N. Elm Grove Rd., #2, Elm Grove, WI 53122
414-821-2125

WYOMING
Catholic Social Services of Wyoming, Cheyenne
P.O. Box 1026, Cheyenne, WY 82003
307-638-1530

APPENDIX IV

Electronic Networking for Adoption

Adoption in the mid-1990s arrived on the Internet with two new adoption information sources:

Precious in HIS Sight: An intercountry adoption photo listing established by Precious in HIS Sight. This listing includes photos and biographies of waiting children. The address is http://www.gens.com/adoption/.

AdoptInfo: A collection of information, research, opinion and policy documents that adoptive or preadoptive families will find of interest. Adoptive Families of America has AdoptInfo as a project as part of its Children, Youth and Family Consortium's Electronic Clearinghouse. For more information on this resource you can send an E-mail message to cyfcec@Maroon.tc.umn.edu, or call (612) 626-1212.

Those adopting will also be interested in knowing that many agencies, parent groups, professional consultants, and therapists who work with adopting families and children are establishing home pages on the Internet. Look under the key words: adopt, adopting, adoption issues, attachment, intercountry adoption, international adoption, and so forth.

ACKNOWLEDGMENTS

The authors are grateful to many people for making this book possible. First and foremost, we must express our gratitude and love for all the children, particularly those in Romania, who inspired this book.

Special gratitude to Michael Vasile, Di Di, Anamaria, Ana Dorr, Alex, Juliana, and Catarina. And to their courageous parents, who endured the process of foreign adoption, lived through the struggles of their children, and finally allowed us to tell their stories so that other children and parents might benefit.

We could not have written this book without the patience, expertise, and wisdom of our editor, Amelia Sheldon of Pocket Books. Nor could we have succeeded without the friendship and advice of our dear friend and agent, Howard Pelham. We are grateful you are with us, Howard.

Others who must be mentioned here include AnnaMarie Merrill of the International Concerns Committee for Children in Boulder, Colorado, who shared her knowledge with us; Rumi Engineer, an immigration attorney with Allott, Engineer & Makar of Littleton, Colorado, who shared his expertise so generously; Ian McKelvey, for his contributions of graphic designs and charts; Janice Tomlin, and her colleagues at ABC who have helped publicize the plight of abandoned children everywhere.

Certainly, no authors of a book such as this can complete their work without the support and understanding of their families.

~

I (Carole) acknowledge the support of my family—George, Ian, Heather, and Justin. George, my partner in life, you have always believed in me and supported my efforts and I couldn't do it without you; I love you. And my dear parents, Francis and Gerri Conner, and my sister and fellow author, Dr. JoEllen Stevens, who has been an inspiration for my midlife career switch to counseling emotionally disturbed children.

I wish to thank my mentor and friend, Connell Watkins of Evergreen, and her colleagues at Connell Watkins and Associates, in Evergreen, Colorado, who labor daily to improve the lives of children.

~

Barbara's gratitude goes:

To my husband, Jim, who has unconditionally supported me for the past two years while I have been writing this and two other books. He is the guy you may see in Denver, Colorado, with a bewildered look on his face and a button that reads: "Be kind to me—I am married to an unpublished writer." If you meet him, be kind to him. It's not over yet.

351

To my adopted son, Erich, who taught me how to be a mother and shared the joys and promises of adoption, the frustration and pain of "special needs" before the phrase was coined. To Fritz, my younger son, who shared the experience, first as a student in Romania, then as our do-everything man for the Brooke Foundation. To my sister Paula, who is the real writer in the family and listens so well. To Taya, who taught me the joy of stepparenting; and Steve, Jimmy, and Vanessa, too. Words are not enough for any of you. Love will have to do.

To the children of Romania—especially Nicoletta (who lived and will continue to live her life in a Camin Spital and who taught me the meaning of survival and friendship), Anamaria (who trusted and has fought so hard to recover), and Vasile (who came first) and Ana, who enriched my knowledge of human potential and demonstrated, time and again, the nonextinguishable human spirit born in all children—and all of us.

To the parents who adopted Romanian children and have taught me what I know about foreign adoption—its upside, downside and upside-down side. I am particularly grateful to Doug and Lissie Mc-Glashen, Lori Eisinger, Greti and Rick Dorr, Lynn and Jim Lansford, and Gene and Susan Goldberg for sharing so much beyond the professional. . . . I stand in awe of the courage that you and the many like you have shown by going public with intensely personal stories so that we all can benefit.

To the ROSES team in Iasi—Alice Vison, Carmen Frunzetti, Melania Ciupurca, Cristiana Dragomir, Mihai Ciongradi, Gheorgetta, John B, the project manager who can solve any problem, all the caregivers, nurse Ani, Mariana, and my dear friend and colleague Dr. Olimpia Macovei. To Alina, Luminitsa, Alex Popescu (now at Taverstock), George Ionita, Sylvia, and Violetta in Bucharest. To Dr. Alin Stanescu and Lumitsa Marcu at the Ministry of Health. To everyone, past and present, on the Romania Adoption Committee. To Timmie Wallace, who shows every one of us what healing is all about, and all the physical therapists like her. To Jane Sweeney, who came three times, and finally brought a dream team of PTs to Romania to help us, teach us, and do the kind of research that needed to be done. To Gale Haradon and Howard and DeWayne Wynn.

To Errol Alden at the Academy of Pediatrics, for everything. To Nina Scribanu, who believed me when I said we could do UAPs in Romania. To my friends and colleagues at UCHSC, especially Richard Krugman, and the PT school. To all the media and press who worked so hard to tell the children's stories; particularly thanks to Janice Tomlin (Phil, too), Tom Jarriel and all the 20/20 crew, Cathy Nolan, Taro Yamasaki and the *People* people, Connie Chung and Brian Unger, Marilyn Greene at *USA Today*, Richard Davies and Robin Groth, and the CBS crew who did *Where Are They Now?*

To singer-songwriter Neil Diamond, who gave us *Childsong*.

~

We thank you all—from our hearts, we thank you.

Barbara Bascom and Carole McKelvey

DEDICATION

We dedicate this book to the memory of Melania Ciupurca, the Romanian psychologist extraordinaire whose healing touch and dedication enabled so many children to "go home, where they belonged." Although her untimely death in February 1996 is almost unbearable, her inspiration and gifts are with us forever. Thank you, Melanie. Go with God. And help us look after the children well so all of them can find their way home.

Index